★ *A Baker's Dozen* ★

★ ★ ★ ★ ★ ★ ★ ★

A Baker's Dozen

★ ★ ★ ★ ★ ★ ★ ★

THIRTEEN
UNUSUAL
AMERICANS

BY

Russel B. Nye

GREENWOOD PRESS, PUBLISHERS
WESTPORT, CONNECTICUT

Library of Congress Cataloging in Publication Data

Nye, Russel Blaine, 1913-
    A baker's dozen; thirteen unusual Americans.

    Reprint of the ed. published by Michigan State
University Press, East Lansing.
    1. United States--Biography.   I. Title.
[E176.N95 1974]   920.073   74-6100
ISBN 0-8371-7495-3

Copyright 1956 Michigan State University Press

Originally published in 1956 by Michigan State University
Press, East Lansing

Reprinted with the permission of Michigan State University
Press

Reprinted in 1974 by Greenwood Press,
a division of Williamhouse-Regency Inc.

Library of Congress Catalog Card Number 74-6100

ISBN 0-8371-7495-3

Printed in the United States of America

For Kay

★

Why should we be in such desperate haste to suc-ceed and in such desperate enterprises? If a man does not keep pace with his companions, perhaps it is because he hears a different drummer.

HENRY DAVID THOREAU

Preface

THE PROPER PLACE to begin is with a series of caveats. Let the reader understand clearly at the outset that the personages who appear herein are the kind usually relegated to footnotes, those whose lives are ordinarily tucked away in library crannies to be exhumed now and then only by the curious. It is difficult to claim that any of them had any major influence on the course of historical events (though, with a twist of direction here and there, some might have) nor is it the aim of the book to prove that any of them did. Neither is this book an attempt to refurbish lost reputations. For the most part, the judgment of history on those who appear here has proved fairly accurate; neither debunking nor glorifying is necessary or intended.

What is offered is simply a collection of sketches of people— a few mavericks, a few eccentrics, a few villains, a few heroes, and a few others who elude easy classification. Some of them are admittedly unimportant; some are simply obscure. Some were notorious in their times; some who were once well-known have been lost in the shuffling of records that occurs when each generation rewrites history. One common factor binds them together. All of them, in one fashion or another, are intrinsically interesting persons.

History is in one sense no more than a record of people. The dull need no biographers, and the famous, important and influential will never lack them, for the demands of the public and the private compulsions of researchers traditionally channel the energy of readers and writers into the study of the great and near-great. A generation ago it was an old joke that every Northern scholar looked forward to his old age so that he could begin his multivolumed biography of Lincoln and every Southern scholar to his so that he could write the definitive life of Robert E. Lee. For British or French consumption, one might substitute Gladstone or Napoleon without destroying the aphorism. There is no argument with this, for there are always new depths to penetrate in the lives of great men, reinterpretations to be made, facets of character to be explored, new sources of information to evaluate—and perhaps even new "major" figures to be discovered as we keep scrutinizing the past for evidences of eminence. And truthfully, we seem not to tire of Washington, nor Lee, nor Lincoln, nor the others of whom, it seems, there is always something more to say.

But the past is more than great men. The bright light focused front and center tends to obscure the playlets being worked out backstage, or perhaps not on stage at all. The audience rarely looks at the bottom of the playbill, where the minor actors and stagehands star in little tragedies and comedies of their own. The closet drama of Harman Blennerhassett, acted out in the wings of Aaron Burr's greater tragedy of imperial ambition, has elements that Burr's lacks, and no less human interest. Clement Vallandigham, who hated war and loved his country, defied a greater man than he and stained his own name with treason in defense of his principles. The social experiment at Brook Farm, because it caught the attention of some New England intellectuals, eclipsed a much more vital and absorbing experiment at Oneida. Simon Girty, who terrorized a frontier, is only a dimly-remembered legend of Indian-fighting days; John Murrell, who terrorized another, is thoroughly forgotten. John Ledyard, who failed utterly at what Lewis and Clark accomplished, never got on the stage of history at all.

Yet the lives of these men, and of others like them, are all parts of the intricate web of interwoven patterns that makes up the fabric of history. These are the men who, as the biographer turns over his notes, he hopes someday to find more about at his leisure. For having pursued them a little farther than usual into their shadowed historical corners, the author makes no apologies.

Contents

★

xi

THE TAINT OF TREASON

★

John Fries

Harman Blennerhassett

John Fries

★

THE RATIFICATION of the Constitution in 1788 did not unite the United States. As the authors of *The Federalist*, that masterful piece of pro-Constitutional political analysis, had already pointed out, the Constitution, though an admirable instrument of government, did not guarantee unity by the simple act of its adoption. There might be "factions," conflicts of self-interest, which could nullify the delicate system of balances and counterbalances by which the document established solidarity in the new republican form of government. Such conflicts, factional disputes, and divisions of haves and have-nots, they fervently hoped, would never occur.

The political nature of Americans being what it is, however, the hopes of the Federalist group faded rapidly during Washington's administrations. The universal respect in which the Virginian was held, as well as the dignified, middle-of-the-road course he steered as President, provided the new nation with a somewhat wavering political unity during his two terms. But there were strains and stresses, even under Washington's leadership. Bankers, shippers, farmers, artisans, merchants, back-country and seaboard, all wanted something from the new government and were determined to get it by political maneuverings. The men who harassed King, Parliament, and Continental Congress had learned their politics in a hard school and knew how to play the game shrewdly. Furthermore, men who had successfully engineered a revolution against centralized "tyranny" in London were determined to forestall the establishment of any such "tyranny" in Philadelphia. Some citizens who opposed the Constitution still preferred the loose decentralization of the now-defunct Articles of Confederation under which, after all, the nation had been governed to their satisfaction for seven years.

The feud between Hamilton and Jefferson, initiated while both were in Washington's cabinet, marked the beginnings of the political factionalism that *The Federalist* feared. The quarrel had its personal element, to be sure, but it reflected a deeper division within the nation over the nature and purpose of government—of creditor versus debtor, of farmer versus city merchant, of strong versus weak government, of poor versus rich. Hamilton represented in the public mind the aristocratic or "Federalist" viewpoint, the interests of merchant, shipper, banker, manufacturer, and seaboard. Jefferson represented the anti-Federalist (or Democratic-Republican) group, the interests of farmer, artisan, debtor, and back-country frontier. Political opinion coalesced about the two men, until by the time of the victory of John Adams, a Federalist, over Jefferson in the presidential election of 1796, the opposing groups emerged as full-fledged political parties. The battle was bitter, in and out of Congress. Adams' stubborn Yankee rectitude would not allow him to bend with the breezes of political expediency, nor would his stern conservatism allow him to compromise with what he considered the dangerously loose radicalism of the Jeffersonians. Whatever he did, his anti-Federalist opponents argued and accused, while his own Federalists criticized him for refusing to play politics harder than he did. John Adams was not a happy President.

Taxes, France, and Jefferson—these were John Adams' three most difficult problems. For forty years America had inveighed against taxes, dumped tea because of taxes, smuggled goods because of taxes, and harried Crown and Federal agents because of taxes. Whether taxes were levied by a King and Parliament, or by a President and Congress, seemed to make little difference; they were still taxes, and nobody liked to pay them. President Washington had the same trouble. The excise tax on whiskey, proposed by Hamilton in 1791, fell heavily on the farmers of western Pennsylvania, who condensed their corn and grain into this easily-shipped and highly-exportable commodity. The result was an insurrection, finally quelled in 1794 by an expeditionary force of militia. Though two of the leaders were convicted of treason, Washington eventually pardoned them, but his mercy did nothing to make taxes more palatable.

France was another problem. The majority of Americans welcomed the French Revolution in its early stages as a sign that the spark kindled by their own had caught flame in Europe. As time passed, some suspected that quite possibly the French were creating not an outpost of freedom in Europe, but an "anarchistic, atheistic" dictatorship whose aim was world domination. American opinion split sharply on the issue, with the Jeffersonians generally sympathetic to the French and the Federalists supporting the British cause. John Adams, when he took office, found it very difficult to hold his own party in some sort of unity while at the same time trying to locate and pursue a satisfactory foreign policy.

By the middle of Adams' term, France, taxes, and politics merged into a single problem. Relations with France deteriorated rapidly, until by 1798 war appeared to be inevitable. Congress passed some twenty acts designed to consolidate national defense, established a Navy Department, repealed all treaties with France, prepared to muster an army, and called Washington out of retirement to command it. The Federalists wanted war, many of them, for the threat of "French radicalism" caused real alarm, verging on hysteria, among American conservatives. After a Congressional committee reported that a network of Gallic "emissaries and spies" planned to "establish new principles of social action and the subversion of religion, morality, law, and government" in the United States, Federalists saw "plots" everywhere. Such fear-mongering gave the Federalists the opportunity to pose as conservators of true Americanism and to label their opponents as conspirators or dupes. Federalist editors found "traitors" and "spies" by dozens, of course, almost wholly among anti-Federalist

Jeffersonians. They uncovered diabolical plots week by week, including one by the Irish, acting under French orders, to burn down Philadelphia on National Fast day. All foreigners were suspect—Irish and French especially—since it was taken for granted that they were all organized into a huge conspiracy to overthrow the government with Jeffersonian help. Thus Congress passed the Alien and Sedition Acts of 1798, which in the interests of national security assumed that foreigners or critics of the administration were either undesirable aliens or seditious plotters. Nearly everyone prosecuted under the terms of these acts was an anti-Federalist.

To finance the expected war, Congress passed several new taxes, among them a direct levy on land, houses, and slaves, that was intended to raise two million dollars. Mindful of the whiskey troubles, Congress planned to collect the property tax on a graduated scale, ranging from two-tenths of one percent up to one percent of the assessed property value, with owners of slaves taxed at a flat rate of fifty cents per slave. The levy was apportioned by states, each state to be divided into districts, a commissioner and assessors appointed by the President for each district. These were patronage jobs, and no Jeffersonians need apply.

Pennsylvania's share of the tax was two hundred and thirty-seven thousand dollars. Slaves were very few in Pennsylvania; their comparative scarcity meant that the tax fell almost wholly on land and houses. Because no set standard of values existed for purposes of assessment, estimates varied wildly, even within the same district. In eastern Pennsylvania the commissioners, Federalists all, decided as a rule of thumb to assess houses by employing the ancient European device of counting the number and sizes of windows. In January, 1799, the government assessors went on the road, and the trouble started.

Eastern Pennsylvania was heavily inhabited by Germans. They were solid folk, comparatively well-to-do farmers, clannish, and violently anti-Federalist, since they had been rather arrogantly treated under the Alien and Sedition Acts and patronized by the Federalist Philadelphians who controlled the state. Many spoke only German. Many read only rabidly anti-Adams German-language newspapers. The majority of them, probably, had only a vague understanding of the new tax laws. The appearance of tax assessors who measured windows and jotted down figures in notebooks aroused a good many old-country memories, recalling particularly the obnoxious German hearth-tax. Tax collectors, to simple farmers only a generation removed from Europe, aroused dislike and suspicion.

Eastern Pennsylvania was divided into the Third and Fifth tax districts, including the counties of Lehigh, Bucks, Berks, Northampton, Montgomery, Luzerne, and Wayne. Adams appointed as commissioners two Federalists, Seth Chapman in the Third and Jacob Eyerly in the Fifth, who set to work appointing assessors. Some of those appointed were understandably reluctant to serve, especially after receiving threatening letters, and a few resigned before the actual assessments began, but within a few weeks Chapman and Eyerly had their districts staffed, ready to begin. The assessors did not have an easy time. In Luzerne and Wayne, settled by English and Scotch-Irish, they found the people reluctantly coöperative, but in the German-speaking counties the assessors reported a great deal of resistance. Some had dogs set on them, some were roughly handled, and a few were doused with boiling water by indignant *hausfrauen*. Stores and taverns in the hamlets bubbled with angry denunciations of the *"verdammt stamplers,"* who took to travelling in twos and threes for protection.

The most troublesome spot was Milford Township in Bucks County, the home of one John Fries. Fries, born in Bucks in 1750, was a cooper, but he worked as an auctioneer, or vendue-crier, more than he did at coopering. He had served as a militiaman in the Revolution, and again in the Whiskey Rebellion. His work took him into all the towns and taverns of Eastern Pennsylvania. He was a familiar figure there, reputed to have the loudest voice in the state. A small, spare man, quick and nervous in speech and move-

7

ment, he wore a three-cornered hat with a white feather, a broadsword, and travelled with his constant companion, a small black-and-white dog named Whiskey.

Fries was a fluent talker, a superb tavern debater after a mug or two of hard cider, and a bitter anti-Federalist. He found good audiences on his trips, because the spring was late and the taverns were filled with farmers waiting for plowing weather. As Fries made his rounds he left irate groups of Germans behind him, cursing the Federalists, taxes, Eyerly, Chapman, and John Adams. The assessors from Milford brought in stories in which Fries' name figured prominently. Mr. Clarke, who had the misfortune to stop at a tavern soon after Fries had left it, was told that "if he set foot in Bucks county again, his legs would be shot off." Mr. Benson heard that if he continued measuring windows he "would be committed to an old stable and fed on rotten corn." Mr. Roderick and Mr. Foulke, pursued by Fries himself and a band of farmers, took refuge in a thicket, from which Mr. Foulke was unceremoniously dragged. Fries, reported Foulke, "snapped his horsepistol at him, looked through all his papers, and exacted a promise that he would not proceed in the valuation of houses." An unlucky peddler, mistaken for an assessor, had his coattails torn off.

That Fries was the focal point of resistance in Bucks was obvious to the commissioners. In fact, opposition to the assessment spread so rapidly to outer counties that Fries and his followers seemed to be successfully organizing a widespread anti-tax conspiracy. Wherever Fries and Whiskey stopped, liberty poles went up in tavern yards and Germans got out muzzle-loaders for target practice; Milford even had a battle-cry: "Damm de President, damm de Congress, und damm de Arischdokratz!" that rang out in tavern after tavern after a round or so of whiskey. Cooler heads were to be found in Bucks, but they seemed impotent in contrast to Fries, who was exercising both an ability to arouse strong feelings and a knack for organization. In February, 1799, Fries called a meeting at his home; it was attended by some fifty men, all

of whom signed a protest addressed to the tax commissioners—
to which they added a statement that they did not clearly
understand the law and hoped someone would explain it.

Convinced that the whole argument arose from misunderstanding, Chapman travelled to Milford in early March to
hold a meeting to explain the law. Unfortunately, as the
meeting was held at Klein's Tavern, hard cider flowed gen-
erously before Chapman and his assessor arrived. When they
did so they found waiting an angry crowd of farmers already
thoroughly exhorted by John Fries. The farmers were "dis-
orderly and threatening," Chapman reported. Much talk
went on in German (which he understood imperfectly) along
with "huzzaing for liberty and damning the Tories." One
man carried a flag crudely lettered LIBERTY, and several
shook muskets in Chapman's face, shouting, "We don't want
any of your damned laws!" Prudently, Chapman left.

The commissioner refused to be bullied. Assessing was
already far behind schedule in that portion of Bucks county.
Chapman felt certain that once the work had begun, most
of the opposition would gradually cease as people came to
understand the law. With Foulke and another assessor named
Child, he took rooms on March 4 at a tavern near Quakerstown, planning to send assessors out into the surrounding
country. The news of his arrival travelled fast. The following day a heated protest meeting met at another tavern a few
miles away in Trumbauersville, and after a few hours of
drinking and argument, it seemed a good idea to the as-
semblage to find the assessors and give them a lesson. Rumor
placed them in Quakerstown, so the Trumbauersville
group, twenty or so strong and a trifle the worse for liquor,
set out down the pike with clubs, pitchforks, a gun or two,
and a fife. While they marched, John Fries and five men were
also on the road to Quakerstown. The Fries detachment
arrived there some hours before the men from Trumbauersville, whose progress was slow and moist. Fries went directly
to Chapman's rooms, blustered a bit, and notified him that
if one assessor went out, five hundred armed farmers would

appear in Quakerstown in twenty-four hours. He would enforce the law, replied Chapman, and if Milford resisted, soldiers would see to it that the law was enforced; Child and Foulke were already at work, and he, Chapman, intended to see to it that they were neither threatened nor disturbed.

The Trumbauersville group arrived at Quakerstown late that afternoon, joining Fries and his five men at Enoch Roberts' tavern. By evening, a witness reported later, the tavern rang with "hallooing, cursing, drumming and fifing, and drinking, with violent denouncing of John Adams."

> *They damned the Alien and Sedition laws, and finally all the laws, the government, and all the laws the present government had made. They damned the Constitution too. They damned the Congress and damned the President, and all the friends of the government. They said they would not have the government or the President, and they would not live under such a damned government. "We will have Washington," others said "No, we will have Jefferson, he is a better man than Adams, huzza for Jefferson."*

Foulke and Child, their assessing done for the day, had to ride by the tavern on their way into Quakerstown. Someone saw them approaching in the twilight, and with a great shout the crowd surged into the road, brandishing clubs, muskets, forks, and bottles. Child pushed on through, but Fries, recognizing Foulke, ordered him to stop. Though Foulke was frightened, he kept his head, pretending not to understand the hubbub, and Fries, having captured an assessor, did not seem to know quite what to do next. He looked at Foulke's papers, cursed him roundly, told him to stay out of Milford, and rather lamely let him go. Then someone remembered Child, who had taken refuge in the nearest house, and Fries went to find him. Child made no resistance while the crowd milled around him (somebody struck him on the side) and finally he, too, was ordered to leave Milford and never return.

He "could raise ten thousand men," Fries told him, "if they should be needed to oppose the house tax, the alien and sedition laws, and fifty other damned laws."

Commissioner Chapman decided to do no more assessing in Milford Township. Meanwhile, in neighboring Northampton County, Commissioner Eyerly, too, found stiff resistance. Fries and his men from Bucks had stirred up the Northampton Germans, who were giving Eyerly's assessors an equally difficult time—at least two resigned hurriedly and several others wavered. Eyerly, who like Chapman believed that much of the opposition to the tax law arose from misunderstanding, also called an open meeting to explain it. About seventy men came, stacked their arms by the door, and sat stolidly while Eyerly carefully analyzed the law. No rowdiness occurred—but the men simply would not obey the law. Things were so bad, they said, "with the government laying one thing and another under taxation," that Adams "will bring us into bondage or make slaves of us" unless someone called a halt to the "stamplers." Any assessors who travelled in Northampton, they notified Eyerly, did so at their own risk. Eyerly retired, but not before he noted that "several wore French cockades in their hats."

Eyerly made the next move, to obtain subpoenas for those Northampton men who seemed ringleaders of the "plot," for by this time Eyerly was convinced (the cockades helped) that there was more to the affair than simple misunderstanding. Judge Henry, a local Federalist, interviewed several witnesses who refused, through fright or sullenness, to talk (more proof of a plot). The Judge then sent a deposition to United States District Attorney Sitgreaves and issued warrants for the arrest of certain parties, presumably those responsible for the tax troubles, to appear in United States District Court in Philadelphia. More than twenty such warrants in all were issued, to be served by United States Marshal Nichols.

Marshal Nichols did not relish the task of arresting his neighbors, but he was brave and dutiful. Accompanied by Eyerly, Nichols rode through the crossroads hamlets, eyed by glowering Germans, to serve his warrants. Near Millarstown a crowd collected to shout at him, but he showed his pistols and went through. He found twelve of his culprits; five more came in and surrendered, and the remainder he simply could not find. The seventeen unlucky men were taken to Bethlehem for confinement before their appearance in Philadelphia. Because Bethlehem jail was too small to hold them, Nichols put them under guard at the Sun Tavern on the outskirts of town.

Northampton and Bucks seethed at news of the arrests. At Milford a loud and angry meeting, steered by Fries—whose threats were horrific—resolved to march immediately on Bethlehem. In Northampton another meeting, directed by one Andrew Shiffert, resolved to do the same. The following day, March 8, both were on the road.

Fries, elected "captain" of the Milford group by acclamation, received word of the Northampton meeting soon after his crowd of marchers left Milford. He had about one hundred and forty men, including two militia companies and a company of cavalry armed with broadswords; Shiffert's column numbered possibly fifty. Both groups picked up recruits at the hamlets and taverns. Fries, whose men had the longer distance to travel, followed three or four miles behind Shiffert. The more frequent the tavern stops, the wilder the rumors grew. At least ten thousand armed men were on the road, the story passed along, coming from New Jersey, western Pennsylvania, and New York; General Washington himself with twenty thousand soldiers was on the way from Virginia to help. Somebody came with a fife, another with a drum. One elderly German who carried "a goot for nossing mustick" explained that he did so because "mebbe I might schkeer somepotty." One man carried a hastily-made flag with five red stripes, representing the five counties of eastern Pennsylvania. With fifing, and drumming, and shouting, and Whiskey barking ahead of Fries on his white horse, the march had an excitingly military aspect that attracted recruits at every crossroad.

Because the progress of Fries and Shiffert was slow, Marshal Nichols had plenty of warning. He conferred with Eyerly, Judge Henry, and the local justice of the peace, and within a few hours he had sworn in enough deputies, he hoped, to resist the invasion. Eyerly meanwhile called his assessors Foulke, Child, and Balliott into the tavern for safety, for all three were known to the local residents and were decidedly unpopular. For safekeeping, he transferred his prisoners to an upstairs room in the Sun, posting guards on the stairway and sending deputies to arrest two local men known to be friendly to Fries, lest they start trouble when the marchers arrived. One or two loafers who gave insolent answers when questioned were quickly hurried into the tavern and confined with the prisoners.

When a rider brought in news that Fries and Shiffert had joined forces at a tavern near Lehigh Bridge, across the river from Bethlehem, Nichols decided to send a deputation to meet them for a parley. He chose four men—two known Federalists and two presumed Jeffersonians—who, after some persuasion, agreed to serve. A half mile beyond the bridge the deputation met a dozen or so armed men, riding somewhat unsteadily toward Bethlehem, and asked to be escorted to their commanders. "We're all commanders here," they replied, and snapped their guncocks. The peace mission hastily retreated to the bridge. There they met a much more tractable group, who had heard, they said, that "two of their neighbors were in jail" and had come to get them out. After a brief conversation the group agreed to send a three-man committee to confer with Nichols at the Sun.

The committee rode back to talk with Nichols, who found them reasonable and sober. Their friends, they claimed, had little to do with the harassment of the assessors, and were guilty of talking threateningly, more than anything else—for that matter, the committee would guarantee their friends' appearance in Philadelphia, if the courts demanded it. The committee seemed honest and sincere, so Nichols and Eyerly agreed to let the two prisoners go, and the group rode away.

On the other side of the bridge the committee met Fries at the head of his column, explained what had happened and informed him they felt sure Nichols would listen to reason. Fries was in no mood for arbitration. "We came for a fight," he shouted, "and if one's coming, we'll meet it!" His men roared their approval and marched on.

The combined forces of Fries and Shiffert arrived at the Sun Tavern in midafternoon. Shiffert, however, was not with them. Somewhere along the road he had lost heart for the proceedings and had decided to remain on the far side of the bridge. Fries was in command, his loud voice dominating the crowd of farmers, who seemed in good order though inclined to be noisy. A great deal of shouting occurred and a great many threats went up. "Them that was Tories in the war is holding the prisoners," someone shouted, and Eyerly, who heard someone say that if "Henry, and that damned Eyerly, and that pot-gutted Balliott were there they'd tear them to pieces," herded his assessors upstairs, carefully staying away from windows. Marshal Nichols, after distributing his twenty-man posse at strategic points throughout the building, sent out word to the milling crowd in the courtyard that he would meet Fries and two others, but no more, for a discussion. Fries stamped in, and the argument began.

Fries, Nichols reminded him, was interfering with the due process of law and "could be severely punished for it." No, replied Fries, he was opposed to the law anyway, to the "alien law, the stamp act, and the damned house tax" inclusively. As for punishment, "the government were not strong enough, for if the troops were brought out they would join him." Fries wanted the prisoners, who, "if they had done something, should be tried in their own courts and by their own people," not in Philadelphia. The prisoners must be released at once. Nichols refused.

"Then we'll take them," shouted Fries.

"If you want trouble," Nichols answered, "you'll get it."

When Fries returned to the innyard and announced the result of his conference to the assembled farmers, a great

roar went up. The men immediately charged the building
while the landlord, with great presence of mind, quickly
locked the taproom, causing "a sudden repulse," reported an
eye-witness, "that maddened the crowd." A hundred men
milled about in the small building, with Fries' powerful voice
rising above the tumult, shouting orders not to fire unless
fired upon. No one was quite sure where the prisoners were,
in the confusion, nor which were guards and which were res-
cuers. The guards on the stairway, unwilling to risk their
lives against a mob, begged Nichols to give up. "For God's
sake," pleaded one of the posse, "deliver the men upstairs
before we are all killed." Nothing was left for the Marshal
to do but surrender. A frightened deputy pushed his way
through the crowd to tell Fries the prisoners would be freed,
and in a few minutes they filed down the stairs. In fifteen
minutes the innyard was empty.

The affair made wonderful tavern talk for several days.
Fries, inclined to be boastful, told the story over and over in
a dozen taprooms, while Northampton and Bucks gloated
over their victory. Nevertheless, a good many of the rebels
had sober second thoughts, once the liquor and exhilaration
had worn off. Decent, law-abiding citizens who had been carried away by excitement and rhetoric began to realize that the
march on Bethlehem was, after all, outright rebellion against
the Government of the United States. Fries himself admitted
he was nervous. He slept badly, and was heard to say he
"would give all he had if the matter were settled and he was
clear of it." On March 15, several Milford citizens called a
public meeting and, after some subdued discussion, appointed
a committee to confer with Marshal Nichols, Eyerly, and
Chapman.

But the affair had long since gone beyond the talking stage.
As soon as he released the prisoners, Nichols sent a full account of the incident to the Federal Judge at Philadelphia,
who in turn transmitted it to Washington. President Adams
discussed the matter with his cabinet on March 11, and on
March 12, three days before the Milford peace meeting, he

issued a proclamation commanding the insurgents to disperse, labelling the attack on the Sun Tavern as "rebellious and treasonable," and ordering military action against the insurrectionists of eastern Pennsylvania.

Adams' proclamation struck Northampton and Bucks like a thunderbolt. The thing was serious. Devilling tax assessors and overawing a Marshal had been exciting, but the penalty for treason was death. The worried insurgents held a series of desperate meetings, sent apologies to Eyerly and Chapman, notified them they would gladly submit to the law, and promised to welcome the assessors. The assessors came, did their work, and left. The weather turned warm, farmers went back to their plowing, and the taverns were quiet.

The machinery, once put in motion, could not be stopped. Nor did the Federalists want it stopped, for memories of the Whiskey Rebellion were still fresh in their minds. The following year was a presidential election year; Jefferson's forces were growing in strength; eastern Pennsylvania was strongly anti-Adams; the insurrectionists were "foreigners." If once permitted to challenge the power of the Federal government, they might do it again and encourage others to do it. Everything pointed, from the Federalist point of view, to the importance of the Pennsylvania incident as a test case. Anti-Federalist rebellions had to be nipped in the bud.

Governor Mifflin of Pennsylvania was inclined to let the matter rest. More as a political gesture than anything else, he asked the Pennsylvania Assembly to investigate the possibility that the affair was provoked by "foreign incendiaries," but he recommended no further action. The Federalists in Washington did not intend to let the affair drop. On March 20, the Secretary of War notified Mifflin that, at the President's order, he should call out five troops of militia to "suppress insurrection in certain counties of Pennsylvania." This Mifflin did, calling the five militia companies to assemble in Philadelphia by March 28. At the same time, remembering how unenthusiastically militiamen had served against their fellow farmers in the Whiskey Rebellion, the Secretary of

War called five companies of regulars and an artillery company from New York. To be on the safe side, he also alerted two thousand New Jersey militia for service if needed. The expedition, commanded by Brigadier General McPherson, a prominent Philadelphia Federalist, left the city on April 4, bound for Northampton and Bucks counties, armed with warrants for the arrest of more than fifty suspected ringleaders.

The Pennsylvania Germans were awed and puzzled by the military might arrayed against them. They had acted rashly, they knew—but they had apologized, the assessors had finished their work, the taxes were being paid. Why the President needed ten companies of soldiers to suppress an uprising that no longer existed was hard for them to understand. Brigadier General McPherson, moreover, was something of a fool. He liked to issue purple proclamations, a steady stream of which preceded his army, calling on "these disaffected citizens to lay down their arms and desist." Since they had already done so some three weeks before, the disaffected citizens were not at all certain what they were being ordered to do.

McPherson definitely meant business. He knew the names of the ringleaders and he had Jacob Eyerly at his elbow to help run them down. Detachments of troops scoured the farms and hamlets and brought the confused and terrified men in, one by one. John Fries, on the road with his dog, went about his business of auctioneering, blustering a bit. He could not do much else. A cavalry troop found him crying a sale at a tavern near Bunker Hill and chased him into a swamp, where Whiskey's excited barking betrayed him. The troopers tied him to a horse, took him to a nearby tavern, and later brought him to McPherson's headquarters to join the others. On April 6, Judge Peters examined Fries and twelve other captives, and bound them over to Federal Court in Philadelphia; thither a cavalry guard took them for confinement in Federal prison.

Thirteen arrests should have satisfied McPherson, perhaps, but he was by no means through. His job was to suppress insurrection, and he meant to do it thoroughly. His army proceeded toward Allentown, making wholesale arrests on the way. Some who had marched with Fries surrendered themselves meekly. Others were hunted down. Bail was not considered; prisoners were manacled, deposited here and there in barns until McPherson was ready to deal with them, and then marched to jail in Bethlehem or Reading. The militiamen, who had not bargained for old men in irons and weeping wives, began to lose enthusiasm for their task. Some militia muttered that only anti-Adams men were arrested; others protested at the treatment of prisoners. The whole expedition was "unnecessary and violently absurd," one officer said, and occasionally the soldiers looked the other way if a prisoner or two escaped. After a few escapes, McPherson turned the chase over to the regulars and the Philadelphia cavalry, who seemed more trustworthy. In Reading, the cavalry took Jacob Schneider, the violently anti-Federalist editor of the German-language newspaper *Adler,* and whipped him in the market place. Then the army marched back to Philadelphia, leaving behind them a bitter, terrified populace.

McPherson sent sixty men in all to Philadelphia, all held without bail. John Fries, as the acknowledged leader of the insurrection, was examined first on April 11, 1799, on a charge of treason. Justice Iredell of the United States Supreme Court presided. Iredell's charge to the Grand Jury was purely partisan oratory, a good indication of how the Federalists intended to proceed with the case. The Government, said Iredell, had been "grossly abused as if it had been guilty of the vilest tyranny" by men who seemed to believe that "the pure principles of republicanism could be found only in the happy soil of France." Next the Judge launched into a long analysis of the constitutionality of the Alien and Sedition laws, closing with a fearsome picture of the "most dreadful confusion" that must ensue if Fries and others like him were allowed to escape punishment. "Anarchy," he thundered, "will ride triumphant, and all lovers of order, decency, truth and justice be trampled underfoot!" Since Fries was neither charged with abusing the Government, nor with violating the Alien and Sedition laws, Iredell's remarks were both irrelevant and shamefully prejudiced. The Grand Jury dutifully returned an indictment within a few hours, charging the defendant with "having maliciously, unlawfully, and traitorously compassed and levied war, insurrection, and rebellion against the United States." Fries pleaded not guilty. His trial was set for April 30. Other indictments followed.

The anti-Federalists provided three good lawyers for Fries— Dallas, Ewing, and Lewis. The government's case was placed with William Rawles, district attorney for Pennsylvania, and Emanuel Sitgreaves, attorney for Bucks and Northampton district. On April 30, Justices Iredell and Chase of the Supreme Court called the case with the selection of a petit jury—all Philadelphians, it turned out, except two jurors from Bucks who spoke little English. None of Fries' three attorneys were satisfied with the jury, but their motion to have the trial transferred to Bucks or Northampton for selection of a more suitable jury was denied. Those counties, Chase pointed out, were still officially in a state of insurrection.

Rawles and Sitgreaves had a strong case. Treason against the United States, Sitgreaves explained, as defined in Section 3, Article 3 of the Constitution, "shall consist only of levying war against them, or in adhering to their enemies, giving them aid and comfort." He did not contend that Fries had adhered to, aided, or comforted enemies of the United States. But he did contend that Fries had levied war against the Federal government, and had witnesses to prove it. Clarke, Roderick, and Foulke told of their brushes with Fries. Nine other witnesses testified to Fries' threats against Congress, the President, and tax collectors in general—threats that might have sounded impressive in Pennsylvania taverns, but which fell a trifle flat in court. Six witnesses recounted the saga of the march on Bethlehem, of which Fries was undoubtedly in command; in fact, said one witness, "he seemed to enjoy it very much, leading the huzzas." Fries himself, whose understanding of English was not great, sat quietly with his lawyers, a visibly shaken man.

Dallas, who presented the main argument for the defense,

did the best he could. The evidence against Fries was incontrovertible, and Dallas took the only possible tack—that what Fries had done did not fall within the constitutional definition of treason. First, Dallas argued, Fries and his followers did not believe in the justice of the tax law and took (regrettably, he admitted) drastic means of protest. This act in itself did not prove treasonable intent. Second, the chief objection of Fries and his friends to the law was the method used in enforcing it, particularly the standard of assessment. Their activities were therefore not treasonable, but rather the result of their manner of objection. The prosecution clearly established that Fries had committed the ʼacts ascribed to him; however, the government had failed to prove that the acts were of "traitorous design." Fries and his men were guilty of something—perhaps riot or incitement to riot, for which they should be punished—but not of treason. Recalling some of the witnesses, Dallas forced several to admit that the affair at the Sun Tavern could have been called a riot as easily as a rebellion.

Dallas, Lewis, and Ewing were not hopeful on May 11, when Justice Iredell gave the charge to the jury. Iredell displayed, one spectator thought, "an evident bias against the prisoner in his looks, speech, and gestures," an impression borne out by the text of the charge itself. The Justice unburdened himself of some twenty thousand words of highly inflammatory and savagely partisan opinion; he breathed fire against the French, condemned rebels, praised the Alien and Sedition laws, and warned against secret plots and conspirators.

Nevertheless, the jury took three hours to find Fries guilty. Court then recessed until May 14, the date set by the Justices for sentence, which, the majority of spectators agreed, could only be death. Fries returned to his cell and his supporters from Milford went home. The old game of baiting the tax men, the tavern threats, the blustering horseplay, seemed destined to end in tragedy. And if they could hang John Fries, they could hang a dozen others just as well.

But one juryman, Joseph Rhoads, had talked too much

and too often. Word came to Lewis that Rhoads, learning that he had been summoned for jury duty in the Fries case, had immediately declared that Fries was guilty and that he would hang him if he could. Lewis and Ewing, with but three days in which to work, hastily questioned, the man's acquaintances, collected sworn depositions, and on May 14, when the Court convened to dispose of Fries, Lewis immediately asked for a ruling of mistrial. Because Lewis' point was perfectly taken, Iredell granted a new trial.

Fries would have been tried again in June or July, but the great yellow-fever epidemic of 1799 that decimated Philadelphia suspended all court sessions. Fries and the other prisoners were removed to jail in Montgomery County. There they were presumably safe from infection, and there they stayed for nearly a year while the epidemic, one of the worst in Philadelphia's history, ran its course.

In spring of 1800 the prisoners were returned to Philadelphia for trial in Circuit Court. Justice Chase chose to replace the absent Iredell with Judge Peters of Philadelphia, who did little in the case. In late April the trials began, featuring Andrew Shiffert as star witness for the prosecution.

Conrad Marks, indicted for treason, escaped with a verdict of not guilty, though the now infuriated Chase declared that "he had no doubt that the prisoner was guilty in a high degree." Then they tried Marks again for conspiracy, obstruction of process, rescue, and unlawful combination—this time Rawles succeeded in getting him two years' imprisonment and an eight-hundred-dollar fine. George Gettman, Anthony Stahler and Fred Haney, all of whom had been in the crowd at the Sun Tavern, each got eight months in jail and a one-hundred-and-fifty-dollar fine. Henry Shiffert and seven others, tried for conspiracy, were sentenced to serve eight months. Only young Daniel Schwartz, a fifteen-year-old boy who had already spent a year in jail, was found not guilty.

John Fries came to trial for the second time on April 29, 1800. Justice Chase was an arrogant, imperious man, a bitterly partisan Federalist with little sympathy for Fries, insurrectionists, or Jeffersonians. Before impanelling the jury he notified the defense attorneys that he intended to hear no arguments over definitions of the law of treason; he had made up his mind, written down his opinion, and would provide copies for the jury as soon as it was chosen. Dallas and Lewis could hardly believe what they heard. Because their entire case rested on an interpretation of treason, proceeding with the trial seemed to them hopeless if the Court had already decided the point, as Chase evidently had. Dallas and Lewis therefore formally notified the Court that they had no recourse but to withdraw from the case. No lawyer, said Dallas, faced with such a pre-judgment, could do otherwise. (The incident later became an item in the articles of impeachment drawn against Chase in 1805, when the Senate very nearly convicted him.) Chase accepted their withdrawal with good grace and notified Fries of his right to have counsel appointed. Fries, ignorant of the law, and only dimly aware of what was happening, asked for none. The trial proceeded quickly, with the same witnesses, the same evidence, and the same result. On May 2, 1800, Justice Chase sentenced John Fries to death.

The yellow-fever epidemic that killed a thousand Philadelphians probably saved John Fries' life. As the year's wait took the case out of the news and gave men on both sides of the case time to think, public opinion swung slowly toward Fries, while tempers cooled. After all, the man had already served a year in jail, which seemed punishment enough for leading an "insurrection" that hurt nobody. Then, too, Fries was a veteran, a man who had stuck his neck in a noose to fight King George. Hanging seemed a drastic punishment for a single slip; a good many farmers at one time or another had secretly wished to run the tax collector out of town. The French no longer seemed so threatening, and talk of "plots" had died down.

Furthermore, the Fries case had political implications. Strong feeling existed in eastern Pennsylvania that Eyerly and Sitgreaves, both ambitious Federalists, had exaggerated the case out of all proportion to its importance, hoping to use the "rebellion" as a springboard to some higher office. Mc-Pherson's heroic march looked something less than heroic in retrospect—"A sergeant and six men," wrote one officer, "could have done as much and better." Certain other inferences also were to be drawn. A Federalist President had sent Federalist troops to arrest and maltreat a poor German' for manly resistance to Federalist tyranny, and a Federalist judge had sentenced him to be hanged. Jeffersonian editors, who began to talk of Fries as "a martyr to liberty," filled their columns with diatribes against Adams, and with invocations of the spirit of '76. The Fries case began to develop a high political temperature.

John Fries had no desire whatever to be a martyr. After a year in prison, he simply wanted to go home to Milford, a humbled and much subdued man who could not understand why he, of all the insurgents, had been singled out as an example. Obviously, no evil existed in the man, and in Northampton and Bucks the Federalists, a little sorry for him, remarked that perhaps the Germans had learned their lesson. Prominent Pennsylvanians came to his support. In the summer of 1800 a petition with a hundred signatures came to John Adams, asking clemency for Fries who, the petitioners assured the President, had demonstrated by his "humility and sincerity" that he was a "penitent offender."

John Adams was thoroughly familiar with the case. At the time of Fries' first conviction, he had heard rumors that the Pennsylvania trouble was not what it seemed. It might be, some Federalists wondered, really what some newspapers implied, an insurrection stirred up by "foreign emissaries." On the other hand, rumors also circulated that Fries was simply a "tool for a person of great consequence" who hoped to embarrass the Administration by fomenting trouble over taxes. The person of great consequence remained a mystery—but it could have been Thomas Jefferson, or so some may have wondered. If Fries, bought with foreign gold, had planned a true rebellion, that was one thing. If he were merely the dupe of high-level anti-Federalist machinations, that was another. Therefore Adams ordered a complete investigation. In the interim between the first and second trials, Adams had kept track of the case. After the second conviction, Adams sent his son Thomas to confer with Attorney Léwis, who gave him the brief which Lewis and Dallas had prepared for the trial. Adams sent the brief to the Attorney General for examination and, on May 20, 1800, took the matter to the Cabinet. No mercy was to be found there. Some thought Fries and all the other leaders ought to swing as a lesson to mobs. Hanging a half dozen Pennsylvanians, thought Secretary of State Pickering (who skirted treason himself a few years later in the War of 1812) would serve "to crush that spirit which, if not overthrown, may proceed in its career and overthrow the government." Others thought Fries' execution alone would suffice to make the point. All agreed that some culprits should hang; the question was, how many?

John Adams was an honest man. He had reservations about the two trials, a great deal of doubt about the wisdom of settling anything by hanging a half-literate, frightened German farmer, and he had good precedent in Washington's understanding treatment of the Whiskey Rebellion ringleaders. Furthermore, a memorandum from Dallas and Lewis concerning the trials revealed things that Adams, a superb lawyer himself, had not known. Iredell's actions were disgraceful in any court of law. The case had been tried in Philadelphia, in an atmosphere dark with prejudice, though the Constitution plainly stated that a trial must be held in the county where the crime was committed. Dallas, chief defense counsel, had been given only five days to examine nearly a hundred witnesses. In both trials, discussion by the defense of pertinent points of law had been curtailed or silenced, while Chase's pre-judgment of the charge in the second trial was almost unprecedented in American law. It was clear to Adams, whatever the political importance of the Fries case, that the man had not received a fair trial. Therefore, on May 23, Adams issued, on his own authority, a proclamation of pardon for Fries and for all those charged with responsibility "in the late wicked and treasonable insurrection in the counties of Northampton, Montgomery, and Bucks in the State of Pennsylvania."

Pickering complained that in pardoning the insurgents Adams "made a fatal concession to his enemies." Others assumed that as 1800 was an election year, his act of mercy was a bid for votes. A few Federalists shook their heads and predicted more and worse insurrections, if Fries went unpunished. The fact of the matter is that John Adams acted as he thought best, politics notwithstanding. To record that he carried eastern Pennsylvania in the elections of 1800 would be pleasant, but he did not. To record that John Fries voted Federalist also would be pleasant, but the fact is that Fries campaigned violently against Adams and led the Jeffersonians to a sweep of Bucks County. Nevertheless, a decade later, John Adams recalled his pardoning of Fries as one of the acts "that I can recollect with infinite satisfaction and which will console me in my last hour." One hopes that it did.

Samuel Chase continued on the bench to earn the distinction of being the only Justice of the United States Supreme Court to be impeached for unbecoming and unfair conduct, though he was not convicted. John Fries went back to Milford and auctioneering. He was never in the news again, and when he died, in 1818, all but a few had forgotten that he was the only man ever to be twice convicted of treason against the United States. He was not much of a rebel, nor was his insurrection much of a rebellion. Had the times been less tense and the Federalists less edgy, the affair in Pennsylvania probably would have been treated for what it was—a mob of tipsy farmers filled with liquor valor and tall talk, out for a little excitement with the law. If Chapman and Eyerly had been as fluent as Fries, or if they had planned their strategy more considerately, the troubles might have been avoided. Fries, of course, was culpable, and deserved his year in jail. A boaster and self-important braggart, he was neither an intelligent nor a dangerous man, certainly not one to threaten national security. Hanging him as the Cabinet advised would have accomplished nothing. Pardoning him, as Adams wisely perceived, achieved much more, by proving that the nation could afford to be both severe and merciful.

John Fries survives in history as an occasional footnote, and his *opéra bouffe* rebellion has been forgotten long ago in Pennsylvania. Yet he had a certain importance, if only as an indication that the Republic was maturing, painfully at times, but also rather quickly, into a nation. For a revolutionary generation to realize that the government was their government, that the "tyranny" they feared could exist only if they created it, was difficult. Fries' insurrection was part of the process by which Americans learned to govern themselves, and to live within the framework of government that they had so recently constructed.

Harman Blennerhassett

★

THERE WERE ONCE an Innocent, an Eden, and a Tempter. The Innocent was Harman Blennerhassett, son of an Irish gentleman, heir to Castle Conway in the County of Kerry. Born in 1767, he studied law at Trinity in Dublin, was admitted to the bar in 1790, and spent a year on the Grand Tour as wealthy young men of his time and station did. But being a retiring and bookish young man, Blennerhassett was not much interested in the law and, after his return from the continent, he found the pleasures of the library and laboratory much more appealing than the hurly-burly of the court. He called himself "a natural philosopher," meaning that he was interested in literature, philosophy, and science, and if he had not met his niece, Margaret Agnew, it is very likely he would have spent his years in the peaceful, meditative life of a scholarly Irish peer.

Margaret Agnew was beautiful, intelligent and young; she was widely read, fluent in French, Spanish, and Italian, and had a practicality and energy that Blennerhassett, some years her senior, did not have. Their marriage seemed unlikely, yet the two—man and girl—complemented each other perfectly—the quiet, shy man of books and the vital, energetic young woman who rode in a gold-and-scarlet coat to hounds and liked to act in amateur theatricals. The difficulty was that some members of Margaret's family, and some of Blennerhassett's neighbors, disapproved of marriages between uncle and niece, no matter how excellent the match. Even the fact that Margaret's father, lieutenant-governor of the Isle of Man, was high in Court favor, failed to make the marriage socially acceptable.

27

The Blennerhassetts therefore decided to go to America. There, they assumed, they might find a freer social atmosphere, a quiet life, and new friends. The Irish estates were sold to Baron Ventry for one hundred thousand dollars, nearly a fortune in the eighteenth century. After spending a good deal of that sum on books and laboratory equipment, the two sailed for New York in early 1797. New York was stimulating, but Blennerhassett wanted to see the West. In the autumn of 1797, he journeyed to Pittsburgh, took a keelboat down the Ohio River to Marietta, and promptly fell in love with the country. In the spring of 1798, he bought for forty-five hundred dollars a one-hundred-and-seventy-acre piece of what was locally known as Backus' Island, lying in the center of the Ohio river two miles below Parkersburg, West Virginia.

This was Blennerhassett's Eden. He purchased some slaves, hired local help, and cleared a hundred acres of land for crops. But most of his time and money, and his wife's, they spent with loving care on their house, which they were determined to make the perfect retreat. It cost him more than fifty thousand dollars, but when he had completed it it was the show place of the Ohio valley. Set at the head of the island, with a commanding view of the broad sweep of the river and the forest as its backdrop, it looked (remarked one observer) "like the Moorish palaces of Andalusia:

> *To the mind of the voyager, descending the river, as the edifice rose majestically in the distance, spreading its wings to either shore, the effect was magical. There was a spell of enchantment about it, which would fain induce the credulous to believe that it had been created by magic and consecrated to the gods."*

Actually, Blennerhassett's Castle, as it came to be called, bore a rather startling resemblance to a modern motel. It was a tastefully-designed two-story mansion with two curved wings sweeping out on either side; it faced a fanshaped lawn set with shrubbery, flowers, and bowers entwined with honeysuckle and eglantine. At the rear of the house was the fruit orchard, with peach, quince, pear, and apricot trees growing on white trellises. To the south were the vegetable garden and "kitchen orchard," with slave quarters, outbuildings, and stables a respectful distance beyond. The house itself Mrs. Blennerhassett furnished richly with velvet hangings, paintings, and much gold leaf, "chastened by the purest taste and without that glare of tinsel finery too common among the wealthy." What more could a man want than this estate, as William Wirt described it in the lush prose of an earlier day?

> *A shrubbery, which Shenstone might have envied, blooms around him; music that might have charmed Calypso and her nymphs, is his; an extensive library spreads its treasures before him; a philosophical apparatus offers to him all the mysteries and secrets of nature; peace, tranquility, and innocence shed their mingled delights around him.*

The Blennerhassetts lived peacefully and happily on their island Eden. Harman, six feet tall, stooped, nearsighted, pottered among his books and in his laboratory with his telescopes, microscopes, and chemicals. He liked to hunt, though his defective vision made him a very bad shot, and he liked to work in his orchard on warm days. Mrs. Blennerhassett reared three sons, ran the plantation, supervised the slaves, and was a charming hostess at frequent dinners, for wealthy travellers on the Ohio often stopped at the island to pay social calls. She rode her favorite horses, wrote poetry, produced Shakespearean comedies in the formal English gardens, and organized musicales at which her husband played the violin and cello extremely well. The local Ohio and Virginia gentry liked both the Blennerhassets. Life on Blennerhassett's Island was a good life—at least until 1805.

The Tempter arrived at Blennerhassett's Island in the spring of 1805, in the shape of Aaron Burr, vice-president of the United States, Revolutionary colonel and slayer of Alexander Hamilton in a duel the year before. On a tour of the West, Burr and several companions were floating down the Ohio on a sixty-foot flatboat equipped with a dining room, a kitchen with a fireplace, two bedrooms, and a good supply of wines. Like other travellers of note, he stopped to visit Blennerhassett's Castle. The master was not at home, but Mrs. Blennerhassett invited Burr and his companion, a Mrs. Shaw, to tea. Charmed by the house and the hostess, the visitors stayed until eleven that night. Later, Burr wrote a letter to Blennerhassett, thanking him for his wife's hospitality, offering regrets at not meeting him personally, and expressing surprise that a man of Blennerhassett's "talents and acquirements" found rustication so pleasant.

Burr had a plan, he suggested guardedly, into which a man of Blennerhassett's accomplishments might fit—Burr needed men of initiative and courage, men qualified for leadership, men interested in turning a little profit. The letter was bait. The Irishman took it. Men of Burr's standing were not lightly refused; furthermore, the Blennerhassett fortunes had been seriously depleted by the high cost of castle-building. "You will not regard it as indelicate in me," Blennerhassett replied, "to observe to you how highly I should be honored in being associated with you in any contemplated enterprise you would permit me to participate in." What Burr had in mind, as Blennerhassett read between the lines, was "not only a commercial venture or a land purchase but a military venture," a prospect calculated both to please and flatter an unmilitary, bookish man.

What plan Burr really had in mind is still not wholly clear. He may have had more than one. At any rate, his planning had to do with the West, particularly with the Louisiana Territory so recently purchased by Jefferson from France. Spain, the original owner of Louisiana, had given Presidents Washington, Adams, and Jefferson more trouble than any other of America's European neighbors. The power that controlled Louisiana and New Orleans controlled the Mississippi; whoever controlled the Mississippi also controlled the trade of its tributaries and all the water-borne commerce of the American West that found its outlet to the sea at New Orleans. The Treaty of San Lorenzo in 1795 had settled some of the navigation and port problems that bothered the Americans, but Spain was still, at best, an unpredictable ally. A year after Spain had ceded the area to France, Jefferson had bought it for fifteen million dollars, divided it into territories, and had opened the Mississippi for navigation to the sea.

The Louisiana Purchase did not make Louisiana American nor guarantee that it would always be American. Many Americans lived in the purchased area, but so, also, did many Spanish, Creoles, and French, to whom American rule was not especially attractive. Those Americans who held French and Spanish land claims in Louisiana feared that the Washington government might disallow them; those who wanted land in the new territory suspected that the Federal government might not be generous in handing it out. For that matter, plenty of feeling against the Federal government existed in Kentucky and Tennessee (admitted as states in 1792 and 1796) and in Mississippi (organized as a territory in 1798) over what Westerners felt was Federal favoritism to Eastern interests. Some influential Westerners believed the West might do better as a separate nation, friendly to, but nonetheless distinct from, the United States—even Washington had remarked that the Western states "stood as it were upon a pivot" where "a touch of the feather would turn them either way," toward union or independence.

The truth was that the American West in 1805 had no sense of union with the East, no strong feeling of nationalism. The Articles of Confederation under which the United States governed itself until 1789 considered the Union a voluntary compact from which sovereign states might withdraw as easily as they had entered. Nor did talk of separation from the Union seem unusual to a generation of men who had just completed a war of secession against an Empire, particularly because reason for holding the East and West together was not then obvious. Communication was slow, trade rivalries were strong, political relations strained and turbulent. Westerners disliked "Eastern bankers" and suspected both Virginia planters and New England manufacturers of loading Congressional dice against them. To substantial numbers of men in the West, therefore, separation of East and West appeared justifiable, profitable, and inevitable.

Aaron Burr—and James Wilkinson—like others, recognized the delicacy of the situation in the West and hoped to capitalize on it. Wilkinson, a Revolutionary officer of doubtful military reputation, was also an ambitious fortune hunter, a slippery politician, and thoroughly untrustworthy. After the Revolution he moved to Kentucky, made a deal with the Spanish to control all Kentucky trade moving through New Orleans, and accepted a yearly stipend from the Spanish for channeling information to them about American policies on Louisiana. He also wanted to get Kentucky and other states out of the union into a Western confederacy, but when the Constitution was ratified and Federal power over the West was strengthened he set aside his plans for the moment. In 1790 he re-entered the Army, rose to the rank of general (while still in Spanish pay) and was sent to New Orleans in 1803 to accept the Territory from the French. Burr and Wilkinson had been friends from Revolutionary days. When Wilkinson was now appointed Governor of Upper Louisiana, they renewed their friendship.

Neither Burr nor Wilkinson, so far as is known, ever put his plans on paper. Wilkinson told nobody (except presumably Burr) what his aims were, though he left both the Spanish and French ministers with the impression that he hoped to see the American West a separate, autonomous nation. Burr gave different persons different impressions of what he had in mind. Judging from later testimony, he may have had one, or more, of three plans. First, he might have planned a filibustering expedition into Spanish Mexico, in an attempt to seize large parts of it, sell the land to American settlers, establish a separate state, and eventually attach it to the United States. If this were his aim, much depended on the state of Spanish-American diplomatic relations, then so strained that many Americans expected war with Spain within the year. This plan, Burr hinted, had the tacit approval of President Jefferson. Second, Burr and Wilkinson might have have planned to seize New Orleans, persuade Louisiana and Mississippi (and other Western states) to secede from the Union and form a separate confederacy. This, the Spanish minister informed Madrid, was the real plan—Burr had already written a Declaration of Independence for Louisiana, and Wilkinson was in touch with revolutionary groups all over the West. Third, they might have planned not only to carve themselves an empire out of the West, but to invade the East, seize Washington, eject Jefferson, and replace him with Burr. A few men claimed that Burr had spoken openly to them of doing so, though not even Burr's enemies, of whom there were many, believed him capable of so wild a scheme.

One thing is certain. Burr talked too much. He loved to shroud his plans in mystery, allowing his rhetoric and his sense of the dramatic to carry him away. He was an extremely persuasive man with the ability to fit his arguments to the temper of the listener, and he therefore found plenty of men ready to listen. To the spirited, he hinted at military glory to be won in action against the Dons. To the conservative, he stressed the profits to be gained from sales of new land. To the ambitious, he spoke of the titles, honors, and positions of authority that might be distributed under a new government. Most of all he talked, until it was evident to everybody that something big was brewing in the West, and that Burr was behind it, though nobody could quite place a finger exactly on what it was. Jefferson knew, for he read the papers and received warnings from prominent Western politicians, but because most of the warnings came from Federalists and Burr was a Republican, Jefferson tended to disregard them.

Burr, on his trip down the Ohio in 1805, was looking for men like Blennerhassett—men with some money, modest ambitions, and the need for more money. On the way from

Pittsburgh to Natchez he stopped frequently, buying boats and supplies on credit, enlisting "recruits" for the mysterious "expedition" with purpose veiled and destination vague. In August of 1806 he was back at Blennerhassett's Island again, with his daughter, Theodosia, and her husband, Governor Joseph Alston of South Carolina. The combined charm of the three was too much for Blennerhassett.

Burr could have moved a stone to enthusiasm; Theodosia was perhaps the most accomplished woman of her time; Alston was a smooth, courtly, very wealthy Southern gentleman. After a day or so of talk, Blennerhassett readily fell in with their plan, which, as he understood it, was to recruit an army to invade Mexico, seize as much of it as possible, and set up a new nation. Jefferson approved of the idea, Blennerhassett was assured, and Burr had heard that two thousand Catholic priests in Mexico were working in his behalf. After the successful *coup*, Burr would be made king, Theodosia queen, and to those who qualified would be given land, titles of nobility, and positions of power at Court. In Louisiana, talk was heard of seceding from the Union, Burr admitted, but this was no concern of his. He would neither encourage nor discourage Louisiana's secession though, if Louisiana seceded, certain benefits would obviously accrue to his new Mexican empire.

Blennerhassett seems to have been thoroughly bedazzled. Burr visited a few prominent men about Marietta, did some recruiting, and moved on, after letting contracts for fifteen bateaux and a large keelboat—Blennerhassett to pay the bills. While Burr paused at Chillicothe and Cincinnati looking for more support, Blennerhassett spread the word. At the signal from Burr (who presumably waited for one from Wilkinson, or vice versa) all the recruits, who were scattered through Pennsylvania, Ohio, Virginia, Kentucky, and Tennessee, were to rendezvous at selected points and begin to move down the Ohio, joining Burr's command somewhere above New Orleans. Blennerhassett's Island was to be the eastern meeting point.

Everybody talked too much. More and more letters came to Jefferson, more and more newspapers speculated about

Burr's plans, while Wilkinson, in Louisiana, shuddered at every fresh bit of gossip. First, his and Burr's chances for success depended on a war between the United States and Spain—or at least continued tension—but Spanish-American relations seemed improving daily. That the administration in Washington would encourage an expedition against a nation (if such were the aim) with whom it was currently working out a peace was highly unlikely. Second, Burr had set rumors flying, all over the country, with Wilkinson's name prominently attached to them. The general was in no position to be investigated, particularly since the salary he drew from Spain might be highly embarrassing to explain. Wilkinson therefore quietly began disassociating himself from Burr. If Burr did succeed, it would not be too late for the general to declare himself in the game. If Burr's prospects looked bad, the general could divulge the whole scheme, lay the blame on Burr, and take bows for his own patriotism.

While Burr moved slowly toward New Orleans, Blennerhassett worked feverishly at home. He wrote a series of articles for the Marietta *Ohio Gazette,* pointing out the grievances of the West and intimating that some decisive action was overdue. He talked expansively to his neighbors, supervised boat-building, and laid in supplies for an army, offering recruits twelve dollars a month, clothes, provisions, and one hundred and fifty acres of free land in the "new territory." He told the Hendersons, a prominent Ohio family (or so they later swore and Blennerhassett denied) that Burr's expedition would seize New Orleans, declare Louisiana a sovereign state, and offer to confederate with Kentucky, Tennessee, and Mississippi. At the same time, Burr was telling Senator John Smith in Cincinnati that the expedition intended to invade Mexico, and that both British and American navies had promised to support him. A few days later Burr told Andrew Jackson in Tennessee that war with Spain was so close he was recruiting soldiers, and needed Jackson's help in attracting Tennessee riflemen to the ranks. Burr also purchased a large tract of land on the Ouachita River, called the Bastrop

Lands; the tract's title was extremely cloudy. Burr made only a down payment, but at least he could now say, in answer to questions, that he was simply recruiting settlers.

By this time Jefferson was well aware that something was shaping in the West. Jo Daviess, the United States Attorney in Kentucky, wrote that he had evidence to show "that all the Western territories are the object of the scheme—and finally all the region of the Ohio—the plot is laid wider thán you imagine." But Daviess was a devoted admirer of the late Alexander Hamilton and therefore politically suspect. Still, the amount of evidence and gossip was alarming, and so, finally, in late 1806, Jefferson took the matter up with his Cabinet. It was agreed to notify the Governors of Ohio, Indiana, Mississippi, and New Orleans, as well as all United States District Attorneys, to keep watch on Burr and to arrest him or any of his men if they committed any overt culpable acts. Jefferson also sent out a private investigator named John Graham to follow Burr's trail.

Actually, the Federal government had nothing substantial on Burr. For Burr to plan a filibustering expedition into Mexico was illegal, but no absolute evidence existed that he did plan one and besides, some support for the idea was to be found among prominent men. If Burr were fomenting internal rebellion, that was different—but again there was no real evidence for a treason charge, though Jefferson would have liked dearly to find it. Jefferson was understandably reluctant to make a martyr out of a political rival who obviously had a good many friends in the West. Therefore Jefferson waited.

In October, 1806, Blennerhassett and Burr met in Kentucky. They returned to the Island for a brief stay, then Burr left for Mississippi. In Kentucky, however, where Jo Daviess had been gathering evidence, Burr was arrested and held for trial. Because he had powerful friends and a good lawyer, young Henry Clay, the Grand Jury quickly discharged Burr, finding in his actions "nothing improper or injurious to the interest of the Government of the United States or contrary to the laws thereof." This was a triumph for Burr, but his last. Wilkinson, hearing rumors that Jefferson intended to remove him as Governor of Upper Louisiana, was nearly ready to give the plan away. Graham, Jefferson's private investigator, visited the garrulous Blennerhassett, who talked very freely about his and Burr's plans, and after Graham interviewed a dozen or so others, he reported to Jefferson that Burr's expedition was very likely aimed at New Orleans.

In November the whole scheme began to fall apart. Burr gave the signal. His recruits in Ohio and Pennsylvania—only thirty of them—converged on Blennerhassett's Island to begin the down-river movement. But Graham had also talked to Governor Tiffin of Ohio. Burr and Blennerhassett, Graham informed the Governor, had a force of thirteen hundred men ready to move on New Orleans, seize the Treasury there and establish a new government under the protection of some European power. Tiffin, extremely nervous and upset, ordered out the militia to seize Blennerhassett's boats and as many of his men as they could. Blennerhassett escaped to Kentucky just in time, leaving his wife to follow; the militiamen therefore missed their quarry. The weather was cold and wet, the militia soldiers were inexperienced and a little scared, and whiskey flowed rather freely as they searched the Island. As a result, they did some damage to the castle, a great deal of damage to the grounds, and frightened Mrs. Blennerhassett by their boisterousness.

Blennerhassett and his men floated down the Ohio while Burr collected another group in Kentucky and Tennessee; the two groups were to meet at the mouth of the Cumberland. The business was tricky, for both Ohio and Kentucky had issued warrants for the arrest of Burr and Blennerhassett, yet, by a combination of speed and luck, they made it. Drilling the men on the flatboat decks, Burr took his band of about seventy recruits down the Mississippi to a point some thirty miles above Natchez. But he did not know, nor did Blennerhassett (who found the trip miserably cold) that the scheme had blown up. Wilkinson, in a remarkable letter to Jefferson, had notified the President that Burr's design was "to seize New Orleans, revolutionize the territory, and carry an expedition against Mexico by Vera Cruz." The patriotic general, however, had already warned Governor Claiborne of New Orleans of the conspiracy and was carefully watching Burr. This was enough for Jefferson. In January, 1807, he notified Congress that Aaron Burr had two objects, joint or separate, both illegal—to sever the Union, and to attack Mexico. Orders were issued for the arrest of Aaron Burr and all his ringleaders.

Burr learned of the warrant for his arrest through a stray copy of a Natchez newspaper. Confused, worried, unable to comprehend Wilkinson's act of betrayal, Burr went to Natchez for confirmation of this news and found it all too true. He had good friends in Mississippi, but nevertheless there was a Federal warrant for his arrest—and there was one for Blennerhassett, too—that could not be disregarded. Burr could do nothing but surrender. Mississippi was filled with Federalists who disliked Jefferson and who had no love for the Spanish. Because Burr claimed that his only aim was to attack Spanish territory, they fêted him as a hero. Balls were held in his honor, with much drinking of toasts and a great deal of social activity. On January 30 Special Agent Graham came into Natchez, hoping to get some sort of statement from Burr, who rejected the whole idea of a "conspiracy" and spoke of settling the Bastrop Lands. For Graham to believe that a man of Burr's shrewdness expected to capture New Orleans or invade Mexico with fewer than a hundred green, ill-equipped adventurers was indeed difficult.

On February 2, 1807, the Supreme Court of Mississippi Territory, Judges Rodney and Bruin presiding, met in Washington, Mississippi, to hear Aaron Burr answer his bill of indictment. Burr, surrounded by well-wishers, was confident to the point of arrogance. He had reason to be, for the following day the Grand Jury simply threw the charges out of court, remarking in the process that they found the arrests to have been made "without warrant . . . and without other lawful authority." Then Judge Rodney did an unusual thing. He refused to release Burr, binding him over from day to day, and Burr thought he knew why. A report was out that a military patrol was on its way from Louisiana to seize him. If he fell into Wilkinson's hands, he was finished. Burr therefore notified his followers, patiently waiting in the flatboats, to sell what they could and take to the woods. Burr himself, though still under bond, then set out for Georgia, followed by a Governor's proclamation labelling him as a fugitive from justice.

Blennerhassett and three others were seized with Burr, arraigned, and released on bond. When the case against Burr collapsed, all five were discharged and Blennerhassett started home, ill, depressed, "with a headache too heavy to ride with." Someone stole his valise in Tennessee, and when he arrived in Lexington, Kentucky, he was suffering from mosquito bites and a bad cold. The news from home was bad. Creditors hounded his wife, the Castle had been attached for debt, his slaves strolled about unsupervised, and two of them had been appropriated by neighbors. He had no money to repair the damage done by the drunken militiamen. Several things had been stolen. Worst of all, he was arrested in Lexington in civil processes growing out of his endorsement of some of Burr's bills and, while he languished in Lexington jail, word arrived from Washington that both he and Burr were under Federal indictment for treason and high misdemeanor. Henry Clay tried to obtain release of Blennerhassett but failed and, in July, Deputy United States Marshal Meade and a five-man guard started out with him for Richmond, Virginia, to bring him to trial. Aaron Burr, captured at Fort Stoddert, was already there, in jail. "Tell the boys," Blennerhassett wrote his wife, "by small and cautious advances. Do not grieve for my situation, as I am not at all discouraged. I feel conscious of all want of law or evidence to convict me. . . ."

He had not much cause for optimism. Jefferson, his mind made up, was determined to crush Burr and Burr's confederates once and for all. Fortunately for Burr and Blennerhassett, Chief Justice John Marshall liked Jefferson no more than Jefferson liked Burr, and the government's case had to rest primarily on the unreliable Wilkinson, who was not at all enthusiastic about testifying. The government could present very little substantial evidence of treason, and Marshall, whatever his politics, was a knowledgeable lawyer. In the weeks before the actual trial, Jefferson and his subordinates bent every effort to obtain better evidence, concentrating on the Blennerhassett Island conference of December, 1806, which the prosecution hoped to prove treasonable. To Blennerhassett it was intimated that if he could give helpful evidence to the government's attorneys, "nothing he should ask would be refused him."

The trial opened on May 22, 1807, Judges Marshall and Griffin on the bench. Burr had beside him a tremendous array of legal talent—Edmund Randolph, Washington's secretary of state; John Wickham and Benjamin Botts, two of Virginia's best lawyers; and Luther Martin of Maryland, who had been a delegate to both the Continental Congress and the Constitutional Convention. The prosecution's attorneys were less able—Attorney General Caesar Rodney, who did little in the case; George Hay, Monroe's son-in-law; William Wirt, a flowery orator, but little else, and Alexander Macrae of Virginia. The reluctant Wilkinson took twenty-four days to reach Richmond, during which both sides polished their briefs.

As the trial opened, the government asked first for the treason charge against Burr. The defense contended that, to make the charge valid, it must be proved that Burr overtly committed acts of war, in the presence of two witnesses, against the United States. This was extremely difficult to establish without Wilkinson's help, and he was glad to help. After he testified, the Grand Jury reported out indictments for treason and high misdemeanor against Burr and Blennerhassett. Though Wilkinson's testimony left much to be desired, and though he was clearly terrified lest he himself be indicted, it sufficed. The general impressed nobody. Crusty John Randolph, the foreman of the jury, said "there was scarcely a variance of opinion among us as to his guilt, and [we] hoped they could try Wilkinson next." The examination of witnesses, nearly sixty of them, continued for more than three weeks. On August 31 Marshall delivered his opinion, which cited more cases, authorities, and treatises than all his other decisions put together. For him to read it took three hours, and when he had made an end very little remained of the government's case against Burr. The next day the jury returned a verdict of not guilty and the indictment against Blennerhassett was also dropped.

Blennerhassett, lodged in Richmond jail while Burr's trial dragged on, rapidly lost confidence in him. The testimony of various witnesses shook Blennerhassett, for, clearly, Burr had told far too many different stories to far too many persons. After "spending much time in painful reflections on the state of my affairs with Burr," he wrote his wife, he realized that the "giddy adventurer" had duped him badly. The trial convinced Blennerhassett that Burr was "as careless with his facts as with his religion," so that "no two persons of his acquaintance understand him alike." Burr was a "strange man," Blennerhassett concluded, "wearing always his mysterious mask, with which he has sought, and still seeks, to disguise his hints." More than anything else Blennerhassett worried over Burr's debts to him—twenty-nine hundred dollars in cash, four thousand dollars in endorsed notes, and more than twenty thousand dollars expended on boats, equipment, and supplies.

Jefferson was not through with Burr nor with Blennerhassett. Though the treason charge had fallen through, the two men were still under indictment for high misdemeanor, based on a 1794 act of Congress that forbade anyone to plot a military expedition against a foreign power with whom the United States was at peace. An excellent chance existed that the government could make this charge stick, for Burr had escaped the treason charge by implying that his expedition was aimed against Mexico rather than the United States. Blennerhassett's own brief to the court, in fact, stated plainly that as both he and Burr believed war with Spain imminent, they also believed that an expedition into Mexico violated no law, though Blennerhassett admitted that Burr had never actually explained this matter of legality to him in so many words. Nevertheless, after a week of testimony, the jury declared Burr not guilty, leaving unanswered for posterity the interesting question—if Burr was not guilty of planning to invade Louisiana, nor of planning to invade Mexico, what had he planned to do with his little army?

The charges against Blennerhassett again collapsed with Burr's acquittal. Indictments were still out against them in Ohio and Kentucky, but these were never pressed and to all purposes the two men were now free. Though Burr, Blennerhassett reported, was in high spirits, "busy in speculations on reorganizing his projects," the Irishman was thoroughly disillusioned. Burr had to defend himself against civil suits to the amount of thirty-six thousand dollars; he was still under indictment for murder in New Jersey, as an aftermath of Hamilton's death; his reputation had suffered badly during his two trials. Whatever the jury's verdict, public opinion still considered him a traitor, and Baltimore citizens burned him and Blennerhassett in effigy, along with John Marshall and Luther Martin for good measure.

Still Blennerhassett hoped to get some of his money back, for he was convinced that Burr had hidden, somewhere, the major share of the funds raised for the expedition. In early September Blennerhassett received word from Ireland that he might have a legal claim on a West Indian estate left by a distant relative. The estate, the solicitors said, brought an annual income of some six thousand pounds a year; this prospect might serve as a means, Blennerhassett hoped, to fool the wily Burr. Therefore, Blennerhassett told his wife, he would play on Burr's vanity. Burr talked of going to England. If Blennerhassett promised Burr letters of introduction to "the first circles" of London society, and if he let Burr know of the West Indian estate, he was sure Burr would repay his debt to keep in favor. The ruse was "a little painful,"

Blennerhassett wrote to his wife, but he considered it justifiable "to bring even a bad man into the path of his duty by artifice." Blennerhassett found an opportunity to mention the matter to Burr before they left Richmond on their way north. Burr immediately saw the point. "[Burr] could not restrain his transports," when he heard of the six thousand pounds, Blennerhassett observed—and the two tacitly agreed that, when Burr paid what he owed Blennerhassett, Burr would receive the letters of introduction. However, when the two reached Philadelphia and Burr had never mentioned payment, Blennerhassett resolved to have it out. Yes, Burr explained smoothly, he did remember the debt, but he had never looked into the matter of payment. He would, soon. Blennerhassett pressed him, Burr lost his temper, and harsh words passed. He had no money, Burr said angrily, nor friends from whom to borrow. He was going to Europe and Blennerhassett could sue and be damned. "I perceived he could give me no hope," Blennerhassett wrote sadly, and the two parted. A few days later Blennerhassett notified Burr by letter that he would get no letters of introduction to London society. "I feel that I could not solicit their attentions to you as my friend," he wrote, "and I should wish to decline doing so on any other ground."

With Mrs. Blennerhassett and her sons in Natchez, her husband began the long weary trip to Mississippi, sick at heart. When he stopped at Marietta in December, he found Blennerhassett's Castle a shambles, his library and laboratory stripped, the gardens trampled, the orchards ruined by floods. Vandals had defaced the walls; the lush hangings and paintings were gone, and even the window casings had been ripped out that the lead sash weights could be stolen. He hired a lawyer to try to reclaim as much of his property as possible, but the lawyer could not do much. After making arrangements to put the island up for sale, Blennerhassett left for Kentucky. In Jeffersonville they put him in jail on the old charges of debt, released him after a few days, and allowed him to go on to

Mississippi. There he rejoined his family in early 1808, about the time Aaron Burr sailed for Europe.

Harman Blennerhassett was a broken man, no longer capable of making decisions. His wife, as charming and intelligent as ever, took over family leadership. By pure luck, they received three hundred pounds from Baron Ventry, the last installment on the sale of Blennerhassett's Irish estates, and a Kentuckian bought Blennerhassett's Island as a place to raise hemp. (Three years later the Castle burned to the ground.) With this money, Margaret Blennerhassett managed to make a payment on a thousand acres of cotton land in Claiborne County, with about two hundred acres under cultivation. She was a good manager, and her husband, in his own way, tried to help, but they began in debt and could never struggle out. The money he had poured into Burr's schemes weighed on Blennerhassett's mind until the thought of it became almost an obsession—if he could only reclaim a part of the money, it might be enough to put the plantation on a financially sound basis.

Blennerhassett brought suit against Burr in the Louisiana courts, but Burr was in Europe and out of reach. Blennerhassett therefore wrote to Theodosia's husband, Joseph Alston, who had been deep in Burr's schemes, but whom the trial had never touched. In August, 1806, during conversations at Blennerhassett's Island, he reminded Alston, Alston had promised Blennerhassett to serve as security for any loans made to Burr. Since there was no way of collecting from Burr, would Alston therefore pay Blennerhassett fifteen thousand dollars at once and the remainder of seventy-five hundred dollars within a year? Governor Alston, he added, might be interested to know that Blennerhassett had completed the manuscript of a book that explained in detail the parts played by all connected with the Burr "conspiracy." If a draft for fifteen thousand dollars arrived within a reasonable time, he might decide not to publish the book. This was blackmail, and Blennerhassett knew it. Bitter, desperate, neck-deep in debt, he could think of no other way. Alston never bothered to reply.

Burr spent four years in Europe trying to raise money for his plan to split Mexico from Spain. The British, who gave him little encouragement because Spain was currently fighting Napoleon, finally ordered him out of England. After some months in Sweden, Burr went to Paris. There Napoleon refused to see him. When the French police refused him a passport to the United States and the American consul gave him no help, Burr, his money dwindling until he was near starvation, stayed on in Paris. Finally, in July of 1811, the French relented, allowing him to leave for Amsterdam and a New York-bound ship. The British captured the ship, took all his possessions, and left him stranded in London until the spring of 1812, when he sailed for New York.

On receiving news of Burr's return, Blennerhassett immediately wrote him a letter. For fifteen thousand dollars, he offered, he would drop any claims on Burr and withhold his book, now tentatively titled "A Review of the Projects and Intrigues of Aaron Burr." But Burr, poor, alone, and unhappy, was past caring. His daughter, Theodosia, the one person in life he really loved, was lost at sea. His name was already synonymous with "traitor," and nothing Blennerhassett could do would damage his reputation more than the Jeffersonians had already succeeded in doing. The two men exchanged a few sharp letters, until Burr broke off the correspondence.

The Embargo of 1812 ruined the cotton market—and the Blennerhassetts. They kept the plantation until 1817, sinking deeper in debt each year until they were at last forced to sell it, to satisfy their creditors. Of how they lived in the following two years, spent next in New York City, no record is known. In 1819, after corresponding with some Canadian acquaintances, Blennerhassett moved his family to Montreal on the promise of a Canadian judicial appointment that never came through. He had been admitted years before to the Irish bar, though he had never practiced; when he opened a law office of his own in Montreal, few clients came. Mrs. Blennerhassett, with all her gentlewoman's education, worked at odd jobs to keep the household together. The West Indian estate still taunted them with hope and, as a last resort, they gathered together enough money and sent Blennerhassett to Ireland in 1822 in pursuit of the supposed inheritance. He had no luck at all. His solicitors informed him that his claim, tenuous at best, had been outlawed some years before. Lord Ross, who held the estate, was a hard, powerful man not likely to make any settlement. Blennerhassett tried to start a boys' school; he tried to publish music; he applied for a post as envoy to Colombia. Everything failed. So Blennerhassett wrote letters, begging his friends for a job—any job, even in India—in government service. Lord Anglesey, his schoolmate, had nothing for him in the Office of Ordnance in London, nor any time to see him. Lord Bathhurst had nothing; neither did Lord Courtney or the Marquis of Wellesley. Blennerhassett's letters were pathetic—the letters of a man desperately trying to keep his self-respect while on his knees, but all his former friends seemed deaf.

Blennerhassett spent three lean years in Dublin and London, living on borrowed pittances, existing on the fringes of the society of the rich and powerful. In 1825 he returned to Canada and took his wife and two younger sons back to England with him. Harman Junior, his eldest boy, who was already turning into an alcoholic, went south, joined the army, and disappeared. In Somerset, the Blennerhassetts lived with the impoverished romanticist's unmarried sister until his failing health made necessary his removal to the Isle of Jersey, where, it was hoped, sea air presumably would improve his lungs. He could do no work; the family therefore existed on the sister's pension. In 1830 they moved to Guernsey. There Harman Blennerhassett, aged 63, died of a stroke on February 1st, 1831.

His indomitable wife came to New York in 1842, six years after Aaron Burr died, to present Congress a claim for the damage done to her home thirty-six years earlier by the drunken Ohio militia. Henry Clay agreed to sponsor her petition, but she died before he could get it out of committee.

Burr denied to the end of his life that he intended to conspire against the United States; as for the accusation that he hoped to separate Louisiana from the Union, he would "as soon have thought of taking possession of the moon." But the taint of treason had touched him, as it had Blennerhassett, and neither could ever erase the mark as long as he lived. Still, it is clear that Burr plotted something—and that the something was technically illegal, at least—though thirty years later a different administration in Washington considered filibustering in Texas high patriotism rather than high misdemeanor. Agile James Wilkinson landed on his feet, escaped a courtmartial by a hairsbreadth in 1814, and spent the last years of his life in Mexico, still trying to promote a revolution. If Aaron Burr deserved punishment for whatever he "conspired" to do, he got it. Ignored, abused, shunned, "severed from the human race," as he put it, he lived out his declining years in sadness. But the more pathetic figure in the affair is Harman Blennerhassett, the innocent led astray by men far too clever and subtle for his simple nature to comprehend. He was not qualified by nature to be a good conspirator, nor did he have any business being one—he simply paid the bills and tagged behind Burr, huddled on a flatboat in the Mississippi mists, with dreams of empires and titles ringing in his head.

Blennerhassett was not a remarkable man, apart from his adventures, nor a brilliant one. He was merely a pleasant, impractical person who asked very little of life beyond the pleasures of home and meditation. Blennerhassett belonged in his library among his books, in his laboratory among his instruments, or in his beloved orchard among his flowering trees. Many times, in the roach-infested jails of America or the scrubby rooms of Dublin and London, he must have cursed the day that Aaron Burr, with his charming manners, smooth tongue, and broad white hat, first saw Blennerhassett's Castle rise into view across the broad reaches of the Ohio river. To die broken and disillusioned on the lonely Channel Islands, far from his Eden, must have seemed to Harman Blennerhassett a high price to pay for a little misdirected ambition.

TWO TRAVELLING MEN

★

John Ledyard

Edward Bonney

John Ledyard

★

JOHN LEDYARD, the third of that name, was born in Groton, Connecticut, in 1751. His grandfather was a London merchant who had emigrated to Long Island in 1717 in search of security and fortune, both of which he found in modest measure. His father, a sea captain in the coastal trade, died at thirty-five, leaving a daughter and three sons, of whom John was the eldest. Grandfather Ledyard, who later moved to Hartford, Connecticut, did not get along well with his sea-going son; they disagreed, argued, and finally became estranged. The old man was rigid but just, and when his son died and the widow remarried, Grandfather Ledyard tried to make amends by offering his help to the rapidly disintegrating family. John the Third went into his grandfather's household at Hartford. William, the sea captain's second son, had the promise of the family farm at Groton. The two other grandchildren—a boy and a girl—remained with their mother at their new home on Long Island.

Young John Ledyard liked and respected his grandfather, a man of some standing in the Hartford community and, on his advice, planned to enter the law. Had his grandfather lived longer, John might well have become a lawyer and the world thereby lost a wanderer. But when Grandfather Ledyard died, young John was shunted to the home of an uncle, Thomas Seymour, of Hartford, who tried to keep the boy reading law. Seymour persisted until it was perfectly clear that the legal profession was not for John nor he for it. Young John was bright enough, mentally alert; he was deeply interested in exploring the woods and sailing a boat on the river—

and thoroughly uninterested in law. If not the bar for John, Seymour reasoned, then the clergy—there were not many other professions open to a New England boy of good family and no bank account. John, who seemed indecisive and rootless, did not appear to care much what he did, preferring simply to fritter away his time in walking and fishing.

John Ledyard, twenty-two years old, was apparently going nowhere. Fortunately, Grandfather Ledyard had a good friend in the Reverend Eleazar Wheelock, founder of an Indian school in Connecticut that he had moved to a new site in New Hampshire in 1770. At Dartmouth, as the school was now renamed in honor of a noble' British contributor to Wheelock's treasury, Wheelock intended to train earnest young men as missionaries to the Indians. This might be a suitable training place for young John Ledyard, thought Seymour, for John was neither prepared for such places as Yale or Harvard nor eager to enroll at either. No record shows that he was enthusiastic about the prospects of missionary life, but in 1772 he nevertheless reported to Wheelock at Dartmouth to begin his studies.

Eleazar Wheelock, the students later sang,

Was a very pious man
Who went into the wilderness to teach the Indian.

Ledyard was not perceptibly pious, as Wheelock quickly discovered. Ledyard was much less energetic at his books than at organizing plays and acting in them—not really the best training for a novice missionary—but he was not a bad student nor a rebellious one. He was simply uninterested in books. What did interest him was the forest, and Dartmouth, at the edge of a vast wilderness stretching far away into the west and north, was no place for a young man who had just discovered the fascination of the unknown. Ledyard spent more time in the woods than in the classroom, and not long after his arrival at college, he simply disappeared into Indian country. He stayed away three months, travelling among the

Six Nations, picking up smatterings of Indian language, and penetrating probably as far as the villages of the Canadian tribes.

Wheelock was furious at Ledyard when he returned, bearded and brown, with tales of the great wild country to the north. Wheelock not only felt a certain personal responsibility for the young man because of friendship with the elder Ledyard and Thomas Seymour; he also felt that John's sudden French leave hardly set a good example for other Dartmouth students. Ledyard explained plausibly that he was primarily concerned with preparing himself for missionary work by acquainting himself with Indians at first hand, but Wheelock suspected (probably rightly) that his motives were less educational than recreational. Wheelock let John off with a reprimand, but it was too late. The taste of adventure was strong in Ledyard's mouth; he knew now that missionary work was not for him.

In the spring of 1773 John Ledyard left Dartmouth for good. He did it somewhat spectacularly by chopping his own dugout from a fifty-foot pine and floating down the Connecticut River to Hartford on the spring flood, ending the hazardous hundred-and-forty-mile trip at his uncle's home in Hartford. Thomas Seymour took him in again, a trifle disheartened, especially after Wheelock wrote to inform him that his nephew lacked "interest and diligence" and would very likely do poorly at any college. So young Ledyard, now almost twenty-four, was once again at loose ends.

Here Dr. Isaac Ledyard of Preston, Connecticut, a cousin, entered with advice. Still convinced that John had potentialities as a preacher, Isaac recommended that he continue to study for the clergy, but this time in private with some tolerant minister who understood his temperament. Without Wheelock's recommendation (which could hardly be expected) Isaac pointed out that it would be very difficult to find a Connecticut minister willing to accept so uncertain a pupil. However, on Long Island, where his mother lived and where theological principles were held a little more loosely than in New England, a sponsor might be discovered for him. Why not, Isaac suggested, find a job teaching school and study for the ministry, too? So Ledyard went to visit his mother and toured Long Island. Clergymen encouraged him and sent him along, one to another, but none wanted to accept responsibility for a young man with no recommendations and a cloudy record.

For New England boys, when everything else failed, there was always the sea. In New London, Connecticut, Ledyard accidentally met one Captain Deshon, a friend of his father's. Deshon's ship was leaving for the Mediterranean. He could use another seaman, no matter how green, and John Ledyard signed the log to ship out for the Barbary Coast. He learned fast and made a good sailor; he had great strength and tremendous physical vitality, though short of stature, and sea life toughened him considerably. He also found the sea as exciting and stimulating as the forests of New England. New lands and strange peoples fascinated him, and even the prosaic task of loading Spanish mules took on a certain romance when done under the lowering cliffs of Gibraltar. Here Deshon almost lost him. When Ledyard failed to return from a tour of the Rock, the Captain, after a search of several hours, found that Ledyard had been shanghaied as a recruit in the British army garrison. To get him released took a great deal of argument.

Ledyard made several more voyages and improved his rating as a sailor. He liked sea life, though advancement was slow and wages were small. Grandfather Ledyard, remembering England with the affection of the immigrant, often had told his grandchildren long stories of his British cousins, of their wealth, station, and standing in British society. If he could not make his fortune on one side of the Atlantic, John thought, he might on the other. Certainly the British Ledyards would be glad to help an American cousin; so, in early 1776, when his vessel touched at Portsmouth, he jumped ship and made his way to London to find the Ledyards. His grandfather's stories were true—the Ledyards were wealthy and socially prominent—but the London Ledyards had no interest whatever in fortune-hunting colonial relations, particularly in view of the day-to-day news that came from the colonies in early 1776.

Ledyard, purposelessly drifting about London, ran into one of the streaks of luck by which his life seems governed henceforth. Everybody knew of Captain James Cook, the explorer who had already made two epochal voyages into the unknown Pacific and who, Ledyard now heard, was preparing for a third voyage, even then taking on recruits. Ledyard traced Captain Cook to the rooms of the Royal Society and presented himself for an interview. Cook liked the eager young American. He liked Americans anyway and, although his crew was already complete, he pointed out to Ledyard that the Marine detachment that was to sail with him was not yet complete. In a matter of hours, Ledyard, with the grade of corporal, was in the uniform of the Royal Marines.

Cook had two ships, the *Resolution* and the *Discovery*, with which he planned to sail around Africa and India into the South Pacific, across to New Albion (the northwestern coast of America) and into those northern waters already touched by Juan de Fuca and Bering. Fuca had thought there might be gold and silver there, possibly an opening to the fabled Northwest Passage. At any rate, both the British government and the Royal Society wanted charts and reports of these dimly-known areas of the northern Pacific Ocean.

Cook and the *Resolution*, with Corporal Ledyard aboard, left England in July, 1776 (news of events in Philadelphia had not yet reached England) to rendezvous with Captain Clerke and the *Discovery* in December off the Cape of Good Hope. The two ships then sailed on to Tasmania, to New Zealand, skirted the barren edge of the Antarctic, and pushed into the Polynesian island chains of the South Pacific. Ledyard was neither a trained scientist nor a philosopher, but he had a speculative mind and knew the importance of what he saw. He observed everything—the strange stone-age aborigines, the exotic costumes of the islanders, the vividly-colored trees and flowers, the scar-faced cannibals, the swift birdlike canoes, and hundreds of other wonders that he described in careful and voluminous notes in his journal. Lieutenant Gore, a friendly Virginian Marine officer, helped him acquire additional information from those who had been there before. Even ramrod-stiff William Bligh, Cook's sailing master (who as a captain was to make a different kind of storied voyage in the South Pacific a decade later) unbent enough to help the young corporal with his notes.

At Tongataboo, Ledyard met a native girl, learned some of the soft native language (jotting in his notes that it resembled Iroquois) and had the backs of his hands tattooed. At Tahiti he found a paradise of tropic beauty that overwhelmed him. At the Societies he felt something of the thrill of real discovery, for here Cook found a new island group which he named after Lord Sandwich, the heartily-disliked First Lord of the Admiralty. The Cook expedition then plunged into the northern Pacific, beating a long slow way into colder waters and violent storms. Finally, in March, 1778, the ships touched New Albion in foul, freezing weather. They sailed up the green, rocky coast to de Fuca's straits (learning of no gold, no Northwest Passage, but only of Indians, snow, and furs), around Vancouver Island, and into Alaskan waters.

The Pacific Northwest, where Cook spent several weeks, was the last unexplored portion of the North American continent accessible by water. The Russians, who had crossed Bering Strait into Alaska, claimed much of the area, but the land itself was virtually unknown and what boundaries existed were vague and uncertain. Even if he were unable to locate the western exit of a Northwest Passage, Cook had instructions to explore and survey the region as fully as he could in preparation of a possible British claim. The Indians were friendly and loaded with furs (this, too, was valuable information), and the British government was not averse to knowing the extent of Russian penetration of the area. Therefore Cook sent out exploring parties when the situation called for it.

John Ledyard was fortunate to be on one of these. At Unalaska Island Cook's men met a few Aleuts who wore trousers and asked for rum (sure signs of contact with white civilization) and when the Indians indicated that white men were on the other side of the island, Cook sent Ledyard to investigate. Ledyard, alone, unarmed, carrying a bottle of brandy, went up an icy river in a kayak, slogged across a barren and marshy plain on foot and crossed a large bay. On the far side of the island he found two white men living in a crude hut—Russians sent out from an Alaskan post to gather skins from the Aleuts. Because they spoke no English and Ledyard no Russian, he gathered little helpful information from them, but in honor of their British guest the Russians provided for him what was surely one of the most fearsome banquets ever faced by any explorer—dried sea horse, smoked bear, salmon fried in oil, boiled whale, and rum.

After Ledyard's return to the ship, a Russian official visited the *Discovery*. He was affable and pleasant, gave out very few data about the fur trade, and seemed reluctant to give Cook any help on what lay farther north. It was no secret, however, that the Russian fur trade was good, very good. Cook's men bought prime skins of "foxes, sables, hares, marmosets, ermines, weazles [sic], bears, wolves, deer, moose, otters, beavers, and a species of weazle called the glutton," Ledyard recorded, for fantastically low prices. Nobody had ever seen furs in such profusion as this, not even in the best days of the Hudson Bay Company.

Cook sailed northward into Bering Strait, found no trace of a Northwest Passage, ran into heavy ice, and turned back toward the South Pacific. Unlike some explorers of his day, James Cook was a humane and sympathetic man in his dealings with natives, but the Sandwich Islanders, on his return visit, caused him trouble. An argument over a stolen ship's boat led to a show of force, language difficulties caused misunderstanding and, almost by accident, Captain Cook died at the hands of a native mob. At Cook's death, command of the expedition passed to Clerke, who turned his ships toward

Kamchatka on the Russian coast. Ice again stopped their progress, Clerke died suddenly, and James King took charge of the expedition. King turned toward Japan, then worked his way along the port cities of the China coast.

Chinese merchants, Ledyard noted in his diary, would pay almost anything for furs. Since skins bought in Alaska as souvenirs could be sold without haggling for thousandfold profits, every man in the crew quickly cleared out his locker. A prime sea-otter skin purchased for a shilling in the Pacific Northwest brought thirty guineas; one sailor sold for twenty pounds a skin that cost him fourpence. The price differential was so great that one could, Ledyard calculated, buy furs from the Russians at their price and resell them in China for triple profits. One shipload of furs, delivered on the China coast, could make a man's fortune for life—a fact that Ledyard and many others most certainly noted and remembered.

At Canton the expedition received news that Britain and its American colonies were at war. England and Connecticut were far away, and his journals contain no evidence that Ledyard held any strong feelings on the subject of war or of independence; furthermore, it was hardly tactful for a Royal Marine on a British ship to express seditious opinions, even in the privacy of one's diary. King brought the ships around India and Africa and arrived in home port in October, 1780, after a voyage of four years, two months, and twenty-two days. Ledyard and the other marines went back to the routine of barracks life, and worst of all, without his multivolumed journal with all its careful notes. But one account of the voyage would be written, explained Captain King—his own official version—and he therefore confiscated all diaries and journals.

Though Ledyard had taken the King's shilling and had displayed no evidences of revolutionary sympathies, he was still suspect as an American colonial. The British intended to release no Royal Marine who might turn up in Continental ranks, so Ledyard therefore stayed in barracks for nearly two years. He would have liked to escape, but the risks were obvious and barracks life was still more attractive than some dank British prison. Two years of inactivity gave him plenty of time to think, particularly about the furs sold to the Chinese; he could not erase from his memory the picture of the rainy, green coasts of the American Northwest. Fortunes were to be made there. New lands were there to see. Sometime during the long, dull months of barracks life he formed the plan that dominated the remainder of his life.

In spring of 1782, with the end of the war in sight, the British deemed it safe to assign ex-colonials to American duty, so Ledyard, assigned to a man-of-war, arrived in Long Island Sound in December, 1782. He promptly deserted. He visited his mother briefly at Southold (a risky business, because her boarding house was still filled with British officers) and then made his way to Hartford to his uncle's home. Here he spent four months reconstructing his lost journals from memory, producing a book which he sold to a local publisher for twenty guineas. It was a good book—the first American account of the unknown Pacific Northwest—though not very many read it. Ledyard had hoped that his stories of the new land and of the fur trade might arouse enough interest among New England speculators and merchants to warrant fitting out an expedition. In this hope he was badly disappointed.

The more he thought about it the more convinced John Ledyard became, and the bigger his plans. An expedition to the northern Pacific, properly organized and financed, would not only open up a tremendously lucrative fur trade but might also well lay the foundations for a new colony in the Northwest. Why not, he reasoned, establish a settlement on the Oregon coast, use it as a base for exploration inland, and then open up the whole western half of the continent? None really knew what lay between the Mississippi and the Pacific. Rumors told of huge forests, millions of acres of arable land, even of fabulous cities of gold left over from the days of Spanish adventurers. Whatever was there, the rewards to those who explored and exploited it were staggering to contemplate. Opening up the great unknown West, Ledyard wrote, could be "the greatest commercial enterprise that has ever been embarked on in this country." A full generation before it happened, John Ledyard saw the vision of the great American conquest of the West, and his imagination caught fire.

Ledyard, like other visionary promoters, found persons who were interested in his project but not interested enough to risk the necessary capital, particularly since the late war had made money scarce in New England. His proposition was simple. You filled a ship with gewgaws and trade goods (chiefly of iron, which the Northwest Indians and Eskimos would give almost anything to get), traded these for pelts, and then traded the furs to the Chinese at an outlandish profit, either for gold or oriental goods which could be resold in Europe or America at even greater profit. Except for outfitting a ship, the investment required was relatively small and tremendous profits were almost automatically assured. It is surprising, in retrospect, that Ledyard's idea of a quadrangular New England-Alaska-China-Europe trade did not find enthusiastic support from some entrepreneur backer, but Ledyard found none in Connecticut and went on to New York in search of some merchant willing to risk it.

The New Yorkers showed little enthusiasm. Like the Yankees, many of them already had heavy investments in the China trade and could see no reason to multiply their risks. Tiring of polite refusals, Ledyard moved to Philadelphia. There he finally managed to meet Robert Morris, supervisor of finance for the Continental Congress, founder of the Bank of North America, and probably the shrewdest financier in the new republic. A natural gambler himself, Morris recognized the potential profits attainable in Ledyard's plan. Morris thought it over in his hardheaded way, looked at the maps, and finally told Ledyard to go find a ship.

Ledyard went back to New England to comb the shipyards for a suitable vessel, a project he found more difficult than he had expected. One brig, offered at a low price, turned out to have a hull full of holes; another was so honeycombed with rot that it barely floated. And before Ledyard could find his ship, Morris sent word from Philadelphia that he felt compelled to withdraw his support. While he had faith in Ledyard and his expedition, Morris wrote, he simply did not have the necessary money readily available.

Ledyard was disappointed, naturally, but Morris' approval of his plan, even though the cash had not materialized, gave him confidence. Since Ledyard had learned by experience how difficult it was to find one man who had sufficient capital, Morris suggested that he try to organize a group of several moderately wealthy men into a stock company. With a recommendation from Morris as his introduction, Ledyard began once more his round of offices and banks. He found twelve rich merchants in Philadelphia who "expressed interest," though not enough to take the plunge. So Ledyard tried New York again, Boston, New London, Hartford, and Salem, and still had no good luck. "Sometimes elated with hope, sometimes depressed with disappointment and distress," he pursued rich men up and down the coast, the memory of those sixpenny furs ringing in his head. Eventually, with most of the American sources exhausted, Morris advised him to try France, where there were plenty of wealthy men interested in new trade routes.

Ledyard landed in July of 1784 at L'Orient, a French trading port where, Morris advised him, there might be merchants willing to listen to him. They listened so enthusiastically that Ledyard nearly refused to believe his ears. The plan was sound, the Frenchmen agreed; they would finance at least one ship, possibly two—but they must wait until the King's permission was assured, possibly until the following summer—"ah these buts!" wrote Ledyard, perhaps with a premonition. Still, there was nothing to do but wait, so Ledyard chafed through the months (in comparative luxury, since the Frenchmen supported him handsomely) using his time in locating a ship, calculating the cost of goods and of outfitting, and rounding up a crew. Suddenly, in February of 1785, the merchants simply backed out, with no warning and no explanation.

An American stranded in France had only one place to go,

and that was Paris. A lively American colony in Paris centered about Thomas Jefferson, who had lately replaced Franklin as American minister and was well-known for his interest in science and exploration. Jefferson liked Ledyard, introduced him into the proper circles, and listened with fascination to his tales of the Orient and the great Northwest. For a young American of Ledyard's charm to exist in Paris on little or nothing was not difficult; he was a welcome guest at salons, with his bright talk, his stories of Cook's expedition, and his tattooed hands. Meanwhile, he lived in cheap rooms in St. Germain, twelve miles out of the city, and walked to and fro daily to bedevil French bankers and American visitors with his project.

Jefferson's interest in Ledyard's plans was real. More than most men, the Virginian understood as Ledyard did the vast potentialities of the American West, and like Ledyard, Jefferson had imagination, daring, and plans of empire. As Ledyard pointed out, a European had discovered America, "but in the name of Amor Patriae, let a *native* explore its resources and boundaries"—a patriotic motivation that Jefferson also felt. Jefferson did not have capital, but he knew men who did. With the American minister's personal recommendation, Ledyard therefore relentlessly stalked the wealthy until he met John Paul Jones, another adventurer at loose ends in Paris.

Jones threw in with Ledyard's proposition at once. Jones had no liquid funds, but he did have a large amount of prize money due him for ships captured in the late war and brought into French ports. As soon as he collected this, he promised Ledyard, they could purchase at least two ships, perhaps more, buy furs in the Northwest, sell them in China for silk and tea, and pile up a fortune. Jones agreed to handle all the shipping problems; Ledyard would stay in the Northwest, develop a colony, and establish a chain of trading posts inland. There was no reason why they should not, Ledyard wrote, control the "entire trade of the Northwest within six or seven years!"

John Paul Jones, snarled in Gallic red tape, never got the

prize money, and Ledyard, having already survived more frustrations than most men meet in a lifetime, might have given up had not Jefferson's enthusiasm pulled him through. If Ledyard could find no ship to carry him to the northern Pacific, Jefferson suggested, why not go by land? "I suggested to him," Jefferson noted, "the enterprise of exploring the western part of our continent by passing through St. Petersburg to Kamchatka and procuring a passage thence in some of the Russian vessels to Nootka Sound, whence he might make his way across the continent. . . ." This meant going east to arrive west, a journey half-way around the world— across Europe and Asia, across the Bering Strait and down the Alaskan coast—but it *was* a way.

Ledyard, Jefferson commented, "eagerly embraced the proposition," wildly conceived though it was. Three years of frustration had prepared him for almost any plan that would land him on the northwestern coast of America, even if it required several thousand miles of travel over the Siberian wasteland. All Ledyard needed was a Russian passport, which Jefferson promised to obtain for him as soon as possible. Empress Catherine the Great, however, was in the Crimea on a long visit. St. Petersburg replied that nothing could be done until her return, though Jefferson pulled all the strings at the Russian Embassy in Paris while Ledyard sat in Paris, living on handouts and charm.

Weeks passed and Ledyard chafed at the delay, until he had a stroke of good luck in August, 1786. A Britisher in Paris informed him that a ship was soon to leave London for the north Pacific; in return for Ledyard's knowledge of Alaskan water, he believed, the captain would land him on the American coast free of charge. Within three days Ledyard was in London. There, somewhat to his surprise, he found the story perfectly true. Such a ship was leaving and the captain would, as agreed, drop him exactly where he wanted to land—on Nootka, Ledyard decided, whence he would strike east, cross the continent, and end his journey in Virginia. In preparation for a trip that would last at least three years, he equipped himself with a dog, an Indian pipe, and a hatchet, ready to face the American continent.

Moreover, the ship did leave London with Ledyard aboard. A few hours out in the North Sea, however, a naval vessel hove alongside, seized the ship's cargo, and ordered the captain back to London. There was some sort of customs trouble, the captain explained, and when the ship would leave again nobody knew, so John Ledyard was back in London, all his few belongings sequestered in customs, his pockets empty. For a full month he wandered about London again, looking for a ship, until his connection with Captain Cook's voyage gave him help when he needed it badly. Sir Joseph Banks of the Royal Society took an interest in him and helped make a purse of twenty guineas for him, enabling him to avoid starvation.

Jefferson's idea still seemed sound to Ledyard. Ledyard had very little money and no passport, but he decided that, if he could not get a Russian passport in either London or Paris, he might get one much more quickly in St. Petersburg itself. Therefore, in December, 1786, Ledyard took passage for Hamburg, went on to Copenhagen, and finally to Stockholm. The route to St. Petersburg lay across the Gulf of Bothnia by way of Abo in Finland, an easy boatride in summer and a short sledge ride across the ice in winter. But the winter of 1786-87 was a hard one in northern Europe; the ice was far too rough for sledge travel and too thick for ships. There was nothing to do, the Swedes said, except wait for spring.

Ledyard had waited too long to be stopped by fifty miles of ice. If there was no other way, he would reach St. Petersburg on his own two feet. So he decided to walk—six hundred miles north through Sweden into Lapland to the Arctic Circle, then south and east for six hundred miles more through Finland into Russia, all in the dead of the northern winter. The Swedes advised strongly against it. "I refuse," Ledyard replied, "to suppose that the seasons can triumph over the efforts of an honest man." In January, 1787, he left Stockholm on one of the epic walks in the history of exploration.

Ledyard had no maps, no knowledge of Swedish or Finnish,

very little money, and no more than a vague idea of the route to St. Petersburg. He got along with French and gestures, spending his nights with hospitable Swedes and Finns who were fascinated by this madman's journey. The weather was bitterly cold (forty below zero at times). The snows were tremendous. Snowblindness was a constant danger. The swampy lake district of Finland, the most hazardous part of his journey, almost killed him—he fell through the pond-ice twice and escaped frozen feet only by good luck and quick thinking. But he got through, and arrived in St. Petersburg with his boots worn out, on March 20, 1787, after a walk of nearly thirteen hundred miles in nine weeks. It was not such a bad experience, he decided. He had found nothing but friendliness for the traveller who had friendliness to give, and "upon the whole," he wrote Jefferson, "mankind used me well."

Though the Empress was still in the Crimea, the surprised Russians, a little awed at Ledyard's determination, managed to cut through regulations to provide him with a paper that apparently allowed him safe passage through Siberia to Kamchatka. This process took two months (fast, by Russian standards) during which he had an opportunity to observe life at the Empress' court. His ease in making friends again proved helpful. Court circles knew few Americans, and the Russians liked the intense young Yankee in threadbare clothes. During his stay, Ledyard kept in touch with Jefferson by mail, reporting weekly on the progress of his battle with Slavic bureaucracy. As Jefferson noted with amusement in his journals, "Ledyard has but two shirts, and still more shirts than shillings. He says that having no money they kick him from place to place, and thus, he expects to be kicked about the globe."

Ledyard's correspondence with Jefferson showed lighthearted confidence, for fortune seemed on his side. Dr. William Brown, a Scottish physician in Catherine's entourage, had to make a journey to the province of Kolyvan in Siberia— would Ledyard care to accompany him? This was real luck. In the first place, it meant three thousand miles of swift travel, expedited by all the authority attached to an official journey. In the second place, Brown, by virtue of his position, could save Ledyard from much of the time-wasting haggling with local officials that always beset the traveller in Russia. Ledyard accepted gladly, and the two men left St. Petersburg in June of 1787.

Travelling by royal coach was much better than walking. They sped through strange and fascinating cities—Vladimir, Kazan, Nishnii Novgorod—while Ledyard filled his notebooks with observations about the people and the country. They crossed the Ural Mountains to Tobolsk, in Siberia, to the wild, primitive plains that lay at the edge of China, a kind of country that Ledyard had never seen. The Russians were interested in Ledyard, too. Many of them had never seen an American and they were fascinated by his tattooing, which Ledyard could never convince them was not the result of an American custom. "I am a curiosity here," he wrote Jefferson from Barnaul, where Brown stopped,—"Those who have heard of America flock around to see me."

The ride with Brown took Ledyard almost half-way across Russia. More than four thousand miles still remained between him and Kamchatka, but fortunately Dr. Brown, by judicious hints to the right officials, obtained permission for Ledyard to ride to Tomsk with the Imperial Mail. After a day's rest, Ledyard started off again into still stranger country, the land of the Tartars with Mongol faces and exotic dress, women with red fingernails and cheeks daubed with red and white, villages with wood-paved streets and domed houses, and always the lonely, immeasurable distances. The mail coach travelled swiftly but in some villages came waits of several days, which Ledyard occupied by making notes in his journals and writing long letters to Jefferson, full of comments on dress, topography, customs, language, and even a mastodon bone he saw on display. As he travelled, Ledyard developed a theory, which he explained at length to Jefferson, that "mankind is all of one race, that what differences there were could be accounted for by differences of climate and surrounding," in proof of which he saw, or thought he saw, actual racial similarities among Tartars, South Sea Islanders, and American Indians. They were all Asiatic in origin, he concluded, with the Indians most certainly the earliest type to develop.

Ledyard resented the frequent delays occasioned by royal business; orders and messages had always to be made ready for the next stop, or reports sent to St. Petersburg. However, the Russians were extremely friendly, too much so for Ledyard's comfort. Russians had a long tradition of hospitality to foreigners, and Catherine's government servants, buried in the Siberian wastes, could not get enough of Ledyard's stories of life at the French court or of the latest gossip from St. Petersburg. He had to make great efforts at times to extricate himself, without rudeness, from overenthusiastic Russian hospitality. "If they hear of the arrival of a foreigner," Ledyard complained, "they load him with their little services. They crowd their tables with everything they have to eat and drink, and not content with that, they fill your wallet." At Tomsk, a wretched city of political exiles, Ledyard suspected that the local authorities deliberately delayed the mails to keep him as long as they dared. It was pleasant, but as he told Jefferson, "my mind ever keeps the start of me." Escaping from Tomsk, he went on to Krasnoyarsk, and another thousand miles to Irkutsk.

The Royal Mail coach stopped at Irkutsk. Ledyard waited there for his luck to take over. Things did not go well at all. After ten days of searching he found a merchant who promised to get him passage from Okhotsk, on the Pacific Coast, to Nootka—if he could get to Okhotsk, another two thousand miles farther. Ledyard was getting closer to his goal. Every day of inactivity stretched his nerves tighter. He even found, in a Russian home, a piece of Sandwich Island cloth that Cook's expedition had traded to the Russians at Kamchatka years before, certainly a good omen, for the next day he found a boat leaving for Yakutsk, fourteen hundred miles down the Lena river. This was not by any means his most direct route, but it would take him within six hundred miles of Okhotsk and that ship for Nootka.

At Yakutsk his luck ran out. The commandant there was gracious, friendly, and not at all helpful. The country between Yakutsk and Okhotsk was harsh and wild, he explained; it was now September, winter was fast approaching, and the journey was impossible. Ledyard would simply have to wait until spring. The commandant's story seemed evasive, though various army officers agreed that the trip was far too hazardous for even an experienced Siberian traveller—but then Ledyard talked with traders who assured him that winter travel on the Yakutsk-Okhtosk route was quite common. He did not know what to think. Arguing with the commandant got him nowhere. He wrote sadly in his journal:

> *I have but two long frozen stages more until emerging from the deep deserts I gain the American Atlantic states. This is the third time that I have been overtaken and arrested by winter; and both the others by giving time for my evil genius to rally his hosts about me, have defeated the enterprise. Fortune, thou hast humbled me at last. What, alas, shall I do?*

There was absolutely nothing he could do. The commandant was pleasant and immovable, and Ledyard, out of funds, resigned himself to a long winter in Yakutsk, finding some consolation in the fact that he could at least make "extensive observations" of the country and people. The commandant gave him quarters with a Russian officer. He entered into barracks life, which gave him a good opportunity to see something of the Russian mind and temperament. He found them hard to understand. The Russians were quick to make friends, he noted, but equally quick to anger. They were insanely jealous—Ledyard's roommate kicked his own dog to death for licking Ledyard's hand—and subject to violent rages, with moods swerving wildly from extreme joy to deep depression. Sometimes they were arrogant, other times so servile and humble as to be contemptible. In all of them Ledyard observed a latent strain of capricious, childlike cruelty.

In midwinter a Russian exploring expedition arrived in Yakutsk, led, to Ledyard's great surprise, by an Englishman named Captain Billings. Billings, too, had served in the *Resolution,* on Cook's voyage, and the two men were overjoyed to meet, deep in Siberia. Billings, Ledyard hoped, might give him help on the Okhotsk journey, but had he given the matter more thought he might have been able to see the reason for his delay. Catherine the Great was well aware of the economic potential of the Alaskan peninsula; Russian expeditions were already pushing a chain of trading posts into the sub-Arctic and down the coast toward Northwest America. The Empress had in mind an even larger expedition than Billings', to which his present trip was but a preliminary, while the newly-formed Russian-American Company, with headquarters in Irkutsk, had plans for expanding trade between Russia and the American continent. It was obviously risky, from Russia's point of view, to have an American poking about in the Canadian-Alaska area, particularly one who talked about starting a colony and founding a fur company. Very probably orders to delay Ledyard had begun to follow him across Russia soon after he had left St. Petersburg.

Ledyard, quite unaware of the Russian wheels turning back in Catherine's court, pinned his hopes on Billings, who promised to do what he could for him if he would accompany the expedition back to Irkutsk. At that city, fourteen hundred miles back up the Lena, the resident governor was waiting with a message from the Empress specifically ordering the arrest of one John Ledyard as a French spy. The charge was absurd, for the French had no interest whatever in Alaska, but it was good enough, and Ledyard, as soon as he arrived in Irkutsk, found himself suddenly a prisoner. He argued and explained. He spoke French, true, but he was an American with letters to prove it; he was simply an explorer and, as Billings could swear, an English marine at that. But with an Imperial order there was no argument. Ledyard was to be put under guard immediately, the order said, and returned as swiftly as possible to Moscow for trial. This was the end of Ledyard's long road and he knew it. "My ardent hopes are all once more blasted," he wrote despondently to Jefferson, far away in Paris. "What secret machinations have been at work?"

The guard of hussars travelled fast on the road back to Moscow, and they were not particularly gentle with their prisoner. Ledyard kept no journal during the trip and never mentioned to anyone what he went through, but it could not have been pleasant. Once, months later, he said, "My distresses have been greater than I ha've ever owned, or ever will own to any man." He arrived in Moscow ill, ragged, semi-starved, and thoroughly depressed in spirit. He had no idea of the charges against him, spoke no Russian, and spent weeks in a cold dark cell. No record of his trial has ever been found, though no doubt one still lies somewhere in Russian files. The court's decision was banishment, on pain of death if he returned to Russia. A hussar guard took him to the Polish frontier, threw him into a thicket, and left him for a Polish peasant to find some hours later. The Poles nursed him to health and finally, "ragged, disappointed, and penniless," he begged his way through Poland and Prussia to England.

John Ledyard, walking the streets of London, could have been pardoned if he had admitted defeat. He had travelled half-way around the world, had been within a few hundred tantalizing miles of his goal, only to be thwarted by forces he knew nothing of. He had seen lands and peoples that few Europeans and no Americans had ever seen, yet the great vision he pursued across four thousand miles of Siberia still eluded his grasp. No explorer could have been more determined or resourceful; none ever was quite so bedevilled by fortune and frustration. He was penniless and dejected, yet the vision of the green coasts of the Northwest and the gray cold Alaskan waters still swam in his head. John Ledyard could not give up his dream.

He still had his charm, at least, and all his enthusiasm.

London acquaintances took him in and Sir Joseph Banks and the others listened to his incredible tale. After a few weeks Banks called him in for a conference. The African Society, a wealthy group enjoying royal patronage, was interested in sending someone to Africa; would Ledyard consent to go? He most certainly would. He knew nothing about Africa, but it was new and strange country and the Northwest could wait a few years longer. His instructions were disarmingly simple—go to Egypt, travel alone across the continent of Africa, and report his findings to the Society within three years. For the first time in his life, Ledyard was adequately financed. He sailed for Alexandria in August, 1788, to spend a month studying languages and questioning traders from the interior. Then he went up to Cairo to hire guides. Here he wrote his friend Thomas Jefferson for the last time:

From Cairo I am to travel southwest about 300 leagues to a black king. Then my present conductors will leave me to my fate. Beyond, I suppose I shall go alone.

John Ledyard never met his black king, for on January 10, 1789, he died suddenly of a tropical fever. The Egyptians buried him outside Cairo, in the same sands that held the bodies of Richard the Lionhearted's soldiers and those of the armies of Louis the Saint. It seemed a fitting resting place for the restless Connecticut Yankee.

John Ledyard's name does not appear on the honored roll of explorers of the American West for the reason that he never got there, though no man ever tried harder. In his next to last letter to Jefferson from Cairo, Ledyard promised that immediately upon his return from Africa he would set out from Kentucky for the Pacific. Ledyard dreamed—before any other American dreamed it—of an American empire beyond the Mississippi, hoping that his name might go down in history as the man who opened the West. With a little luck it might have, but some perverse fate always drove him in another direction. Throughout his life he carried in his head his memories of the Northwest, of the rocky headlands, the snowcapped mountains, the pine forests crowding the shore, the vast reaches of wet green land that he saw once and never saw again.

What Ledyard hoped to do, others did while his body lay forgotten in the Egyptian sands. Captain Vancouver (another one of Cook's men) reported twenty-one ships in Nootka Sound in 1792; the American Robert Gray that same year explored the Oregon coast and discovered the Columbia river; Sir Alexander Mackenzie a year later found and explored part of the Fraser. Ledyard was hardly in his grave before the same London and Boston merchants who had turned him away with polite answers were scrambling to equip expeditions to the fabulous land of furs, exactly as Ledyard had begged them to do. Thomas Jefferson, a scant fifteen years after Ledyard died, sent Meriwether Lewis and William Clark into the Northwest, exactly as Ledyard had planned. Ridden by his "evil genius," John Ledyard had dreamed his imperial dream a little too early.

Yet, failure that he was, John Ledyard had in him the true stuff of the explorer—the drive to see what lay beyond the horizon, the burning response to the challenge of the new and unknown. He was, said a friend, "adventuresome beyond the conception of ordinary men," and, in a sense, he did not really fail. Fame and recognition eluded him, yet he lived the kind of life he wanted to live, the only life that his urgent, wandering, rootless nature would let him live. He once wrote, in a kind of epitaph, "I have trampled the world under my feet, laughed at fear, and derided danger." What man could say more?

Edward Bonney

★

I F THERE IS A SINGLE central hero in the American folk myth, it is the frontiersman. James Fenimore Cooper and his multitudes of followers wove the figure of nature's nobleman, the brave, taciturn, buckskin-fringed pioneer, deep into the pattern of the American myth, with the result that such men as Boone, Crockett, Kenton, and their Western counterparts Cody, Hickok, Carson, Bridger, and others, became in their own lifetimes near-legendary figures presumably encompassing all the frontier virtues. And as the historian Frederick Jackson Turner pointed out a half-century ago, the frontier did have its virtues—self-reliance, optimism, energy, equality, and other traits associated with conditions of life in the wilderness, the plains, and the mountains.

In real life, the frontiersman had his vices as well as his virtues. Individualism and self-reliance could turn into plain lawlessness. Justice on the frontier was likely to be primitive and self-administered; "lynch law" too often replaced the courts. Without the restraints of organized society, the frontier could be, and sometimes was, ugly, brutal, and unruly, far different from the romanticized picture stereotyped on the American consciousness by generations of novelists and scenario-writers. Theft was common, murder or rape not unusual, eye-gouging and ear-biting fights almost normal in log-town life. Until the arrival of the church, the school, and the pioneer wife, until the establishment of law enforcement agencies and other organizations of social control, a frontier community hung suspended between civilization and disorder. in a transition stage which fortunately did not last long.

The Northwest Territory, organized in 1787 and speedily settled after the turn of the nineteenth century, changed in the short time of fifty years from an imperially-sized wilderness to frontier territory, then to the five thriving, populous states of Ohio, Michigan, Indiana, Illinois, and Wisconsin. Their stories were much the same—at first trappers and Indians, replaced by squatters and farmers, forests cleared and game gone, hamlets growing into towns and towns to cities, the plank road laid over the forest path, the canal and railroad pushing into the hinterlands. The process was rapid, the westward flow of population amazingly swift. In 1850 Wisconsin had men who had already moved five times, each time farther west; Lincoln's father liked to tell a tall story about a pioneer family that moved so often the chickens were trained to walk to the wagon, lie down, and put their feet up to be tied for the next trip. Ohio entered the Union in 1803, Indiana in 1816, Illinois in 1818, Michigan in 1837, Wisconsin in 1848. So rapid was the cycle of change from frontier to statehood that some of Chicago's first settlers were still alive when it became one of the nation's six largest cities.

The terms of the Northwest Ordinance established three stages of government for the area north of the Ohio River and east of the Mississippi. In the first, the territory was to be ruled by a governor and three judges appointed by Congress. When the population reached five thousand free persons, a territorial legislature could be elected and a delegate without vote sent to Congress. The third step was reached when the population in any of the districts that were to become states numbered sixty thousand free persons; then a constitutional convention could be held and the prospective state could apply for admission to the Union. The transition from Federal control to self-control for each of the new states thus moved in easy stages from frontier to organized statehood, as Congress gradually relinquished authority and the states assumed it. Theoretically neat and simple, the process involved certain awkwardness, particularly in the enforcement of laws. Federal marshals and their deputies had tremendous areas to cover. Territorial legislatures, which set up the machinery of legal control, often had trouble in making it function properly. Sheriffs and constables were acutely conscious of the political winds that blew through pioneer state politics. The new states themselves, only a few years removed from the wilderness, found it hard to adjust to the rapid change of frontier to state, from a society of bowie knives and pistols to one of sheriffs, judges, lawyers, and courts. Growing out of a heritage of every-man-for-himself and devil-take-the-hindmost into a civilization of law and order took time, and sometimes, to the early citizens of the Old Northwest, the process proved painful.

Edward Bonney, a middle-aged lawyer in Montrose, Iowa, found it painful in 1844. A transplanted Easterner, Bonney had settled in Montrose, slightly south of Fort Madison on the Mississippi, about ten years earlier, and had seen it grow from a crossroads village into a respectably-sized small town in which he was regarded as a leading citizen. He was a dignified, quiet, capable man of orderly habits, perhaps a little stuffy, but known and respected through eastern Iowa and neighboring Illinois. There was nothing unusual about him. He was simply a solid citizen, a believer, he wrote, "in law human and divine, peace and quiet, and sufficient judicial power."

Many respectable men like Bonney lived in the Northwest, and there were many less-desirable citizens too, a vicious element left by the backwash of the wave of settlement that had just passed west. Lawyers, judges, and clerics with ruffled shirts and tall hats rubbed shoulders in the street of the raw new towns with petty thieves, drifters, and booted thugs in leather jerkins. The banker's mansion on the bluff, with its imported piano, often overlooked the squatter's squalid shack on the river flats below. Bonney and those of his class (and class distinctions, whatever the theory of frontier equality, were sharp) despised the crude, lawless element that surrounded them while they waited for the country to grow out of its awkward age. They were not frontiersmen, not men of

75

fist and gun, but civilized, law-abiding, literate men intent on developing a decent society in the Northwest.

Theft and robbery were common crimes in the Northwest of the forties. Bonney handled a good many such cases in court. In the fall and winter of 1844, however, he noted an unusual increase in the number of robberies, spread through northern and central Illinois and eastern Iowa. The Frink and Wells Stage, carrying money from the Dixon land office, was held up and robbed in Lee County, Illinois. A few weeks later, Mr. Mulford, who lived north of Dixon in Ogle County, was held up, badly beaten, and robbed of four hundred dollars. Someone broke into McKinney's store in Rockford and stole seven hundred dollars. A peddler named Miller was waylaid and robbed near Troy Grove. Two men who attempted to rob a house near Inlet Grove were driven off. Some robberies occurred in Montrose and several more in Nauvoo, the Mormon town across the river in Illinois, which, unfortunately, local Gentiles considered a robber's roost.

In January of 1845 Sheriff Estes of Lee County, Iowa, made a lucky arrest. He picked up a smalltime thief named West, who not only confessed to the robbery of the peddler but also talked more than Estes had hoped. West said five or six men were creating the crime wave; some of them he knew, some he did not. One was a thirtyish, dark, small, slightly built man named Fox. Another was John Baxter, a young German who had been an accomplice of West in the Troy Grove robbery. Another was a man named Robert Birch (who also went by the names of Blecker or Bleecker, and Harris) whom West had not seen but whom he had heard mentioned. Old Mr. Mulford, he added, had been robbed by Baxter, Birch, Fox, and two Iowa men named Bridge and Oliver. Estes arrested Bridge and Oliver and they, with West, were sentenced to serve eight years behind bars.

The capture of West and his two companions seemed to have no effect on the incidence of thefts. Until May, 1845, crime was limited to thefts, but on May 9 two strangers appeared a few miles from Montrose searching for a yoke of oxen which, they claimed, had strayed away a week before. They stopped at the farm of John Miller, found no trace of the lost oxen, and moved on. On the night of May 10 Mr. and Mrs. Miller had overnight guests, Mr. and Mrs. Liecy. At midnight Miller was awakened by someone hammering on his door; when he answered it, three men forced their way in. Miller put up a fight, but fell with six knife wounds. Meanwhile Liecy, aroused by the commotion, attacked the robbers. Bleeding from twenty wounds, he knocked one man out through the doorway, but while he struggled with the other two the worsted attacker shot wildly through the door and brought Liecy down. Then the criminals fled into the darkness.

Mrs. Miller saddled a horse and rode to West Point, the county seat. Sheriff Estes and a posse returned with her at dawn to find Miller, a bowie knife still in his back, dead in his own front yard. Liecy, though badly wounded, was still conscious. It had been too dark for him to identify his attackers, he told Estes, but the Sheriff found a cloth cap, trimmed with fur, in the field across which the men had evidently escaped toward the Mississippi and into Illinois. When Edward Bonney heard of the Miller murder at ten o'clock the next morning, the story of the cap interested him. Three weeks before he had seen such a cap, he thought, on a man named Hodges in Nauvoo.

Bonney determined, therefore, "to track up the fatal cap." Inquiries in Nauvoo revealed three Hodges brothers, Amos, William, and Stephen, none of savory reputation. Amos had been in Nauvoo on May 9, but William and Stephen had been seen in a skiff crossing the river that afternoon, with a man named Brown. Furthermore, William Hodges, who owned a fur-trimmed cap, appeared on the street, wearing a hat rather than a cap, on May 11. This was all evidence of the most circumstantial sort, but enough for Bonney. He reported his suspicions to the captain of the City Watch in Nauvoo, who on May 13th arrested all three Hodges.

The two Hodges brothers, William and Stephen, came up

for examination the following week. They were Mormons, and their arrest on the charges of an Iowa Gentile created some feeling in Nauvoo. Rumors reached Bonney that the Hodges had an army of friends ready to testify to their presence in Nauvoo on May 9, 10, and 11, and Bonney's evidence, admittedly somewhat flimsy, therefore might not hold up in a Mormon court before a Mormon magistrate. Bonney consequently extradited the two brothers to Iowa, prosecuted them himself in June, won convictions and saw them hanged.

The third man in the case, Brown, seemed to have disappeared. The few in Nauvoo who knew of him believed he came from Quincy, so Bonney set out for Adams County. Sheriff Pitman of Adams knew something of Brown—he lived eighteen miles north of town in a shack on the river flats. Questions asked of Brown's uncommunicative neighbors brought out only that Brown had red or auburn hair, was "a hard case," and had not been seen for weeks. Sometimes, one neighbor recalled, Brown went to St. Louis, so Bonney, too, went there. A saloonkeeper there remembered a redhaired man who said he was on his way to Memphis. Bonney went to Memphis, spent three days, and found nothing.

Despite the capture and execution of the Hodges, the robberies continued. On June 7, aged Jeremiah Strawn slept at his home near Hennepin, Illinois, more than a hundred miles northeast of Montrose. At midnight three men broke in his door, robbed him of fifteen dollars, and beat him severely because he did not have more. On June 15, three men robbed the law offices of Knox and Dewey in Rock Island, Illinois, a hundred miles upriver from Montrose, of six hundred and forty dollars. On June 25 an attempt was made to rob Mr. Beach, a Quincy merchant, but Beach fought his assailant off. Beach, fortunately, could identify two of the bandits— one was known as "Judge" Fox, the other as Bleecker. When he read the newspaper account of the attack on Beach, Bonney remembered West's confession—mentioning Fox and Bleecker —and stored the names in his mind.

One of Bonney's closest friends was Colonel William

Davenport, who lived at Rock Island, Illinois. Davenport, aged nearly eighty, had made a small fortune as an Indian trader in the early days and had retired thirty years earlier to live in some splendor in a magnificent home on Rock Island's western shore. On July 4, 1845, Davenport's family and servants attended Independence Day celebrations in Rock Island, leaving the old man at home. In midafternoon, as he sat reading, three men suddenly burst into the room and, as Davenport reached for his cane, one of them shot him in the thigh. Then they dragged him into his bedroom by his hair, which he wore long in the eighteenth-century fashion, and demanded that he open his strongbox. Davenport, faint from loss of blood, did so, and the men poured its contents, some seven hundred dollars, into a bag and demanded more. He had no more, Davenport protested. He must have, they said, but they could not beat his secret out of him. They left him for dead, with three broken ribs, a shattered leg, and a serious gunshot wound. The old frontiersman, however, was tough and clung to life. He was still alive when his family returned, and before he died, that night, he described in detail the three men who had robbed him.

The murder of Davenport aroused northern Illinois to anger. The Davenport family offered, for capture of the murderers, a reward of fifteen hundred dollars, to which Governor Ford of Illinois added six hundred dollars. Bonney, a hundred miles downriver, heard on July 8 the details of Davenport's death. Pieces of the pattern fell into place in his mind. A dark, slight man (Fox?), a square, red-haired man (Birch—Harris—Bleecker?), and a tall, "middling-built man" (possibly one John Long, who had served as a defense witness for the Hodges Brothers). In every case since the robbery of Mulford, the descriptions of two men tallied— so as to point at Fox and Birch. The single exception to the pattern of descriptions was the murder of Miller, in which a third man participated, and he might have been the elusive Brown. Birch was known in Rock Island, Bleecker in Quincy, Harris in Dixon, Brown in Nauvoo. So Bonney did the obvious

thing. He went to Nauvoo—Brown, Captain Markham told
him, had red hair. He went to Quincy—the Sheriff said
Bleecker had "auburn hair." He went to Rock Island—yes,
Birch had red hair. He went to Dixon—same story, Harris
had red hair. After some four hundred miles of travel Bonney
knew that Brown, Harris, Bleecker, and Birch were all the
same man.

Bonney had a family and a law practice to look after. Con
victing, not catching, criminals was his business. But Miller
was dead, Davenport dead, Liecy a hopeless cripple, and Bon
ney was therefore angry. So were others, angry enough to hold
a mass meeting at which it was determined that someone
should go after Fox, Birch, and other members of the gang
track them down, and bring them to justice. The citizens
choice was Edward Bonney. "I declined," he wrote,

> and plead my situation as an excuse. I had a wife and
> children, and failure in the attempt was likely to mean
> certain death. But the vision of Davenport, his gray
> hairs clotted with blood, cried out to me. After careful
> thought and reflection I came to the decision that the
> duty I owed my fellows, as one of the great social com-
> pact, was superior to all other considerations.

Thus Edward Bonney, middle-aged lawyer, honest man, and
angry citizen accepted the job.

Bonney had little information to go on, but his precise
lawyer's mind sorted out and added up what he knew. Robert
Birch, William "Judge" Fox, and probably John Long were
the key men in the gang, if there was such a gang. Their
method of operation, as Bonney figured it, was clever and
simple. One, or two, or all three of them travelled from place
to place, making contacts with local criminals, committing a
crime, and then moving on to the next town to make another
contact. Now and then, as in the case of the Hodges brothers,
the local culprits might be caught, but when they were, Fox,
Birch, and Long were already gone. The only way to nail

the trio down, Bonney decided, was to track them through their own contacts, something most likely to be accomplished by joining the circuit himself. He would make a rather improbable criminal, Bonney realized, but the chance was worth taking. In August of 1845 Bonney started out on the trail. The sheriff of Rock Island County deputized him, Sheriff Estes deputized him, and various judges armed him with letters of introduction. First he went to Dubuque, talked to his friend Judge Wilson of the Miner's Bank, and obtained a dozen sheets of the paper used by the bank in preparing its scrip. This bank-note paper seemed, to the inexpert eye, the next thing to money. Then Bonney went to Galena and took passage on the steamer *War Eagle* for St. Louis. On the riverboats, he theorized, he might find someone who knew Fox or Birch, or perhaps Long, who came from Galena and who, like Birch, often visited St. Louis. As a concession to the presumptive need for disguise, Bonney put on a fancy vest, hung about the ship's bar, and tried to act suspiciously.

Luckily, Bonney flushed game the first day out. Soon after the boat left Galena, a sporty young man introduced himself. "My name is Young," he said, "Granville Young. I think I saw you last winter in Nauvoo."

Bonney's heart dropped. Could it be that this youth knew him by name? When it was apparent that Young did not, Bonney felt better. His name, he said, was Brown, and he *did* occasionally visit Nauvoo. After a few free drinks, Young began to talk freely, and Bonney threw out the bait.

"I think," he said, "that you're a fellow of the right stripe. What kind of speculation are you in, these days?"

"Oh, I'm working in Galena," Young replied. "A while ago I was on a little operation up near Prairie du Chien."

"Well," said Bonney, "I think you're the right stripe. What do you think of this?"

The bank-note paper made Young's eyes pop. It was "a damned good article," he said, and when Bonney said he could lay his hands on fifteen thousand dollars worth, Young looked at him with respect. Bonney said he wanted help of some sort in passing counterfeit notes printed on this paper; perhaps Young knew of some contacts he could make. As it turned out, Young was thoroughly hooked. A natural braggart, he babbled to Bonney for the next two days, helped along by free drinks and adroit flattery. Young knew just the men Brown needed—"Judge" Fox, John Long, and Bob Birch. In fact, he knew their contact in Nauvoo, "Old Grant" Redden, a name Bonney filed away in his mind. Young knew Long's father, Aaron, who served as contact in Galena, and the man to see in St. Louis was a stable-owner named Reynolds. John Baxter, who lived in Jefferson, Wisconsin, worked with Fox, Long, and Birch on jobs in Wisconsin, and Ed Logan did the same in Memphis, Tennessee. Shack Phips, near Terre Haute, was contact man in Indiana. Birch's father lived in eastern Illinois, in Clark County— Birch might be found there, perhaps. Young knew of the Miller and the Davenport cases (more than he should, Bonney thought) but he could get no specific information on them. At any rate, by the time Bonney reached Nauvoo he had nine names and a working knowledge of the framework of the whole organization. Young left the boat at Nauvoo and, as his usefulness was now ended, Bonney turned him over to the police, went back aboard the *War Eagle*, and proceeded to St. Louis.

Bonney found the stable-owner, Reynolds, at his place of business, as Young had told him he would, but Reynolds refused to talk until he saw the bank-note paper. Reynolds pronounced it "the best imitation he had ever seen." His tongue loosened considerably. Reynolds knew Long and Fox, and they would certainly be interested in Bonney's "counterfeit" paper. In fact, he told Bonney, Long and Fox had left St. Louis only two weeks before, headed east with a third man, whose name Reynolds did not know, but who had red hair. Bonney thanked him, promised ten thousand dollars worth of bank-note paper, and left for Springfield, Illinois.

Putting together what he now knew, Bonney began to get a clearer picture of the men he was hunting. Long was physically powerful and intelligent; both Young and Reynolds seemed to regard him as the strong-arm member of the trio. Fox was a trifle stupid, but "the most energetic fellow," Reynolds said, "I ever knew." The shadowy figure of the red-haired Birch, however, interested Bonney most. Birch was always there, always in the background, known here by one name and there by another, really known well by none. Certainly whoever had planned and organized the travelling crime-circuit had brains, and Birch, Bonney suspected, was probably the man. His trail led, apparently, across the entire Northwest, perhaps into Kentucky, Tennessee, and Ohio as well. It was a cold trail. Obviously Bonney needed help, so in Springfield he called on Governor Ford, from whom he obtained, somewhat irregularly, but in the interests of the public welfare, blank extradition papers for the whole tier of Northwestern and border states, with the exception of Michigan.

Birch's father, according to Young, lived in Marshall, Illinois, near the Indiana line. Because the three men had headed east, Bonney took the stage for Marshall. There he found that Sheriff Bennett of Clark County knew the Birches well. The family's local reputation was not high. John Birch, the father, known as "Old Coon," was suspected of receiving stolen goods. Sixteen-year-old Tim Birch had already served time for horse-stealing. Robert Birch had not been home, so far as the sheriff knew, more than once or twice in seven years. With the sheriff's help, Bonney called on "Old Coon," who lived nine miles away in a dirty log cabin, deep in the woods. The elder Birch, an ignorant, slovenly old man, was in bed and did not want callers. He feigned deafness, then stupidity, but Bonney kept talking until mention of his son's name brightened his eyes. Perceiving that old Birch was proud of his son, Bonney led him on. Robert was a "smart fellow," the old man bragged, "always making money." All his boys made money, but

Robert was smartest. Tim was just out of jail, the eldest son, John, Jr., had been hanged in Texas, but Robert "had heaps of money and never got caught." Unfortunately, Bonney learned that Robert had not been home in eleven months.

Because nothing more was to be learned from "Old Coon" Birch, Bonney went on to Terre Haute. There he picked up a piece of good news. William Fox and Shack Phips reportedly were in jail for horse-thievery at Bowling Green, Indiana, only twenty-five miles away. Bonney hurried to Bowling Green to find, however, that both men had been out of jail for two weeks, on bail put up by Fox's father. Neither man had left a trace.

Bonney was disappointed, but he had a strong feeling that his luck was about to turn. Certainly, by just missing Fox, he had proved he was on the right trail. Phips lived in Owen County, perhaps twenty miles away, in sparsely-settled forest country. Bonney decided to see if he could find him. After two days of riding on a borrowed horse he found the place, observing at once that if Phips were a professional criminal, he had "certainly not done well at his profession." Phips lived with his wife and mother-in-law in a fourteen-foot-square log cabin, doorless, dirty, and furnished with only a three-legged stool, a plank table, two miserable beds, and a broken chair. The old woman was "a meagre specimen of humanity," but fifteen-year-old Mrs. Shack Phips, Bonney noted, was a strikingly beautiful girl beneath the dirt.

Neither the old woman nor the girl was communicative. Phips was not there, they said; he "had been gone for weeks." Bonney talked of his own friendship for Fox, spoke glowingly of Birch (apparently they did not know him), and watched the old woman gradually thaw. Finally she said, "Do you want to see Shack real bad?"

"I do," replied Bonney, "with some good news."

"Well," said the old woman, "I'll holler him up." Then she climbed to the roof of the cabin and shouted at the top of her voice.

Shack Phips, a small, meek little man, appeared from the

woods a few minutes later. Bonney struck up a conversation, dropping names to which Shack responded only vaguely. He was not sure he knew Birch, he said; he knew of Long, and he did not like Fox at all, for Fox had trapped him into the stolen-horse affair and had left him to hold the bag. Bonney sized him up as a weakling, and finally broke in roughly. This "confounded nonsense," he said, was useless. The facts were these; Fox and Phips were out on bail, eight hundred dollars worth. As a friend of Fox's, Bonney had a plan that would help them both. Because he came from Illinois he could easily pose as the real owner of the horses. If he claimed ownership of the horses and took them away, then Phips and Fox could go back to Bowling Green, collect the bail, and go off scot-free. Who could convict them, with the evidence gone? Bonney's plan pleased Phips very much. The horses, he explained, had really been stolen in Illinois by Long, Fox, and a red-haired man who had turned up at his place a month ago. After Long and his companion—the red-haired man—had gone, a posse had picked up Fox and Phips with the horses and jailed them—thus Phips' aggrieved innocence.

The point of Bonney's plan was to locate Fox, who, Phips told him, was hiding somewhere in Wayne County, near Indianapolis. Bonney was confident he could lure Fox out and arrest him for his crimes in Illinois, but catching Fox would still leave Long and Birch at large. None of the three suspected that someone was on their trail, and none had any reason to suspect that their part in the murder of Colonel Davenport was known. If Bonney arrested Fox for it, Birch and Long probably would never be seen in the Northwest again. What Bonney wanted was Fox safely in jail on some other charge, and information of the whereabouts of the other two. If Fox could be tricked into returning to Indiana, he might be trapped.

So Bonney went searching for Fox. Fox's father lived on a farm near Centerville, Indiana. There questions revealed that the son, William, was indeed in the area and had been seen working on his father's farm. At the farm, old John

Fox, obviously lying, claimed he had not seen his son for weeks. Bonney left a letter, signed John Brown, referring guardedly to a matter of horses ("to excite curiosity," Bonney wrote, "and induce him to call upon me in Centerville to see who I was") and rode back to his hotel.

At ten that night a man walked into the hotel, inquiring for Mr. Brown. Bonney, keeping out of sight, hurried to his room, threw himself on the bed, and pretended to be asleep. Someone knocked, and Bonney, after lighting a candle, opened the door.

"Is this Mr. Brown?" Fox asked.

"Well," said Bonney, "not exactly."

Fox peered at him a moment in the candlelight, and then said, "I think, Mr. Brown, that you are Mr. Bonney from Nauvoo."

Of all Bonney's tense moments, this instant was the worst. Within a few seconds he had to judge, weigh, reject, and choose among alternative plans, trusting to luck. He still had his bank-note paper; it was a long chance and he took it.

"That's my name at home," he replied carelessly, "but it's Brown when I'm on the road."

Fox was puzzled and suspicious. He knew Bonney the lawyer had helped hang the Hodges in Iowa, yet here Bonney was, in Indiana, calling himself Brown. By sheer luck, Bonney had struck Fox's weakest point—his inability to think quickly—and Bonney produced the bank-note paper.

"Look at this," he said.

Fox examined, admired, and asked questions. The uncompleted scrip looked like the real thing; where did it come from? From Cincinnati, Bonney told him, and he could get thousands more. Reynolds in St. Louis had told him that " 'Judge' Fox was the man to see to pass the queer stuff," and as Bonney talked, he could see Fox relax. Was he surprised, Bonney asked, to find that Bonney the lawyer was "one of the boys"?

"You are the last man I'd have suspected," Fox admitted. "You've made a damned good move. Bonney at home, Brown on the road. I don't wonder you do your work in Cincinnati."

The Hodges, Bonney explained, were a different matter. The Hodges had committed murder, and he did not like murder, for "there are enough ways to get money without murder." Therefore he had hanged the Hodges and they deserved it; counterfeiting was a clean game. To this Fox agreed, and by midnight the two men were fast friends. The plan about the horses Fox regarded as extremely clever—his father wanted the bail money back, and he, Fox, wanted to leave Indiana with no charges against him. At one o'clock he left, leaving Bonney to an uneasy sleep, but he turned up the next morning ready to start for Bowling Green.

On the long stage ride Bonney found out what he needed to know. Long and Birch, Fox said, were in Delaware County, Ohio, near Columbus, at a small town called Berkshire. They had several "jobs" planned in the area with a man named Royce, after which the three were to meet in northern Illinois to begin the circuit again. Long, according to Fox, was "a first-rate fellow," brave, strong, smart. Birch was intelligent, conceited, and a bit of a fop. He dressed well, insisted on being called "captain," and expected Fox and Long to do the work while he did the planning. Still, Fox admitted, Birch was very shrewd; he had never been caught and perhaps never would be caught. He had planned the Frink and Wells robbery, the Mulford robbery, and most of the others.

At Centerville, Bonney had to improvise swiftly, for Fox had to be arrested. Bonney did not exactly know what the charge should be. Again Bonney's luck held, for Fox left the stage at the edge of town, saying he wanted to see a friend and promising to meet Bonney at the hotel later in the morning. Bonney hurried to Sheriff Gentry and outlined his scheme. Gentry was to arrest both Bonney and Fox for counterfeiting and Fox also for stealing a horse in Missouri (which, Fox had told him, he had). The double charge should hold Fox for some time; meanwhile Bonney could "escape," locate Long and Birch, and when he did so extradite Fox to Illinois for murder. Fox turned up at the hotel on time, Gentry appeared on schedule, found the bank-note paper, arrested both men, placed them in separate cells, and

Bonney "escaped" that night. At dawn he was on the stage bound for Columbus.

Edward Bonney was tired, but he felt that the end of his long road was in sight. He had, including Baxter in Wisconsin, nine men staked out in four states, with none of them aware of it. Only Long and Birch remained at large.

Two days later Bonney arrived in Columbus. Berkshire, a small town twenty miles northwest, meant another day's ride. At Berkshire a few questions established that two men named Henderson and Bleecker (undoubtedly Birch) had stopped for a day two weeks before, stayed with a man named Royce, and had then taken the stage for Pittsburgh. Though disappointed at the news, Bonney was heartened to find this much of Fox's story verified. Royce was not hard to find and the "counterfeit banknote" device convinced him, as it had the others. Henderson and Bleecker, said Royce, were not in Pittsburgh at all, but somewhere in central Ohio. They were planning to rob a reputedly wealthy farmer in the northwestern part of the state, and then undertake the far more ambitious project of holding up the South Bend, Indiana, bank.

Bonney, who stayed in Berkshire, spent a restless night. "Sleep departed from me," he wrote, "notwithstanding the great fatigue of travelling day and night." He was close, very close to his quarry, and terribly afraid that one false move might send them into flight. It would be easy enough, of course, for the South Bend authorities to pick up Long and Birch if they really intended to rob the bank—but there was no guaranty that that was actually their plan, or that they might not change it. Bonney wanted them tried and hanged in Illinois for murder, not imprisoned in Indiana for an attempted robbery. He therefore intended "to endeavor by proposing a more brilliant operation than the one they had in view, to detach them from its pursuit on the ground of its little comparative importance."

Royce was easy to convince. Counterfeiting involved little risk as contrasted to bank robbery, and he agreed with Bonney that Henderson and Bleecker would be eager to forget about South Bend if they had a chance to make thousands in an easier way. Royce would, he promised Bonney, contact both men within a few days and ask them to meet him at a predetermined time and place to discuss the formation of a five-state bogus-money ring. Why not Adrian, Michigan, Bonney suggested, since that was on the stage route to South Bend? Royce promised to get word to his two friends at once and, to whet their appetites, Bonney gave him a supposedly counterfeit ten-dollar bank note on a Missouri bank, with the promise that he could get ten thousand dollars more.

Bonney was weary, anxious, and involved in an extremely complicated game. On his way back to Columbus he realized his mistake—he had no extradition papers for Michigan. Since he had them for Ohio, it was absolutely necessary that he change his plans quickly, yet a sudden change might easily arouse Royce's suspicions, or Long's, or Birch's. The men had to be caught before they left Ohio. In Columbus, Bonney made a hasty visit to the State House, obtained Ohio warrants for Long and Birch, and began a long evening of letter-writing.

His net was nearly ready to be drawn. He had Baxter located in Wisconsin, Young in Illinois, Phips in Indiana, Fox in Indiana, and various smaller fry throughout the Northwest. They could all be connected, in one way or another, with thirty-two thefts and two murders in four states, while Long, Fox, and Birch (perhaps one or two others) could be indicted as the murderers of Colonel Davenport. To arrest a few of them meant frightening away the remainder; his trap had to be shut on all at the same time. Therefore Bonney wrote to the sheriff of each county that harbored a suspect, outlining his plan, and asking that in each case the arrest be made on Saturday, September 18. Then, at one o'clock in the morning, he went to bed for another restless sleep.

Bonney explained his problem to Sheriff Thrift of Knox County the next day. Birch and Long were somewhere in central Ohio. If Royce made contact with them, as he promised, presumably both of them would be on the way to Adrian, Michigan, within the next few days. If they were together, they could be intercepted and arrested somewhere in Ohio, before they crossed the Michigan line. But if they were not together, they might (and here Bonney could only hope) meet in Ohio and continue toward Adrian. Depending on their starting points, their possible stage routes might lead through Mount Vernon, or Mansfield, or Marion; however, the shortest route to Michigan lay via Marion, Upper Sandusky, Tiffin, Sandusky, Perrysburg, and Maumee. North of Marion, Bonney believed, he and the Sheriff ought to be able to pick up the trail and make the arrests before the two reached Michigan. Thrift promised complete coöperation, and himself sent letters to various county officials in northwestern Ohio, asking that a lookout be kept for men answering to the descriptions of Long and Birch.

Bonney and Thrift left on the stage the next morning. They received no word at Delaware, none at Marion. However, it was race week at Little Sandusky. A stranger in town resembled Birch, the town constable reported, and Bonney found the stranger on the racecourse. Bonney had never seen Birch, but the red-haired man closely resembled Birch's description—and he was wearing, stretched across his waistcoat, Colonel Davenport's watch chain and seal. Long was nowhere in sight. Bonney followed Birch all day. Birch seemed always alone.

Bonney must have spent some anxious moments that day in Little Sandusky. Had Royce contacted Birch? Where was Long? A word from Bonney, and a murderer was caught; the wrong word, and the whole intricate plan collapsed. Better to leave Birch, Bonney decided, and trust to luck that he and Long would meet somewhere else and ride toward Michigan into the trap. So Bonney and Thrift, with some misgivings, left Little Sandusky for Tiffin, hoping to find word of Long. At Upper Sandusky there was no news, none at Tiffin, and none at Sandusky. Weary and dispirited, Bon-

ney went on to Perrysburg, Ohio, the last stage stop below
the Michigan line. There he stayed two days, simply waiting.
At eleven o'clock of the evening of the nineteenth of September, a messenger arrived in Perrysburg from Sandusky,
"bearing the welcome intelligence of the arrest of Long and
Birch at that place, by a posse under the direction of R.
Dickinson, Esq., at the Railroad House." Both men, the
messenger reported, denied any connection with the murder
of Davenport; both, in fact, denied they had ever been in
Illinois. Bonney arrived in Sandusky the next morning to
make the identifications, which must have given him pleasure. Birch was still wearing Colonel Davenport's watch and
chain and that undid them. Confronted with the evidence
engraved on the watch, "Henderson" and "Bleecker" admitted to being Long and Birch, and Bonney had the great
satisfaction of informing them that he intended to see them
hang in Illinois.

On September 21, 1846, Bonney left Sandusky with Birch
and Long safely in irons. Birch was brash and confident,
Long silent. Both were thoroughly puzzled by the fact that a
lawyer turned counterfeiter, named Bonney but alias Brown,
had caused their arrest for a year-old murder some six hundred miles away. Bonney told them nothing and, on the
stage to Detroit, Birch suggested a bribe. On the railroad
from Detroit to St. Joseph, he made threats. On the boat from
St. Joseph to Chicago, he warned Bonney his "friends would
free them before the stage reached Dixon." Between Chicago
and Dixon, Birch raised his bribe to ten thousand dollars,
claiming he had more than that hidden in a cave along the
river flats near Galena. By this time Bonney had had enough.
"Gentlemen," he said,

*you must make no more threats or attempts to bribe
me. If you do, I will put a hundredweight of iron on
you and loop you from head to foot. I intend to treat
you well but I shall keep you safe. Believe me, you
will go to Rock Island dead or alive.*

And on September 29, Edward Bonney, "worn by fatigue and constant watchfulness," but true to his promise, delivered his prisoners to Sheriff Lemuel Andrews of Rock Island County.

Bonney's trap caught all but one. William Fox broke jail at Centerville, Indiana (Bonney was sure he had bribed a jailer) and was never heard from again. The arrogant Birch broke down after a week of confinement, made three separate confessions, and implicated two more men. Long stolidly refused to say anything. On October 6 the Grand Jury at Rock Island indicted Birch, Fox, John Long, Aaron Long, Baxter, and Young, for complicity in the Davenport murder, and on October 19, the two Longs and Young, who had been tried first, were hanged, as Bonney recorded, "under a clear blue sky, and as the drop fell, they swung off into another world." Baxter was tried, sentenced to be hanged, and later had his sentence commuted to life imprisonment. "Old Grant" Redden went to prison, and Shack Phips served six months in Indiana. Royce (in Ohio), Reynolds (in Missouri), and Logan (in Tennessee) all served short sentences.

Robert Birch put up a shrewd fight. In each of his confessions (and he seemed willing to confess to anyone at the slightest provocation) he told a variety of confusing stories, reducing his part in the murder more and more each time. With Fox gone and Long dead, it was extremely difficult to pin down his lies and inaccuracies. His lawyers, who apparently were good ones, obtained two continuances, finally succeeded in having his case transferred to Knox County, and in a burst of inspiration swore out a warrant for Bonney's arrest on charges of counterfeiting under the alias of "Jack Brown." It took Bonney some weeks to straighten this out. By that time, Fox's trail, which Bonney was eager to follow, was lost. Bonney made a trip to Indiana and Ohio, trying to pick up Fox's trail again, only to find on his return that Birch, too, had broken jail and disappeared. Bonney never saw Birch hang as he had wished, but he did have the pleasure of receiving, some months later, news that the red-haired murderer, with a sort of poetic retribution, had himself been murdered in Alabama. "Thus," Bonney wrote with finality, "terminated the disposition of the members of the banditti responsible for the murders of Miller and Colonel Davenport."

With these words Edward Bonney disappeared into the obscurity of smalltown Iowa life, his job completed. It was a nasty, dangerous job, but one that someone had to do, he wrote, "as a duty to the community." Bonney did not consider himself a hero, nor did he think of what he had done as adventure. If his part in the affair had not been "misrepresented and misunderstood," he explained, he would never have considered it worthwhile to write a book about it. But the counterfeiting charge, nonsensical as it was, had to be answered by "a true statement of the affair" to set the record straight among his friends and neighbors.

Because Edward Bonney was not an imaginative man, much of the charm of his story lies in what he fails to say. Taken at face value, the facts of his tale are exciting enough, but behind them lies an even more engrossing tale of high adventure that Bonney could not tell because, being the man he was, he did not realize that he had lived it. The stuff of the picaresque novel is there, the thrill of pursuit, the satisfaction of justice done and malefactors punished—but Bonney doggedly plods his way through his "plain, unvarnished tale" without heroics, without emotion. What must have been his feelings when, after months of pursuit, he came face to face with the red-haired killer, a dead man's watch chain across his vest, swaggering about the racetrack in Ohio? What did he feel when finally the trap dropped and John Long, as Bonney wrote with a fine sense of the cliché, "was launched into eternity?" What did he feel in that tense few seconds when Fox, peering at him in the candlelight, called him by name? If Bonney had feelings, he gives no hint of them to anyone.

In the last analysis, it is stolid, sober, unimaginative Bonney—not his story, that sticks in the mind. His is the story of a plain, honest citizen suddenly jerked out of the rut of his daily routine into a wildly adventurous pursuit of a band of brutal, lawless men he had never seen. If Colonel Davenport had died quietly in his bed, Edward Bonney would have lived out his life in a dusty law office in a sleepy Iowa river town, instead of spending thirteen months wandering on rail, stage, and horseback over three thousand miles on the trail of murderers. His story is an epic, in its minor, quiet way, of the ordinary men, dozens of them, who civilized the frontier.

A BRACE OF VILLAINS

★

Simon Girty

John A. Murrell

Simon Girty

★

D URING THE EIGHTEENTH century the frontier, that vast
area that stretched from the Atlantic to the Mississippi,
was a land of almost constant warfare. England and France
contended for its ownership throughout the first half of the
century, extending into the American forests the same struggle for supremacy that was fought out on the battlefields of
Europe. Later in the century, as the colonies broke away
from Britain—and even after the young Republic had won
its independence—Americans and British fought over the
same ground again for control of the empire of forest, farm-
land, and furs, the possession of which meant so much wealth
to the possessor. In this century of war, the Indian became
a kind of pawn, used by both sides, trusted by neither, his
ultimate fate the concern of none.

In the mid-eighteenth century, Indians crowded the Ohio
basin and the Northwest, some of them protecting their
ancestral homelands, others driven there from the East—
Shawnees, Delawares, Senecas, Wyandots, Miamis, Mingoes,
Ottawas and lesser tribes. They were willing to fight for or
against anybody, for the good reason that there was little
else they could do and no other place to go. The Shawnees
had already been driven from the South to Pennsylvania then
to Ohio by the inexorable advance of white settlement; the
Delawares had been driven from the Atlantic seaboard, and
other red refugees from the East and South. They were all
useful allies, though capricious, to the English, French, and
Americans who were eager and willing to use them.

The so-called "Indian Wars" of the eighteenth century in

America were in reality not Indian wars at all. They were, rather, wars between white men in which the Indian served as a weapon, or instrument, by which the white man settled the fate of the Indian's homeland. Much of the fighting was done by Indians; much of the war was carried on at their level of military tactics and ethics. Much of it was savage and cruel war, for fighting against or with savages, white men found, made war cruel and savage. The traditional military codes of Europe broke down in the Northwest. Massacre and torture were not unusual, women and children were fair game, traitors ordinary, truces often meaningless, hatred and cruelty toward one's enemy much more common than chivalry or respect. Frontier warfare was total war, fought as the Indian defined it.

The Indian wars exposed the seamier side of frontier life. The frontier, with all respect to its salutary effects on the development of American character and institutions, could be, and often was, a violent, lawless place. Along with the Godfearing and industrious who went West to make their fortunes, went the human dregs of Europe and the East, men anxious to escape the mores and morals of civilization. If the frontier marked the outer boundary of civilization, it marked also the boundaries of savagery. The line was not sharp and clear. In sparsely populated forest country where houses were few and huts rude, where a rifle, a pig, a few rows of corn and a trap line represented his food supply and his capital investment, the pioneer's life-line to civilization was slim and tenuous. Where a yearly trip to the nearest fort, for salt, powder, lead, whiskey, and cloth was his only contact with civilized life, the frontiersman found himself closer to the Indian than to the white life he had left. Sometimes the environment was too strong for the man. It was easy, very easy, to cross the line that separated red and white, after a few years in the wilderness had blurred distinctions.

More than a few white men crossed it. A deerhide shirt, a pair of moccasins, a few Indian friends, firewater sprees, an Indian wife as solace for wilderness loneliness—and the step was taken before they knew it. Those who had been captured by Indians, particularly as children, were even more suscepti- ble. The Indian custom of stealing white children and adopting them into their tribes created dozens of "white Indians" who, after a taste of savage life, were often reluctant to return to their own, and who, if they did, never fully adjusted to it. And there were the shiftless, the indolent, the refugees from justice or service, the drifters and failures who found the red man's society a welcome haven from the com- petitive bustle and hurry of Eastern civilization. Simon Girty was one of these.

Simon Girty, senior, his father, came to America from Ire- land in the early eighteenth century, to settle in Lancaster County and later at Fort Hunter in Pennsylvania. In 1737 Simon Girty, senior married; he fathered Thomas in 1739; Simon, junior, in 1741; James in 1743, and George in 1745. Life on the fringes of the forest was hard and violent, and Simon the elder fitted it perfectly. A drunken, shiftless fel- low, he was killed in 1751 in a fight with an Indian named The Fish. Girty's friend John Turner avenged him by kill- ing The Fish. Not long afterwards Turner married the Widow Girty, took over responsibility for her four sons, and in 1754 she bore him one of his own, John Turner, junior.

Western Pennsylvania, during the fifties, was a dangerous place. Marauding bands of Indians, led, supplied, and en- couraged by the French, raided the outlying settlements, burning, looting, killing, and taking captives. The entire Girty family was unlucky enough to be captured in one such raid in 1756. John Turner, senior, was burned at the stake after three hours of torture, while his wife and children watched. When the Indian forces separated, Mrs. Turner, George, and young John went with the Delawares; Thomas escaped; James went with the Shawnees, and Simon with the Senecas.

The Senecas treated young Simon as one of them. The pres- ence of young white captives in Indian settlements was not unusual; the captives themselves did not find much difficulty in slipping into tribal ways. Simon Girty learned the Seneca's language, formed friendships, and became an excellent woodsman and hunter. In 1758, when General Forbes took Fort Duquesne, one of the terms of the peace treaty signed with the French forced the Indians to return their captives, so in 1759 Simon, George, and James were reunited with their mother and brothers at newly-named Fort Pitt. All of them, except Thomas, were unaccustomed to civilized life after the free and easy life of the forest. Bustling, energetic Pittsburgh had few attractions for them. Simon, James, and George had lived out their adolescent years in an atmosphere of drunkenness, violence, and irresponsibility; they were trained for no trades nor were they possessed of any particular ambitions. Nearly four years of life among the savages were hardly calculated to develop the finer traits of a growing boy's character. The Girty brothers were rough, hard young men in a rough, hard frontier country. Furthermore, their mother simply walked out of their lives about 1760, never to be heard from again.

Simon, George, and James, who knew various Indian languages nearly as well as they did their own, took about the only jobs open to them—translators for the Army. Thomas, the eldest, traded with the Indians and by dint of shrewdness and hard work was soon on the way to becoming a respectable and perhaps a prosperous merchant. His brothers, known and liked by the Indians, spent much of their time outside the fort in the Indian camps, finding among Indians an acceptance and friendliness they did not find in white society. By 1770 Simon Girty was nothing more than one of the numerous hangers-on about Fort Pitt, a thick-necked, illiterate, worthless young man who drank too much and had a reputation for a bad temper.

The Indians of the Ohio valley, temporarily pacified in 1758, were becoming more restive and warlike, particularly as streams of white settlers pushed into the rich lands of the Ohio-Kentucky-Illinois country where the tribal hunting grounds lay. In 1774 the Virginians, under Governor Dunmore, sent an expeditionary force of militia against the Shawnees and Mingoes. Simon Girty—with George Rogers Clark and Simon Kenton—went along from Fort Pitt as a scout and an interpreter. "Lord Dunmore's War," after a few skirmishes, produced a peace treaty and for his services Simon was commissioned a second lieutenant of militia.

If Simon Girty had hopes of a military career, excellent opportunities existed for him at Fort Pitt. Talk of independence from England filled the air and there was much uncertainty among the military authorities at Pitt. Loss of Fort Pitt, the most important of frontier posts, to the revolutionary colonials would mean a severe blow for the forces of the Crown. Therefore the political affinity of each military person was carefully tested and listed, with Simon, who in accepting his commission swore fealty to King George, listed as "loyal." After Lexington, Simon changed his mind. Because his knowledge of Indians was considerable, he was a valuable acquisition to the revolutionary faction at Fort Pitt, which sent him as an emissary into Wyandot country to gather information about Indian attitudes towards the impending struggle between Crown and colonies.

The Continental Congress, hoping to extract a pledge of neutrality from the Northwest tribes, created three Indian Departments to handle diplomatic relations with the red men, with headquarters at Fort Pitt. Girty, when he returned from his mission to the Wyandots, in 1776, received an appointment as interpreter to the Senecas, his old captors. Unfortunately, his job lasted only a few months and his hopes for military preferment went with it. Discharged for "ill behavior" (probably brawling) he used his lieutenant's commission as a means of regaining grace, serving as a recruiting agent for the Continental Army. His record evidently did not inspire confidence in the authorities, however, for when the troops left for the war in the East, Simon was left behind, still a lieutenant but with neither command nor responsibilities.

The years of the Revolution were murderous in the Northwest. General Henry Hamilton, the British commandant at Detroit, deliberately embarked on a campaign intended to stir up the Indians against the Americans, organized Indian raiding parties, supplied them with leaders, and provided them with arms and equipment. His aim was, he notified his superiors in London, "to create a diversion on the frontiers of Virginia and Pennsylvania," using Ottawas, Wyandots, and Mingoes to harry the Americans while trying at the same time to woo the Shawnees, Delawares, and others to the British cause. There is no real evidence that Hamilton was a "hair-buyer," as the legend had it, who paid his Indians a bounty for American scalps. But no doubt whatever exists that Hamilton was happy to see scalps brought to Detroit. Nor did he express any sympathy for the victims of Indian tortures or for the women and children they captured. This was Henry Hamilton's way of making war for his King. As the Mohawk Joseph Brant and the renegade John Butler scourged the East at the urging of Sir John Johnson, so, in the West, Hamilton hoped to do the same.

The Americans at Fort Pitt tried to neutralize Hamilton's efforts by negotiating new treaties with the Indian tribes. The declaration of war on the United States by the powerful Seneca-Iroquois confederacy pulled many Western tribes with them; the murder by Americans of the peaceful Chief Cornstalk of the Shawnees aroused others. All the major Northwestern tribes, with the exception of some Delawares, eventually threw in their lot with the British. The friendly Delawares allowed the American forces, fortunately, to build Forts Laurens and Mackintosh in eastern Ohio as bastions against Hamilton's marauders.

General Hand at Fort Pitt sent out expeditions of his own against the hostile tribes. Simon Girty went with one of them—in which five hundred militiamen succeeded in killing three squaws—and brother George joined another into Mississippi. But Simon, who had already changed sides once, was ready to change again. At Fort Pitt one Alexander Mc-Kee, a shrewd Tory, secretly organized a party to escape to

Detroit and the British. Hand suspected McKee and ordered his arrest, but not soon enough. He had already recruited Girty, who joined him for reasons that were never clear. Simon gave later a good many explanations, none of them convincing, but it is established that he received no bribe. There were, of course, a number of reasons why he might have succumbed to McKee's arguments. His military career on the American side had certainly not been brilliant, nor could he expect much more advancement than he had already received. He had been left behind by the regiment he helped to enlist; he had been fired summarily from the one job he had held; and he had most certainly cared little for the American authorities at Fort Pitt. Pique may have played a part in this decision, and the British pay of two dollars a day may have been a temptation. Most of all, Simon's entire background was not such as to instill in him a strong sense of either honor for, or loyalty to, anything. Girty himself was never quite sure why he switched his allegiance to the British.

At any rate, McKee, Girty, an Irishman named Elliott, two Negroes, and two others left Fort Pitt on March 28, 1778, headed for Detroit. Because both McKee and Girty were influential men among Indians, their defection aroused both trepidation and anger in Pittsburgh, and a good many threats of reprisals. The Tory group reached Detroit in June.

Hamilton welcomed them, made McKee a captain as well as deputy Indian agent, and appointed Girty to an interpreter's post. Two months later James Girty came in, followed shortly by George. Not long afterwards, the Supreme Executive Council of Pennsylvania condemned them all to hanging for treason.

Hamilton and McKee made good use of the Girty brothers. Simon and James went to Ohio to organize the Shawnees and Mingoes against the Americans and to lead raids into southern Ohio and northern Kentucky. The raids themselves were matters of a few dozen Indians, a few burned farmhouses, a wrecked supply train or so, and some dead frontier families, women and children included. Militarily, from the point of view of Continental Congress, such Indian raids were merely irritating diversions in the major war being fought to the East and South. To the frontier, however, they were anything but unimportant, and the frontiersmen clamored to Congress for protection. Virginia and Pennsylvania called up such military forces as could be spared, and with George Rogers Clark in command, the expedition pushed west. Boone was with him, and Simon Kenton. While Clark's army went on to capture Kaskaskia and Vincennes, Kenton was captured in a small engagement in Kentucky. After surviving several beatings, three gantlets, and a march without food into central Ohio, he was sentenced to death at the stake.

Simon Girty's band of Indian marauders was returning from Kentucky when it encountered the war party that held Kenton captive at the Shawnee village near Upper Sandusky. Hearing that the Shawnees had a white captive, destined for the stake, Simon asked to see him. He did not recognize Kenton, who sat in a darkened tent, bloody with beatings, his face blacked in the Shawnee death sign. Girty merely looked curiously at the white man. Kenton recognized Simon, identified himself, and was overjoyed when Girty rushed to seize his hand. The renegade, by Kenton's account, nearly wept at the sight of his old companion and promised to intercede for him with the Indians. After some heated discussions the Shawnees agreed to release Kenton to Girty's custody, but the arrival of another band of Indians, fresh from Kentucky, started the argument all over again. This time Girty lost, shrugged his shoulders, and walked away. The Indians bound Kenton once more, beat him, blacked his face, and started him on his way to Upper Sandusky to be burned. Fortunately, a white trader at Upper Sandusky helped Kenton to escape.

Clark's successes in Kentucky and Illinois worried General Hamilton. Indians were easily-discouraged allies, and to counteract Clark's victories Hamilton planned to increase British activities throughout the Northwest. The British needed a few victories of their own. Simon Girty, Hamilton knew, was perhaps the most skilful of his white guerrilla leaders, so McKee sent him and seventeen Mingoes to scout about Fort Pitt, where they harassed the American settlements and scouting parties. It was not an important expedition, but Simon and the Mingoes posed a threat to the garrison at Pitt, tomahawking a farmer here, ambushing a scout or so there, disappearing into the forest at the first sign of pursuit. Girty's reputation was growing and his name spreading, though other white renegades among the British forces had been equally active. Particularly at Pitt the feeling against him ran high. Simon was not a sensitive man, nor did he believe that he was doing anything dishonorable in leading Indians against the Americans, but as word came to him of the threats from Pitt a real hatred for Americans began to stir in his slow brain. The Americans, he heard, offered eight hundred dollars gold for his scalp; Colonel Gibson at Fort Pitt ordered him shot on sight, and another officer offered to trepan him when he was caught. The Girty legend was forming, and Simon was ready to live up to it, sending word to Pitt that he "expected no mercy from the Americans and would give none."

The British at Detroit gave Girty plenty of opportunity to live up to his growing reputation. He accompanied the Indian leader Captain Bird in an unsuccessful attack on Fort Laurens, and he took mixed parties of Mingoes and Shawnees on a protracted series of raids into western Virginia and Ohio in 1779. The raids were not militarily damaging to the American cause, but their frequency helped to foster the impression on the American frontier that Girty was everywhere. They also helped to enhance his reputation for cruelty. His Indians, like the others, scalped, burned, and tortured. There are no eye-witnesses to Girty's participation in actual tortures, but at the same time it is obvious that he could not lead Indians in battle and refuse to do as they did—for to refuse meant cowardice in Indian eyes. British officers, sickened at the Indians' treatment of captives, seemed nevertheless able, with a little experience, to overcome their repugnance and Girty, who as a boy had seen his own step-father die at the stake, had much more experience than they. Until 1781 Simon, George, and James lived almost exclusively with the Indians, visiting Detroit occasionally to supply the British with information about the Ohio tribes. That year George Rogers Clark's expedition into the Northwest, led by the best Indian fighter on the frontier, brought Simon into action again as a scout attached to the British forces sent to intercept Clark. His term of service was cut short by an ignominious wound. Joseph Brant, the Mohawk, tomahawked him during a drinking bout and nearly killed him. After three months of inactivity during his recovery, Simon returned to the Wyandots again, leading small war parties into eastern Ohio and western Virginia. According to the Moravian missionaries who saw him occasionally, he was drinking heavily and developing vicious fits of temper.

In 1782 Pennsylvania and Virginia sent another expedition west, a force of nearly five hundred frontiersmen under the command of Colonel William Crawford, aimed at wiping out the Wyandot raiders in upper Ohio. The commandant at Detroit, Major De Peyster, countered with an expedition of his own, including Simon Girty with his Wyandots, George with the Delawares, and James with Captain Snake's Shawnees. The two armies met near Upper Sandusky, fought an inconclusive engagement, and separated. Crawford and eight others, however, were captured by the Shawnees.

The Shawnees marched their prisoners toward Upper Sandusky, the Half-King's town, tomahawking all but two of them on the way. At every village the squaws and children came out to beat Crawford and the other remaining captive, Surgeon Knight, while the braves slapped them in the faces with the wet scalps of their dead companions.

Dr. Knight, who later escaped by incredible luck and fortitude, left a complete account of the affair, one of the most hair-raising of frontier documents. At the Half-King's village, the two men saw Simon Girty, astride a white horse, watching while the Shawnees stripped them, clubbed them, and then whipped them with hickory rods. Crawford called to Girty, asking if the Indians intended to torture them to death. Girty replied simply and impassively, "Yes."

The fact that Girty watched for the next five hours is enough to condemn him to perdition. Crawford was tied to a stake by a rope about his waist, with enough slack to allow him to walk around it several times. The Indians fired powder from unshotted guns into his body—perhaps a hundred discharges, Knight counted—until his skin was black. The squaws, after slashing off his nose and ears, built a fire about the stake and forced Crawford to run around and around until he fell, poking him with burning sticks until he got up again. Crawford, too weak to stand, and suffering horribly, begged Girty to shoot him as he lay in the coals. Girty laughed at him, replied that he had no gun, and translated the joke to the Indians for their amusement. For two hours more the Indians poked the dying man, until finally, as he fell, a brave leaped on his back, scalped him, and poured live coals on his head. Crawford roused, staggered a few steps, and fell for the last time into the fire. For hours into the night, long after Crawford was dead, the Indians heaped coals on the charred body and danced in the firelight. Simon Girty stayed to the end. When Dr. Knight arrived at Pitt, nearly naked and half-alive after days of wandering, the Americans swore to draw and quarter Girty the moment he was captured. But no one captured him, and for the rest of the war he continued his hit-and-run raids in Ohio and western Pennsylvania.

When the Revolution ended in 1783, the three Girty brothers were with the Indians in Ohio. Simon, at the signing of the peace, returned to Detroit as an interpreter on half pay, but James and George elected to stay with the Indians. Within the year Simon married a white captive girl named Catherine Malott, who had spent four years with the Indians and may have chosen Simon as a somewhat more desirable alternative to an Indian husband. Whatever the motive, it is unlikely there was much romance in the courtship, with the bride a girl of twenty and the groom a surly, hard-drinking forty-two. In recognition of his wartime services, the British gave Simon a plot of ground in Canada, near Amherstburg not far from Detroit; there he settled down to a sort of shiftless farming. Since the Revolution was over, there was nothing else for Girty to do but drink and wait until he was needed again.

The Revolution may have been over, but the Indian wars were not. Though the United States signed treaties with the more troublesome tribes in 1785, friction between Indians and advancing white settlers continued almost without interruption. Over the span of years from 1785 to 1796, England, France and Spain embroiled themselves in a struggle for power, involving the New World as well as the Old, with the American West as part of the stakes. The British, though they had agreed to evacuate the Northwest posts by the terms of the Treaty of Paris, hung on, hoping by some maneuver to save their fur-trade empire and extend the Canadian boundary southward. Detroit, in particular, the British hated to give up. The center of a thriving trade and a key to the control of the Great Lakes, the city was the most important of the Northwest posts.

Lieutenant-Governor Simcoe of Canada extended the traditional British policy of using the Indians in the Northwest as a tool for creating disturbances. He was certain in his own mind that the United States, once it had obtained the frontier posts, intended to use them as bases for an invasion of Canada. Lord Grenville, in London, saw the Northwest posts as part of a somewhat larger plan. If the Indians could be kept at war, it might be possible to erect a neutral Indian buffer state between Canada and the United States in the area stretching from the Ohio River to the Great Lakes. The Canadian border would then, in effect, be pushed south to the Ohio, American westward expansion blocked, the British fur trade saved. The Indians already claimed rights to all the land north of the Ohio, and the British saw to it that the Indian claim stayed alive.

Simcoe and Grenville reasoned if the British could form a coalition of Indian tribes to hold back the Americans until they wearied of the wars, the whole Northwest territory might drop into British laps like a ripe plum. Yet since the United States and Britain were at peace, and since Britain had extremely pressing military and diplomatic problems in Europe, the British dared not risk an overt act that might precipitate war. The Americans, well aware of British intentions, worked swiftly to negotiate treaties with the hostile tribes before they could be welded into an effective confederacy. From Britain's point of view, it was essential that the leaderless and disorganized tribes be kept at war, and organized into some semblance of anti-American unity. Because this kind of thing was Simon Girty's specialty, the British called him out of his rural retirement.

For six years after the Revolution, Girty spent much of his time away from home, travelling among the Indians and stirring up resentment against the United States. He was undoubtedly of extreme value to the British, and had real influence among the Ohio tribes. A captive white boy, who saw him once at an Indian settlement, reported that he wore deerhide clothes, Indian style, a handkerchief around his head, and carried a silver-mounted pistol and a short dirk. The Indians showed great respect for him; they treated him as a chief. A word from Girty eased the boy's captivity considerably. By 1790, with the help of Girty and others like him, the British had created a brisk though limited war in the Ohio country. Simon himself led small war parties year after year, working mainly with the Wyandots. At least once he equalled his performance as an impassive onlooker at Crawford's death.

Girty's Wyandots, besieging a small fort in Ohio, captured one of its defenders, a luckless man named Abner Hunt. They beat Hunt brutally, then sent him to the fort under a flag of truce with the message that, unless the garrison surrendered, the Indians would torture him to death. Hunt begged his commander to surrender, but Wyandot promises were not to be trusted. The commander, weighing one life against many, refused, and the Wyandots led Hunt away. Girty kept their word. His Indians tortured Hunt to death that night, while the garrison listened to his screams until dawn and watched the glow of the Indian fires.

Girty's raids against the scattered American settlements and forts kept the Northwest in terror, until bitter complaints from the frontier led Congress in 1790 to authorize President Washington to organize a militia expedition against the hostile Indians. The British, well aware of the plan, redoubled their efforts to form an alliance among the various tribes. After some six months, Governor St. Clair led fifteen hundred men, drawn from Pennsylvania, Virginia, and Kentucky, into the Ohio country. A part of St. Clair's army, under General Harmar, was caught moving slowly up from Cincinnati by Blue Jacket and Little Turtle near the present site of Fort Wayne. Harmar's men were soundly thrashed, their relieving force ambushed, and the expedition halted. Girty, who had been working hard at consolidating the Indian confederation, fought there with his Wyandots.

Arthur St. Clair, after Harmar's failure, planned to take out a larger force himself and to build a chain of forts across Ohio to support it. But building forts and organizing an army was slow work. While St. Clair gathered his militiamen, Girty and other British agents from Detroit scattered among the tribes, trying to keep the wavering Indian alliance together. In October, 1792, the Indian chiefs, under British sponsorship, held a great conclave near Maumee, drawing delegations from even the faraway tribes beyond the Mississippi. The topic of discussion was war or peace with the United States. The Six Nations advised peace; Little Turtle and the Ohio Indians wanted war. The only white man allowed to attend the chiefs' council was Simon Girty, who earned his British pay that day—and more—by helping to persuade the Shawnees and Miamis to stay on the warpath. St. Clair's expedition ended in disaster when Little Turtle caught St. Clair's green army napping and almost demolished it.

Simon Girty by 1792 was a man for the Americans to reckon with. He had great influence with the Shawnees, Wyandots, and Miamis, the most troublesome of the Northwest tribes. Of all the renegades employed by the British, he was the most successful at leading raids, and while he had neither the skill nor the intelligence to make military policy, he was particularly effective as a liaison between the British Indian agencies and the Indian chiefs. He was, it is true, a drunken, quarrelsome man, and a problem to his British superiors, who at the same time recognized his usefulness as a tool to stir up Indians. Yet Girty, who reached the highest point of his influence at the conclave of 1792, was nearly finished, for British-American-Indian affairs in the Northwest were rapidly approaching a climax.

Though both the United States and Britain had carefully avoided any overt acts of war for nearly ten years, Governor Simcoe in 1792 overstepped the line. Sending an expeditionary force a hundred miles southwest of Detroit, he built a fort on the Maumee River in the center of Indian country. British agents, working among the tribes, promised the Indians support—possibly military support—for their continued resistance against American encroachment and provided them with blankets, arms, food, even vermilion for warpaint. The attempts by Girty and others to consolidate the Indian tribes began to show success. Little Turtle's Miamis, Black Wolf's Shawnees, the Chippewas and Ottawas under Blue Jacket, even Sacs and Foxes from Wisconsin and Minnesota gathered on the Maumee in the heaviest concentration of Indian strength yet seen in the Northwest.

The United States answered Simcoe with Anthony Wayne, "Mad Anthony" of Revolutionary fame, who took charge of military affairs in the Northwest in 1792. No fumbler like Harmar, and a professional soldier as St. Clair was not, Wayne took a tough, expert army, the "Legion of the United States," into Ohio in 1793. There he drilled it, taught it woods warfare, and after hardening it through the winter, marched it into Indian country on the lower Maumee. Then he built a fort under the noses of the British, named it appropriately Fort Defiance, and stayed, daring Indians or British or both to fight. The British did not dare to accept his challenge, for to do so meant open war with the United States. Wayne parleyed with the Indians, failed to win them over, and the chiefs returned to the British fort. Simon Girty was there, with the Wyandots, to lend his weight to the argument for war and to lead his Indians in a sortie against a part of Wayne's army near Fort Recovery. The attack was beaten off—as Girty fought for the last time against Americans— and on August 20th Wayne began his offensive. The Indian forces took cover behind a tangled mass of fallen trees, but Wayne's troops routed them in less than an hour of hard fighting. The Indians fled to the shelter of the British fort, pursued by dragoons; the British commander, cannons loaded and matches lit, warned the American troops off. Wayne almost stormed the fort, changed his mind, and turned away. Then his men systematically laid waste the Indian villages and cornfields for miles around, destroying anything that might serve to support Indian resistance. Girty and his Wyandots, stationed somewhat removed from the area of concentrated fighting, saw the battle turn against the Indians and took no part in it whatever. The battle was lost, and neither Simon nor the Wyandots could see any reason to fight without winning.

The Battle of Fallen Timbers broke the back of organized Indian resistance in the Northwest. Tired of war, discouraged and defeated, the Indian chiefs refused to respond to British urgings and signed the necessary treaties with the United States in 1795. They could do nothing else. The British finally agreed to vacate the military posts in the Northwest, and in 1795 and 1796 the Americans took over Fort Miami, Detroit, and Michilimackinac. There were no more British, no more scalping raids, no more council fires along the Maumee, and there was no more work for Simon Girty. After Fallen Timbers he simply left for his Canadian farm. James Girty married an Indian wife and took to trading with the Indians. George went back to the Delawares and lost himself among them, turning at last completely Indian.

Simon's life after 1795 was a long anticlimax. He made a bare living from his farm, occasional interpreting jobs, and his half-pay pension from the British. He visited Detroit now and then, less frequently as the time approached for the Americans to take over. The legend persists that he was in Detroit as the last British soldier left, and that as the Americans entered the city, he jumped his horse from the river bank and swam to Canada as a gesture of defiance to the occupying troops. In Amherstburg he was a local celebrity, known as a violent, boastful man, given to periodic wild drunks. Local children remembered the frightening figure of the half-blind old man reeling home in the night from the saloons, cursing at those who got in his way and slashing at the air with his sword. His wife, tired of beatings, left him in 1798 and took their four children with her.

During the temporary occupation of Detroit by the British during the War of 1812 Simon Girty visited the city a few times. When Harrison's American expeditionary force crossed to Canada in 1813 to occupy Amherstburg, Girty prudently left well beforehand to live with the Mohawks. Ironically, Simon Kenton, who was with Harrison's company of Kentuckians, spent a night quartered in Girty's house—had the troops known who the owner was, they undoubtedly would have burned the house to the ground. Girty came back to his farm in 1816, almost totally blind, ill, and somewhat less vicious in temper. His wife returned to stay with him until his death on February 18, 1818. He was buried in the iron cold of Canadian winter, and in spring no one remembered to put a marker on his grave.

The four Girty brothers make an interesting study in atavism. Thomas, the least affected by his Indian captivity, was a somewhat stolid man who was always embarrassed by his surname, which gave him a great deal of trouble in his business dealings around Pittsburgh. The other three never lived down the effects of their stay with the Indians. James and George preferred Indian life and eventually chose it in preference to white society. Both of them, unlike Simon, dressed like Indians, married Indians, and found Indian life much more suitable than white. Simon, the middle brother, was a blend of red and white, an unpredictable combination of civilization and savagery, unable to make up his mind on which side of the line he really belonged. He watched and encouraged the torture of fellow white men (and may have helped) like an Indian. At the same time, in four authenticated instances he gave assistance to white captives held by Indians; he seemed to have an especially soft spot for young white boys. He did save Kenton from death—once—but walked away from him the second time. It is also noticeable that until he recognized the doomed captive as Kenton, his only reaction was one of idle curiosity. And most of all, he simply stood by while Crawford and Hunt, and probably others, died horribly.

Simon Girty was not an admirable or pleasant man. He had enough white in him to know what he was doing, and enough red to do it. The line of demarcation between savagery and civilization was indistinct to his mind; he could cross and re-cross it easily, living with Wyandots one year, moving back to white society the next, finding no difficulty in the transition. At one moment he could be the white leader, admired and respected by the lesser savages who followed him, at another the cruel, capricious, amoral savage, a red man with a white skin. The truth is that Simon himself probably did not know which he was.

Though there were other renegade white men as cruel as he, and several others who played more important parts in the Indian wars, Simon Girty by 1779 had become the frontier's symbol of the White Savage. The Americans thought of him as a devil; "a wretched miscreant," one contemporary called him, "a savage in manner and principle, who spent his life in the perpetration of a demoniac vengeance against his countrymen." Stories of barbaric tortures clustered about his name from New York to the Carolinas and far into the

West. Any white man seen with Indians was automatically identified as Girty; any rumors of renegade cruelty were readily attached to him; balladeers chronicled his misdeeds. American soldiers, officers and rank-and-file, hated him fiercely and frontier settlers vowed horrible vengeance upon him.

Yet, in contrast to his reputation, Simon Girty was rather small fry. He never held a responsible military post, nor did the British ever entrust him with any mission that required intelligence or trustworthiness. His fellow turncoats, McKee and Elliott, both held much more important posts in the British Indian agency than he and had much more to do with the shaping of Indian policy. They had no illusions about Simon; they used him for what he was—a cruel, half-savage lout who knew Indians and had a certain skill in forest warfare. But the Americans needed heroes and villains for their frontier war. For heroes they had Kenton, Boone, Clark, and later Anthony Wayne. Simon—along with Captain Pipe, Dumquat the Shawnee Half-King, and Hair-Buyer Hamilton—was made over from an ordinary brute into a fearsome symbol of villainy. Of everything that war in the wilderness meant to the frontier, he became a convenient personification.

John A. Murrell

★

THE DRIVE WESTWARD at the turn of the nineteenth century created a southwestern as well as a northwestern frontier. Paralleling the stream of trade and settlers that poured into the Ohio-Great Lakes basin, another stream flowed southwesterly toward New Orleans, French Louisiana, and Spanish Mexico. Congress, in 1798, created the Territory of Mississippi, garrisoned it with troops, and gave it a territorial capital. In 1803, with the Louisiana Purchase, the United States opened the Mississippi, turned New Orleans into a major seaport and began to survey the land preparatory to sale. In 1812 Louisiana entered the Union, and two years later Arkansas became a territory. The Southwest became a booming frontier.

It was a different kind of frontier, however, from that of the agrarian Northwest. This was cotton and slave country, dominated by the rich black cotton lands, the slaveholding planters, and the Mississippi River—especially by the big river. To the farmers and planters of Ohio, Kentucky, and Tennessee the river provided the only really feasible route of commerce, and New Orleans the only outlet to the sea. From Pittsburgh, and from the Ohio and Kentucky towns, the Ohio led to the Mississippi and New Orleans; from Tennessee the Tennessee River and its subsidiaries led there, too. After 1800 the rivers were thick with flatboats carrying the produce of the West to market, later with steamboats magnificently churning the waters with paddlewheels. Memphis, Vicksburg, and Natchez mushroomed into bustling port towns, while New Orleans, the focal point of it all, turned from a quaintly moss-hung old-world city into a brawling commercial metropolis.

The difficulty with the Mississippi was that it carried traffic in but one direction. Flatboats could go only downriver, and until the development of the steamer this one-way trade had serious disadvantages. Flatboats were usually broken up and sold for lumber in Natchez or New Orleans, leaving the boatmen and traders to get home overland as best they could. There was no efficient channel for northwardbound trade; roads were few, and virtually impassable.

The demand for roads created the Natchez Trace, developed from an old Indian trail, running northeast across Mississippi, following the Big Black and the Pearl Rivers to the Tennessee, and continuing to Nashville, where it met Boone's Wilderness Road. In 1806 the Federal government declared the Trace a post road, placed it under the authority of the Post Office Department, and sent soldiers to widen and improve it. From 1801 until 1835 the Natchez Trace carried settlers southward, and boatmen and traders northwards, by the thousands.

The stream of wealth flowing down the Mississippi and along the Natchez Trace lured half the thieves, gamblers, prostitutes, and petty criminals in America to the Southwest. Men travelling alone with money in their pockets, either on the Mississippi or along the Trace, were not good insurance risks. On the river, until the steamers came, pirates preyed on the flatboats. From outlaw nests like Cave-in Rock, near the mouth of the Wabash on the Ohio, New Madrid, and Wolf Island, organized bands of killers attacked passing boats with impunity for nearly a decade. Even the steamers, when their day arrived, were infested with crooks and cutthroats; more than a thousand gamblers alone, it was calculated, worked the river from 1835 to 1850. The river towns developed districts given over entirely to criminal elements, "sinks of crime and corruption" lined with saloons and brothels, such as Memphis' "Pinchgut," "Natchez-under-the-hill," and New Orleans' "Swamp." Law enforcement in the raw Mississippi towns was nearly nonexistent. When affairs became unbearable for honest men, the Regulators or Vigilantes might take over and hang a few of the worst criminals, but the roaring lowlife of the river towns never really stopped.

The Natchez Trace was no safer than the river. For three hundred miles after leaving Natchez the road stretched through a virtual wilderness of swamp, canebrake, and forest, with only an occasional squatter's cabin, an inn, or a ferryman's hut to break the desolation. Traders returning from Natchez or New Orleans with the proceeds of slave or cotton sales in their saddlebags travelled in pairs or groups whenever possible, and even then found little safety in numbers. Settlers bound from Ohio for the newly-opened delta lands and carrying all their belongings with them, provided particularly lush pickings for the Trace brigands. Because there was no other way for men to travel overland to New Orleans or back except by the Trace, the "land pirates," fully as murderous as their river brethren, made it a bloody and dangerous trail.

The Harpe brothers, "Big" and "Little," were the first to prey on the traffic of the Natchez Trace. Homicidal maniacs both, shunned by other outlaws as abnormal killers, they were responsible for at least a hundred murders along the trail. "Big" Harpe was caught by Vigilantes, decapitated, and his head nailed to a tree on the banks of the Cumberland. "Little" Harpe escaped to join Samuel Mason, who had been commissioned a justice of the peace and sent to Mississippi to bring some law to the territory. Mason found the temptation too great; he himself became an outlaw and lived as one until he was tomahawked by "Little" Harpe, who in turn was caught and hanged when he tried to collect the reward offered for Mason's head. Joseph Hare, a graduate of the Eastern city slums, spread terror along the Trace for several years—but Hare, a moody man, dreaded the silence and loneliness of the wilderness, began to have hallucinations, went to pieces, and was captured and hanged.

The Harpes, Mason, Hare and lesser criminals like them

along the Natchez Trace were outlaws plain and simple. They operated alone or with small groups, planning nothing, moving from one killing to the next, one step ahead of the vigilantes. They were vicious, cunning, but not intelligent men who did no more than nibble at the wealth moving along the Trace. None of them lasted more than a few years, and none of them ever displayed talent for anything more than simple brutality. The first man to recognize the real potentialities of crime in the Southwest, the twisted genius who hoped to carve out a huge outlaw empire from the new frontier, was John A. Murrell of Tennessee. The others were merely a prelude.

John Murrell was born in middle Tennessee in 1804, probably near the town of Columbia, some fifty miles from Nashville. His father, who kept a roadside tavern, seems to have been an honest and industrious man (at least Murrell said so) but his mother was of a different sort. She taught all her children to steal, and by the time he was ten years old John was expert at cleaning the pockets of sleeping guests. At sixteen he left home, joined a gang of horsethieves, learned the rudiments of gambling and robbery, and dabbled in a little counterfeiting. A year or so later he made the acquaintance of Harry Crenshaw, an older and more experienced criminal who had once shipped with Jean Lafitte. Crenshaw, who liked young Murrell, suggested they make a team. Murrell quickly accepted, and with a few stolen horses the two men made for Georgia.

From Crenshaw, Murrell learned how easy it was to kill. In the Cumberland mountains they fell in with a trader named Woods who was returning to South Carolina with some cotton money. One blow with a weighted whip butt, and Crenshaw and Murrell were twelve hundred dollars richer. However, Woods was stunned, not killed, so Crenshaw calmly threw him over a cliff and rode on. In Georgia they sold the horses and worked their way into the Carolinas and back across Alabama to New Orleans, robbing travellers here, stealing horses there, while Murrell learned his trade.

Crenshaw needed to teach him very little, for Murrell was a born killer with neither conscience nor compunction. "There is but one safe way in this business," he said later, "and that is to kill." Unlike the Harpes, who killed because they enjoyed it, Murrell murdered because murder was to him a good business. On the swing through Georgia and Alabama with Crenshaw, Murrell learned his first rule— "Never rob a man, unless by stealth, without killing him, and never rob by violence where the person robbed cannot be killed."

The two men ended their trip in New Orleans' Swamp district. "We frolicked for a week or more," Murrell said, "commenced sporting and gambling and lost every damned cent of our money." With empty pockets Murrell then set out for Tennessee, sold his horse in Natchez, and began the long walk along the Trace. After four days of walking he met a traveller, stripped him, shot him, and rode away on his horse with four hundred dollars and thirty-seven cents. Murrell did it coolly and efficiently. His victim, he said, "looked wishfully up and down and at last he turned from me and dropped on his knees and I shot him through the head. I could not help it. I had been obliged to travel on foot for the last four days." He also evolved his second rule of robbery—never leave a corpse behind. His method of disposal, one he followed the remainder of his life, was to disembowel the body, fill it with stones, and sink it in a stream. So a week later, with money in his purse and fine new clothes, Murrell was back in Natchez.

John Murrell was an intelligent man with a facility for learning from experience and observation. For one thing, he knew that the days of freebooters like Crenshaw were numbered; they robbed and killed casually, but sooner or later they ended up dangling from a tree or with their heads nailed to posts. They were rough, brutal men, obviously thugs and easily identifiable as such. Murrell, on the other hand, "possessed a quick mind and a remarkably pleasant and gentleman-like address." He neither talked, looked, nor acted like a criminal. Nearly everyone who knew him re-marked on his "genteel manner," a quality he could easily turn to his advantage. He learned how to use it from a man named Carter in Natchez. Carter, who had a smattering of Bible knowledge, travelled as an itinerant Methodist preacher, making the campmeeting circuit. When he was ready to go on the road again he invited Murrell to join him. Murrell and Carter for the next few months wandered through Tennessee and Alabama, conducting revivals. Car-ter's specialty was counterfeit money, and through him Mur-rell learned a good deal about what Carter called, in the argot of the day, "passing the queer." Murrell specialized in robbery, which was not difficult during the excitement of a frontier campmeeting, while he learned at the same time, he said, "to quote scripture, shout hymns, and preach a damned fine sermon." After the trip he drifted to Natchez again to work along the Trace to Tennessee and back, sometimes alone, sometimes with a companion or so. He was clever enough not to be caught, though he was once fined fifty cents for riot (considered an unimportant misdemeanor on the frontier) and another time a few dollars for gaming. Never-theless, Murrell was not satisfied. He was still a minor, petty crook; his status was exceeded by his ambitions.

The turning point in Murrell's career came in 1825. That year he was caught stealing horses in Tennessee, convicted, flogged, branded on the hand with HT (Horse Thief) and jailed for near a year. For a proud man to be convicted as a common horsethief was bad enough; flogging and brand-ing were worse. Murrell spent his time in jail thinking and studying. He read some law, particularly the rules of evi-dence so he would not be caught so easily again, and he studied the Bible, the better to authenticate his ministerial pose. And he also fed on his bitterness against those who had imprisoned him—"When they turned me loose," he said, "I wanted to kill all but my own girt (*kin*)."

When they did turn him loose, Murrell had the rest of his career carefully charted. The old days of casual banditry were over. The frontier towns were growing swiftly; frontier society was organizing against land pirates just as the river towns were mobilizing against the river pirates. To be successful in the new society of the Southwest, the criminal had to be respectable. He had to have a wife, a home, property, community standing. He had to dress well, speak well, appear as a substantial citizen among citizens. Then, too, the new criminal had to plan. He should have a storehouse for his loot, men of semirespectable position to dispose of it for him, friends among law officers or prominent citizenry to help him out, even a disciplined gang so that crime could be coordinated for greater efficiency and better returns. Organization was the key—"I soon began to see the value of friends in this business," he said. Murrell recognized the advantages of diversification. There were other ways to make money beside armed robbery—counterfeiting, slavestealing, horsethievery, selling stolen goods, and so on. Murrell had the brains, the motive, and the ability to become a major criminal. When he was released from jail in 1826 he set about doing so.

The first thing he did was to establish a horse-stealing ring in Tennessee. This time he supplied the organizational skill and let others do the work. He was eminently successful, enough so that he could purchase a good farm near Denmark, in West Tennessee. He brought a wife there (a girl he picked out of Memphis' Pinchgut) and settled down in the community, where he soon was known as a man of substance. He lived quietly (though frequently away from home), kept fine horses, and wore tailored clothes. His calfskin boots he had specially made; his coat had gold buttons; his hats he had shipped from Philadelphia.

Murrell also expanded his interests. On his trips, posing as a Methodist preacher, he still passed counterfeit money and occasionally robbed a traveller. But since slaves were valuable property, even more so than horses, he branched out into slave-stealing. A persuasive talker, Murrell found it easy to convince some simple Negro that he was mistreated and that he would be better off under a new master. Then, with a single slave or a group, he would make his way to some distant plantation, sell the Negroes, and start all over again. Here his ministerial manner helped him, for who could suspect a sanctimonious man of the cloth of dealing in stolen slaves? If pursuit came too close, Murrell killed the Negroes, loaded them with stones, and sank them in a river. When he found a coöperative or particularly gullible slave he developed a variation on his scheme, restealing and reselling the same Negro over and over until someone recognized him. Then Murrell shot him and found another. How many slaves he stole and sold Murrell never really knew, and how many he killed he never bothered to count. Sometimes, too, in his various operations, Murrell killed unfortunate witnesses. "No man should live," he said, "who can implicate me without implicating himself."

By 1830 John Murrell was a wealthy man. He had horse-stealing and slave-stealing rings in operation, a successful counterfeiting business, a good organization for disposing of stolen goods, connections with every corruptible law officer in the Southwest, a host of shady friends who asked no questions, and a number of highly respectable friends who suspected nothing at all. "All were fish that came to Murrell's net," wrote a contemporary, "men of all classes, including many persons of wealth, judges, lawyers, militia officers of high rank, merchants, etc." Everywhere he went he asked about thieves, counterfeiters, swindlers, or criminals of any kind and, if they seemed likely prospects, he looked them up for his organization. He could offer steady work and protection; they could provide him with the manpower he needed to maintain his expanding enterprises. And they were expanding. John Murrell was well on the way to becoming the first gang overlord in American history.

Murrell's power grew fast. During the early thirties, a contemporary wrote, "the citizens of the Southwest lived in apprehension." The Natchez Trace, always dangerous, now seemed doubly so. Slaves disappeared by the dozens. Banks and stores took in bales of queer money. If one of Murrell's horse thieves or slavestealers were hauled into court, witnesses had a way of failing to turn up or of refusing to testify. Sheriffs let prisoners escape; helpful juries gave verdicts of Not Guilty; complainants received threats and decided not to prosecute. Meanwhile John Murrell, impeccably tailored and gentlemanly of manner, rode through Tennessee and Mississippi directing his enterprises. Nobody could touch him, though by this time a good many suspected him. The Southwest was literally afraid of him, for Murrell's men were far better organized and much more efficient than the forces of the law.

Murrell's success lay in his gift for organization. He had, he claimed, a hundred or more criminals of one sort or another working for him. To enforce discipline and maintain organization he founded a secret society known as the Mystic Confederacy, or The Clan, to which each of his employees belonged—a silly scheme, perhaps, but one exactly fitted to the minds of the characters he attracted into it. The Clan had initiation ceremonies, two degrees, plenty of mumbo jumbo, and various signs. The sign of the lower degree, that of "stryker," was a wave of the hand with the wrist bent; the higher degree, that of "grand counsellor," had as its sign a handshake with certain fingers closed. Any Clan member, on receiving a recognition sign, was supposed to go to the aid of the one giving it. Nor did Murrell neglect the desires of those who joined his Clan. In his new headquarters, which he established in Arkansas, he provided whiskey, gambling, refuge, and finances for trips to the river-town brothels. To those who violated their oath of secrecy he promised torture and death—and occasionally he carried it out.

John Murrell had great ambitions, imperial aims that far surpassed the creating of a successful gang to befuddle the law and intimidate his victims. He studied and analyzed the structure of the frontier society of his time, familiarized himself with its strengths and flaws, and evolved a way to shatter it. What he really wanted to be was ruler of the Southwest.

The most vulnerable point of Southern society, Murrell knew, was its almost pathological fear of slave rebellion. Nothing panicked the South more than the thought of another Nat Turner. On his trip with Crenshaw into the Carolinas as a boy he had seen what the mere rumor of a slave uprising could do to a Southern town—deserted streets, frightened people, frantic preparations, complete collapse of community organization and morale. What an opportunity a slave rebellion might give a bold, unprincipled, intelligent man! Why not, Murrell reasoned, engineer a real revolt, take over the Southwest, and build his own empire of Negroes and Clan outlaws on the ruins?

Exactly when Murrell conceived his "great conspiracy" is hard to determine; possibly it was in 1832 or 1833. The plan was in many ways fantastic, one that in the end would have failed inevitably, but Murrell's vaulting ambition blinded him to its weaknesses. In his favor he had certain advantages— a well-organized gang of his own, the morbid Southern fear of the Black Terror, slow communications between widely-scattered towns, poorly mobilized local militia to oppose him, an inefficient group of law officers who were usually unable to cope with anything more than simple thievery. An alliance of outlaws and slaves in the Southwest would pose a real problem for any but Federal troops, who were thinly scattered and far away. And before the Southwest could recover from a well-planned attack, Murrell's men could loot, burn, and plunder at will; perhaps he could establish his own dictatorship before anyone could stop him. At any rate, Murrell seems to have believed in his plan and to have convinced others of its chances for success. He held a three-day council at which the whole scheme was worked out, and "then determined to undertake the rebellion at every hazard."

First Murrell intended to send his men among the plantation slaves, stirring up dissatisfaction and hatred—here he could use antislavery societies and their agents as a cover. Next, the slaves would be sworn into The Clan with a long and fearsome ceremony, involving "a monstrous picture of a great devil, to teach them obedience, and the skeleton of a man, to show what will happen if they are unfaithful. . . ." The Negroes would then be organized into regiments, a trusted white Clan member at the head of each, with Murrell as Supreme Commander. At a given date would occur simultaneous uprisings through the entire Southwest, with attacks in force on Natchez, Memphis, and other key cities where local Clan members stood ready to assist. The towns would have no opportunity to organize. With his Negroes sweeping through Tennessee and Mississippi, his Clan beside him, his friends working from within, and outlaws ready to join him at every village, John Murrell would scour the countryside, killing, pillaging, and burning, until the Southwest called him its master. Then Murrell himself, at the head of his outlaw army, would smash New Orleans—the city the British could not take, but Murrell could.

Murrell worked at his scheme for months, calling councils, laying plans, choosing his officers, storing arms, and establishing routes and communications. He had, he said, eighty officers and about three hundred white men in his organization by the close of 1833. He even had chosen his target date, with a sense of irony, as Christmas Day, 1835. Then his vanity betrayed him.

The agent of Murrell's downfall was a fresh-faced Scots boy from Georgia named Virgil Stewart. Stewart, born in Jackson County, Georgia, migrated to West Tennessee when he was twenty years old, farmed a while, and then sold his property in 1833 to move to the Choctaw Purchase lands in Mississippi. He settled at Tuscahoma, Mississippi; there he joined a man named Edward Clanton in running a store, a business he liked so much that he decided to give up farming. Soon after Christmas, 1833, he decided to travel back to Tennessee to visit acquaintances in Madison County, particularly Parson John Henning, whom he counted as his best friend. Henning and his wife welcomed young Stewart and told him their troubles—someone was stealing their slaves. One had disappeared some time earlier and now two more were gone—prize field hands worth a thousand dollars apiece. The Parson suspected John Murrell.

Henning had no good reason to suspect Murrell, who lived quietly with his wife and younger brother on a farm not far away. But Murrell's wealth (more than his farm produced), his frequent absences, and his too-smooth manner made his neighbors vaguely suspicious of him. Murrell knew it. He even knew that Henning suspected him of slave-stealing, and he had written Henning a pleasant letter explaining that though he was leaving on a business trip on January 25th, he would be glad to allay the Parson's suspicions as soon as he returned. The Parson was not put off by smooth talk. He still thought Murrell guilty, and with Stewart devised a plan to trap him. Murrell did not know Stewart. Why not have Stewart meet Murrell "accidentally," ride with him on his trip, and see if Murrell could be pumped? So Stewart hid in Henning's house for two days, and on the twenty-fifth rode out in the early dawn to find Murrell.

Stewart waited by a toll bridge at the town of Estanaula, where Murrell was likely to cross the river. Traveller after traveller passed, until a dark, handsome man, immaculately dressed, a brace of silver-mounted pistols at his side, his face pitted with smallpox scars, rode up on a blooded horse. This was John Murrell. Stewart caught up with him a mile down the road and began conversation. His name was Hues, he said, Adam Hues, and he was looking for a lost horse. Murrell did not seem particularly interested, but Stewart was a friendly fellow and as he chattered on Murrell warmed up a trifle. They rode the remainder of the day together, with Stewart providing an audience for the older man. By nightfall, when they bedded down at an inn, the two were good friends.

Stewart was exactly the sort of person to strike Murrell in his weakest spot, his vanity. He liked the young Scotsman who listened wide-eyed to his talk and who obviously hung on his every word with admiration. Murrell had no son of his own, and perhaps the boy appealed to him. Stewart seemed especially interested in tales of crime and criminals, and Murrell began to brag a bit, subtly at first, then more openly. Speaking of rogues, he said—he knew a pair of brothers who were "the slickest rogues in Tennessee," particularly the older one. This man had killed, robbed, stolen, done everything, yet none could catch him. He had stolen "half the niggers in Tennessee, and most of the horses," killed dozens of men on the Natchez Trace, robbed on the river boats, "passed the queer" at a hundred campmeetings, and bought sheriffs and lawyers like cattle. They rode the next day and the next and Stewart listened. At night when they stopped Stewart made notes in a book he carried in his saddlebags, filling page after page with names, dates, crimes. After three days young Stewart had a record that frightened him. If half of what Murrell said was true, he was by all odds the most vicious criminal in the Southwest. This man was a cold killer.

Virgil Stewart was involved far more deeply than he cared to be. Starting out to see if he could find some evidence on stolen slaves, he was now in possession of information that jeopardized his life every moment Murrell was at his side. If Murrell found out his real name or real purpose, Stewart realized he would live no more than thirty seconds. The longer he stayed with Murrell, and the more Murrell talked, the more Stewart knew and the less his life was worth. Yet if he aroused Murrell's suspicion by leaving on some trumped-up excuse, he knew Murrell would track him down relentlessly and kill him. So Stewart rode on, listening with sick fascination while the whole life story of crime and murder unfolded, taking notes at night with shaking fingers, hoping during the day to meet no one who could call him by his right name. And still Murrell talked on, drawling out his tale, until finally he grinned and said, "I might as well out with it. I am that elder brother I was telling you of."

Stewart knew the next move, and inevitably it came.

"Look here," Murrell said, "I am going to Arkansas. Why don't you come along with me?"

Though Stewart pleaded the lost horse, lack of money, friends who expected him, he knew he dared not protest too much. "I'll guarantee you a better horse than the one you're hunting," promised Murrell, "and I'll learn you a few tricks if you come with me!" Still Stewart hung back, until Murrell, losing his temper, shouted, "Damn it, you must go!" So Stewart and Murrell turned toward Arkansas and The Clan's headquarters.

On the way to Arkansas Murrell explained the Mystic Confederacy, and before they reached the Mississippi he had outlined his slave-rebellion conspiracy. He had almost four hundred by now in the Clan Council, he claimed, and six hundred "strykers," who "did those things we are not willing to do." By rebellion day he hoped to have several thousand slaves sworn in, and he talked enthusiastically of the rebellion, how it would be organized, how his men would lay waste the Lower Mississippi valley, leaving behind them "one common scene of devastation, smoked walls, and fragments," until he rode into New Orleans, master of the Southwest. "By God, Hues," he said, his eyes shining, "I want you to be with me at New Orleans the night the niggers commence their work." Stewart did not have to pretend interest. He listened in horror while Murrell talked, and rode on with a cold chill in his bones.

Stewart's only hope lay in getting a message to someone who might believe his incredible tale. With Murrell at his side there was small chance of doing so, until at Champeon's inn, just before they crossed the Mississippi, Stewart had an opportunity to blurt out the whole story to the innkeeper, who promised to send word to Parson Henning. The innkeeper, Stewart felt, no more than half-believed him, yet he had to take the chance. The next day Murrell and Stewart crossed the river and landed in Arkansas. Murrell led the way through the swamps along a dim trail until they came to a hut. Four men were there, rough-looking heavily-armed fellows who talked confidentially to Murrell about four stolen slaves who sat mute and huddled in a corner. Then the two pushed on. Finally Murrell pointed ahead to a grove of trees. "That is the Garden of Eden," he said. "That is headquarters."

Murrell's robbers' nest was a long, low, log building, well-hidden in a clump of cottonwoods, dirty, littered with whiskey bottles and trash. A dozen or so men waited to greet Murrell, and much discussion followed of stolen horses and slaves. Late that afternoon Stewart was initiated into The Clan, the drinking began, and the building roared with brawling, drunken thugs. Stewart wanted to get out, as fast as possible, but Murrell, claiming that they were sending out for some "Arkansas girls and the fun was just beginning," wanted him to stay. Well, said Stewart, there was a girl he'd met at Irvin's plantation—and Murrell, half-drunk himself, laughingly let him go, on his promise to meet Murrell at Irvin's later.

Stewart, "breathing easily for the first time in four days," reached Irvin's and told his story to the plantation owner. Though Irvin found the tale hard to believe, he promised to watch Murrell's goings and comings and try to catch him with some stolen slaves. A day or so later Murrell turned up, as he had promised, and Stewart rode off with him. Pleading the necessity of going to Yalo Busha, Stewart left the trail, rode hard ahead, and arrived in Madison County a day before Murrell did.

Stewart and Henning, working around the clock, aroused the entire countryside. When Murrell rode into his farmyard a group of armed farmers met and arrested him. When Stewart appeared in the crowd, Murrell nearly collapsed. "For the first time," wrote Stewart, "Murrell lost his spirits and fortitude. He appeared as though he would faint and they gave him water several times before he recovered." They then bound him and took him off to Jackson to jail.

Though Murrell was in jail, Stewart was by no means safe. The charge against Murrell was slave-stealing, but the only evidence against Murrell was Stewart's word—and Murrell had a good many friends in high and low places. If

Murrell were not convicted, and turned loose, Stewart's life was worth nothing. And Stewart knew that Murrell knew that if Stewart did not survive to give evidence at the trial, there would be no conviction. It seemed impossible to find corroboration for Stewart's story, try as he could. The Jackson County Sheriff led a posse to the Arkansas hideout; it was deserted. Another posse tried to trace the slaves Stewart had seen in the hut, and lost them. Guards were posted at various plantations and slave markets to see if some of Murrell's agents might appear, but none did. Meanwhile Murrell stayed in jail, talking with visitors, blandly denying everything. In a way he convicted himself. He escaped, but not for long; a posse captured him near Muscle Shoals and brought him back. The indictment was drawn and trial set for July, 1834.

Murrell was worried, and so were many others. Stewart had a list of names (more than three hundred) of corrupt officials, dishonest merchants, conniving innkeepers, and major and minor criminals scattered over three states. Stewart also knew the whole story of The Clan and of the conspiracy, all of which, Murrell and his confederates realized, the trial would reveal. Therefore, it was clearly necessary to destroy Stewart. Simply to murder him was a trifle too bold. Therefore stories about Stewart began to circulate—he was a horse thief—he had been run out of Georgia for robbery—he had been thrown off the river for gambling—he was a disgruntled rival of Murrell's out for revenge. Murrell himself wrote letters from jail, accusing Stewart of counterfeiting and enclosing sworn statements of those who claimed to know of Stewart's crimes.

The campaign had its effect. Some of Stewart's acquaintances began to avoid him in the street and he received a few threats. Finally, feeling as if he were on trial himself, he decided to go back to Clanton's store until July. Clanton, however, was not at all glad to see him; the Vess family, with whom he had boarded in Tuscahoma, wanted nothing to do with him. Clanton, Stewart heard, had been hired to make charges of embezzlement against him and Vess (with his wife's permission) to charge him with adultery. A few weeks later a man turned up in Tuscahoma looking for Stewart, saying that the Grand Council had ordered him killed. Luckily, Stewart gave him the name of "Tom Goodin" and convinced the not-overly-bright assassin that "Stewart" had left the state. The point may simply have been to frighten him, for he never saw the man again. Nevertheless, he slept with pistols at his side from that night on.

On the charge of stealing slaves, John Murrell was tried in Circuit Court, Jackson, Tennessee, in July of 1834. John Read and Milton Brown (later a Congressman) served as lawyers for the defense, General Bradford and Major Martin for the prosecution. As Stewart anticipated, he was on trial as much as Murrell. He told his incredible story, reading from his notes and repeating whole conversations from his ride with Murrell while Murrell's partisans hooted. The "great conspiracy" was met with amazed silence. Nobody really believed it, and neither Martin nor Bradford attempted to make much of the fantastic story. Attorney Brown did his best to destroy Stewart's reputation, citing all the gossip, repeating all the rumors, dragging the young man's character back and forth through the mire.

However, it was not quite enough. The jury believed Stewart, or at least sufficiently to find Murrell guilty as charged. The Court sentenced him to ten years of hard labor at the Nashville Penitentiary. A few weeks later at Nashville, the great phrenologist, Professor O. B. Fowler, after examining the bumps on his head, gave out the opinion that Murrell had "the natural ability, if it had been rightly called out and directed, for a superior scholar, scientific man, lawyer, or statesman." At about the same time Stewart met Attorney Brown on the street in Jackson and if spectators had not intervened would have had the satisfaction of horsewhipping him.

But the trial and the gossip left Stewart with few friends in Tennessee. After one attempt on his life, he decided to move to Lexington, Kentucky. Still feeling it necessary to vindicate himself, he wrote an account of his experiences, including his lists of names, his story of the "great conspiracy" and the Clan, and attached sworn affidavits from all those who had seen or talked with him during his eerie ride with Murrell. Unfortunately, Stewart's story was too good. It had all the makings of a dime shocker, and immediately the hack writers seized it and made it into one. Murrell's tremendous design of conspiracy and rebellion was simply too big to be believed. Stewart's document made wonderfully lurid reading, much like other popular stories of Rattlesnake Ned or The Brigands of the Plains, and eventually it ended up as a *Police Gazette* extravaganza. Furthermore, people remembered that Stewart himself had taken an oath and broken it. Did such a man deserve to be believed?

In June, 1835, a Mississippi planter named Latham uncovered what he believed was a plot among his slaves. Latham told his neighbors, who questioned their own slaves, and the protesting Negroes, under the whip, confessed to some vague knowledge of a conspiracy to revolt. A young slave named Joe finally talked at length; there was such a plot, he said, led by several white men, among them two "steam doctors" (practitioners of a current form of medical hydropathy) named Cotton and Sanders. The planters hanged the Negroes and reported their findings to the authorities at Livingston, the county seat. The Livingston Committee of Safety promised to probe into the matter.

What they found rocked Mississippi. Cotton was brought in, claiming innocence, but Sanders collapsed. There was a conspiracy, he admitted, headed by Cotton—he, Sanders, had joined it, changed his mind, and now wanted simply to get out of the whole thing. Meanwhile more evidence piled up. A Negro identified Cotton as the man who suggested he run away; another testified Cotton had questioned him about a rebellion. How much of the Negro testimony can be believed is an open question, since much of it was obtained after repeated lashings, but the point is that Cotton himself eventually broke and confessed.

"I am one of the Murrell Clan," he admitted, "a member of what we call the Grand Council." The plan, he continued, "was to excite the Negroes to rebellion, not for the purpose of liberating them, but for plunder." The rebellion had been "conceived and plotted by Murrell, and embracing the slaveholding states generally—a large number of desperate and unprincipled white men were engaged in the plan, and they contemplated, if not the total destruction of the white population, at least the possession of most of their wealth." What Stewart had said, Cotton went on, was true. Though Murrell's arrest and Stewart's book had botched the plot, the Clan Council had decided to carry it out anyway, choosing July 4, 1835, as the day of uprising. Thirteen white men were involved in Mississippi, Cotton said, and he named them. Then he signed his confession and that afternoon, on the gallows, repeated his guilt with the noose around his neck.

Mississippi was badly frightened. The Committee of Safety in Livingston, digging deeper, lashed about while Vigilantes picked up where the courts left off. They hanged Sanders, Albe Dean, Lee Smith, and a man named Donovan. Two men escaped, while Hall, Benson, and Barnes, against whom nothing could be proved, were flogged and banished on pain of death. The Earl brothers were caught and tortured; one hanged himself in his cell and the Vigilantes hanged the other. Rual Blake, a man of wealth and some standing in the community, was captured in Natchez, brought back, and hanged despite his claims of innocence. Meanwhile the terror spread. A report (unconfirmed) from Nashville that an attempt would be made to rescue Murrell from prison simply added fuel to the blaze. Governor Runnels of Mississippi, recognizing the emergency, issued a proclamation of warning on July 13 and authorized each town to establish "active and efficient patrols," while townsmen and planters, riding from house to house and farm to farm, searched out surly Negroes and suspected whites. "I have not slept two hours out of twenty-four for six days and nights," wrote one exhausted Mississippian, "and I have been on horseback more than four-fifths of the time." "A great excitement exists among the whole white population," the Clinton, Mississippi, *Gazette* reported, and *Niles' Register* reprinted hysterical accounts from Southern papers with the comment that "alarm among the females was truly distressing and the excitement of the males was intense." In Mississippi, and then through the entire South, men went armed and women stayed indoors. After a few months the excitement died down, the lynchings lessened, and the South decided that "the great conspiracy" had been scotched.

In a sense, the Mississippi scare partly vindicated Stewart. After Cotton's confession, Stewart's story seemed to ring somewhat more true. As the Lynchburg *Virginian* remarked, when Stewart's book had appeared, "so startling was its character that we placed but little confidence in it." Now, said the *Virginian*, "we can no longer doubt its truth," nor could many others in the South. Cotton was on Stewart's list; so were some of the others hanged in Mississippi. And the more one read of the reports of the Committees of Safety, the more the evidence seemed to fit into the pattern of Murrell's plan of operations as Stewart had recorded it. It is not known what Stewart said, if he said anything. Nor did Murrell, serving his term in prison, say anything either. But Stewart's book and Cotton's confession, taken together, seemed sufficient proof that John Murrell was guilty of something far greater than stealing slaves.

Murrell tried an appeal, which the Tennessee Supreme Court denied in 1837. He served out his ten years, but by the time of his release he was past caring, ill, and mentally deranged. His wife had long since disappeared, his property was gone, and he had only a short time to live. He died of tuberculosis and was buried near Jackson, but the legend attached to his name was still so strong that some curiosity-seeker dug up his grave, took his skull, and put it on display in a museum, where it remained for some years. What happened to Virgil Stewart no one knows.

Yet what Stewart had begun gathered impetus. The Southwest had had enough of disorder and lawlessness. Up and down the Tennessee and the Mississippi and along the Trace bands of Vigilantes cleaned out the hoodlums' nests, hanging those hardy ones who stayed to fight. "Every town along the river," wrote one commentator, "had its Vigilant committee and patrol. . . . Committees were formed in every community from Cincinnati to New Orleans that had suffered from the thief and the cutthroat, and general notices issued for them to leave in twenty-four hours." Rangers and Regulators patrolled the streets, questioned strangers, and dealt out quick justice in doubtful cases. The Gut, the Swamp, the Natchez-under-the-Hill were doomed. The Southwest was growing up.

In Vicksburg the respectable citizens decided that they "had borne with their enormities long enough." Gathering their forces, they descended on the gambling houses and after a pitched battle hanged five gamblers and chased the remainder out. The police at Clinton, Mississippi, posted a notice that all thieves and swindlers found in the city after noon the following day would "be used according to Lynch's law." As a warning to crooks, Vigilantes in Rodney, Mississippi, tarred and feathered one malefactor, whipped him "until he was insensible to pain," and then dipped him in turpentine before riding him on a rail out of town. A mass meeting in Natchez ordered out all members of "the black-leg fraternity;" in August the captain of the steamer *Mogul* reported sighting "two flatboats of females" bound downriver after being evicted from the stews of Natchez-under-the-Hill. Within a year the river towns were not yet fully civilized, but in them a man could at least walk the streets without fear, meeting only normal temptations.

John Murrell came a little too late. Civilization was closing in on the frontier when he began his career. A decade earlier, perhaps, and it might have been different, but by his time the Southwest was maturing too fast and organizing itself too well for any such plan as his to succeed. Murrell should have known this. His desire for power, his overreaching ambition that approached megalomania—the same qualities that lifted him out of the class of ordinary brigands—these undid him. He liked young Stewart, his vanity mounted to his head, and he talked too much.

If Murrell had not stolen Henning's slaves and begun the chain of events that led him to prison, what he might have accomplished is interesting to conjecture. His conspiracy was bound to fail. The Vigilantes would eventually have beaten him, the troops would have arrived, the criminals in his own command could hardly have maintained any unity of purpose or discipline for very long, even under Murrell's iron leadership. No one can seriously believe Murrell could have created his pirate empire of slaves and outlaws. Yet no one can doubt that in his attempt to do so he would have left behind him a path of blood and terror unmatched in American history. Had he not met young Stewart that January day at Estanaula bridge, John Murrell's name might appear in larger type in the books, and in something more than a mere footnote.

LIMITED UTOPIAS

★

John Humphrey Noyes

James Strang

John Humphrey Noyes

★

THE AMERICAN of the early nineteenth century faced the
future with a great deal of self-assurance. "There is at
hand," thought William Ellery Channing of Boston in 1830,
"a tendency and a power to exalt the people . . . , a devotion
to the progress of the whole human race." The Shaker
prophetess Paulina Bates thought that the "present age" was
the beginning of the "most extraordinary and momentous
era that ever took place on earth." In this spirit the men of
Emerson's and Jackson's time confidently awaited the arrival
of a better society (perhaps the perfect one) and a refined,
repaired, and redirected way of life. Some of their attempts
to create this perfect society were intelligently planned; some
were naïve but sincere; some showed more than a trace of
the eccentric; a few bordered on the lunatic. But all of their
experiments, James Russell Lowell remarked, had in them
"a kernel of deadly explosiveness, and a struggle for fresh
air."

The kernel so identified by Lowell was the age's belief in
the perfectibility of man. In the process of shaking off the
shackles of eighteenth century Puritanism, men of Emerson's
time found a new respect for themselves and for their potentialities. Men could make progress—of this they were convinced—and man's horizons were unlimited. Thus the social
reformers of the eighteen-thirties and the eighteen-forties
planned their utopias, aided by a wave of evangelism that
inundated the decades with a renewed, aggressive religious
confidence. If men were intelligent beings, they could surely
order their lives better than they seemed to be doing. Was

poverty really necessary? Were unemployment, depression, and instability always to be society's lot? Could not men so arrange their lives so that all humanity could live together in security, peace, and plenty? The age strongly believed that they could if they tried.

During the three decades preceding the Civil War there appeared in the United States a profusion of "communities" or "societies" which, their founders hoped, might serve as pilot models of Utopia. Some of them, following a tradition as old as Christianity itself, turned to the Bible as a guide, banding together to live according to Gospel injunction and New Testament ethics. Others evolved complicated economic and social schemes which, they were supremely certain, would solve the problems that had plagued men since they emerged from caves into civilization. Almost any man you met in the street, Ralph Waldo Emerson wrote in his journal, "had a plan for a new community in his pocket." Granting an allowance for Emersonian hyperbole, he was not far wrong. Between 1825 and 1860, sixty-one experimental communities were founded in the United States, thirty of them during the banner years of 1843 and 1844.

These experimental communities fell into three general classifications. The Frenchman, Fourier, attracted a number of American followers who divided themselves into "phalanxes" and "series" of "compatibles," split up property, work, and profits, and lived out their principles in a dozen or so shortlived and turbulent colonies. The disciples of Robert Owen, the intrepid Scots socialist, set up a large settlement at New Harmony, Indiana, and thirteen small ones scattered through New York, Pennsylvania, and Ohio. Religious communities, based on various interpretations of Christian social ethic, were more numerous and durable— Zoar, Amana, Separatists, Icaria, Bishop Hill, Bethel, the Wallingford group and others.

Whatever their origins, only a few of these colonies could be called successful. The average life of an Owenite community was about eighteen months, that of a Fourierist phalanx less than three years. The religious societies, with three or four exceptions, usually did not last much longer. One of the exceptions, and by all odds the most interesting, was John Humphrey Noyes' community in Oneida, New York.

Noyes was born in Putney, Vermont, in 1811. His father was a Congressman, his mother an intelligent, educated woman from the same New England family that produced President Rutherford B. Hayes. Young John Humphrey, after good schooling, was sent to Dartmouth to prepare himself for the law. Nothing about the youth marked him as anything more than a staid, conservative New England boy. After his graduation from college in 1830 he settled down at home to read law, as the custom was, with a local attorney. Less than a year later an evangelical revival completely altered the course of his life.

In 1831 the great evangelist Charles Grandison Finney and his disciples, preaching a new kind of religion, blazed across New England, leaving behind them hundreds of "converted" young men and women. Men could be perfect, Finney proclaimed, here and now; men could be saved from sin, and saved, could live as God meant those to live who had attained salvation. What Finney and his adherents said fired the imagination. What his converts did shocked and disturbed orthodox Congregational and Presbyterian ministers and their congregations. Finney allowed women to "testify" in public meetings; he instituted an "anxious seat" for sinners; he allowed "posturing and groaning" in his revivals; and occasionally (though not often) the emotions released at his meetings led to conduct not in good taste. Nevertheless, there was much in Finney's "perfectionism," as it came to be called, to attract and inspire young men like John Humphrey Noyes, who decided almost overnight to quit the law and become a minister himself.

Noyes enrolled at Andover, the most conservative of the New England theological seminaries. There he found little to interest him. Debating eschatology and searching one's soul bored him, and furthermore, he simply did not believe the orthodox theology he was supposed to believe. The next year he shifted his studies to Yale. He did better there, though he was regarded as a brash, rebellious student and a most puzzled one.

What Noyes learned at Andover and at Yale did not square with what he had absorbed from Finney's perfectionism, which seemed to contradict orthodox Calvinism at several vital points. The most difficult doctrine for Noyes to accept was the Calvinist principle of original sin—the dogma that men were born sinful and remained so until by God's grace and Christ's intercession they attained salvation—which separated Calvinist sheep from unregenerate goats. Young Noyes had too much enthusiasm and self-confidence to be a good Calvinist. Try as he could, he could not feel properly sinful. There must be a theological reason why this was so, he decided, a reason unaccounted for by either Andover or Yale theology.

The reason came to him in a flash of inspiration during the summer of 1833. Reading a passage concerning Christ's Second Coming, he suddenly realized that quite possibly the Second Coming had already occurred. The more he thought about it the more convinced he was that it had—about 70 A.D., to be exact, when sinners and saved had been divided as the Bible said they would be. Talk of "inherent sin" was therefore simple nonsense. If he were one of the saved (as undoubtedly he and many others were) it was perfectly clear how, under Finney's guidance, he had been made aware of spiritual salvation as an accomplished fact. And if he were saved he was therefore perfect, free from sin now and forever. After he notified several fellow students of this fact, the word went round that "Noyes says he is perfect," and soon changed to "Noyes is crazy."

John Humphrey Noyes received his license to preach, although the examining board spent a good deal of time questioning him and granted the license with some hesitancy. Back home in Putney he had time to ponder his discovery and its implications, which were extremely broad. What he had done was to attack orthodox Calvinism at its knottiest point; once he slashed the knot, the whole skein of close-woven logic fell apart. Calvinism said in effect that men attained salvation only by a hard, slow, process, and that no man could be absolutely certain of the result. Noyes said the election of the saved had already been made. Man *is* saved, if only he chooses to recognize it, and once saved he is perfect. Thus it followed that the man who has attained perfection is no longer subject to those restraints placed upon him by an imperfect society; laws are for the unsaved, not the perfect, who can never sin again.

Noyes was enough of a Vermonter not to be carried away by his theological speculations. While he considered himself literally free from sin forever, he was willing to grant that even perfectionist men (who were after all human) "always had room for improvement." Yankee commonsense indicated that he still had to live in an imperfect society that put men into jail for breaking its laws. "All things are lawful for me," he wrote, "but all things are not expedient"— a sort of temporary compromise with an unedified world. As a result he decided to live within the law for practical purposes, while at the same time refusing to concede that the law had any pertinence to him and reserving the right to break it if he wished.

The elder Noyes, a patient and understanding man, tolerated his son's theology, though many in the community frankly believed him insane. Noyes' next step confirmed their belief. If he and others were saved, he said, it was entirely possible for them to create a life on this earth very close to that described in the Bible as Heaven. The Calvinists said that the reward of salvation was a perfect life in the hereafter; Noyes saw no reason why one had to wait. The country was dotted with experimental communities, all of them seeking the same goal, but only he, Noyes thought, had grasped the real principle that lay at the bottom of the perfect Christian social and economic order. So at Putney, Vermont, in

1834, John Humphrey Noyes set out to make the Kingdom of Heaven come true on earth.

Noyes did not rush in blindly. He read Robert Owen, Fournier, and Albert Brisbane, Fourier's chief American disciple. He studied the Shaker communities, visited others, and spent a long time analyzing the flaws of those he saw or read about. His own "holy community" did not look very promising at first. The best he could do was to convert his brother, and later his two sisters and their husbands, which kept the experiment confined within the Noyes household. Noyes himself (recently jilted by his childhood sweetheart) married Harriet Holton, a Vermont girl of good family, after a singularly uninspired courtship that resembled two soldiers enlisting for battle.

After a few more joined, and the elder Noyes left his children twenty thousand dollars in his will, they formed the Putney Association in 1840 for "a few families of the same religious faith, without any formal scheme or written laws." The Association, they made clear, was not patterned on any other current experiment nor was it to be confused with Fourieristic, Shaker, Owenite, or other colonies. Putney, Noyes said, was "Bible communism." It represented a new doctrine of religious faith combined with a new concept of the social order—"Revivalism and Socialism working together for the Kingdom of Heaven." All that its members asked was "to be able to preach Christ without being burdensome to any, and to act out as far as possible the family spirit of the Gospel."

Noyes was an excellent organizer. His community, with the help of the legacy, prospered and grew. It did adopt the principle of community ownership of property because, as Noyes said, "A spirit of love naturally led us unto a sort of community of goods," though he warned that he would retain the principle "only so long as it was expedient to our present circumstances and objects." The women did the cooking and housework, the men labored in the fields, an elected treasurer administered community funds, and all were happy. Putney's prosperity, combined with Noyes' persuasive proselyting, attracted more converts, until in 1845 the community had seventy members, five hundred acres of farm land, seven houses, a small store, and a newspaper called *The Witness.*

The Putney group led a carefully organized life. Members worked ten hours a day and in the evening sang, prayed, and debated. They studied Hebrew, Latin, and Greek, read widely, and held highly intelligent discussions. Women found the life particularly pleasant, for Noyes (who was a strong believer in women's rights) insisted upon complete equality of the sexes in all community affairs. The group had but one established meal each day—breakfast—after which the women did the housework and were free until the next morning. The group held regular financial meetings at which a woman's vote was as good as a man's, and men and women alike set the rules for community living.

Noyes revealed his real genius for administration by the institution at Putney of what he called "mutual criticism." The chief reason for the failure of similar experiments in communal living, he knew, was the dissension that usually appeared after a few months of intimate, regimented, and sometimes arduous living. Recognizing the failings of human nature, he suggested that the best thing to do was to force petty arguments and individual differences into the open, where all could comment and advise, providing a needed escape valve for the pressures that were bound to build up within a tightly-knit group. A Putney member with a grievance, therefore, or one who was uncertain of the exact state of his soul, might request a hearing before the group, which heard his story, discussed it candidly, and suggested a solution. From simple group discussion, "mutual criticism" developed into a formal, organized system, with regular weekly hearings before a chosen board. Clashes and disagreements occurred at Putney, of course, but through "mutual criticism" the community escaped the eruptions of spite and hatred that blew so many contemporary colonies apart.

Noyes was not a man who liked to stand still. Though he had a successful, expanding community, his orderly mind saw a good many other things to do with it. Because he regarded the usual social patterns as unnecessarily binding on those who had already attained perfection, he expressed himself rather strongly about various accepted social institutions, chiefly marriage. By 1845 he had worked out the whole problem.

Love, Noyes thought, was a communal emotion that ought to be controlled and channeled within the social order. There was no such thing, really, as "individual love." Talk of "being in love" with another person was irrational, the so-called process of "falling in love" illogical. Love between two people, and only two ("exclusive love") was anti-social, for mankind possessed "natural amativeness" that extended far beyond couples. If people were born to love one another, as the Bible said, why should a person "be required to love in all directions, and yet be forbidden to express love except in one direction?" Logic and love therefore required that any man and woman might live together as man and wife, if they so wished, without legal sanction.

This system of matrimony Noyes named "complex marriage." It was not "free love," he hastened to explain, but a relationship governed by rules established by the community at large and "rooted deep in the community religion." It was also perfectly adapted to communal living. "There is no intrinsic difference," he remarked, "between property in persons and property in things," thus carrying the principle of communal ownership to its ultimate conclusion.

Complex marriage, however, created certain obvious problems. Harriet Noyes had given birth to five children in six years, four of them stillborn. Noyes, a kindly man who hated the fear and pain attendant to childbirth in the early nineteenth century (for childbed fever made motherhood a dangerous venture) vowed that he would "never again expose her to such fruitless sufferings." Noyes understood and respected the theological injunctions against contraceptive devices, yet he found nothing in the Bible to prevent relationships between the sexes without conception. Furthermore, he believed that sex had an important social function, distinct from the propagative—it was, after all, the highest act of love. The answer, he announced, lay in the principle of "Male Continence," that is, *coitus reservatus,* by which "amativeness can have its proper gratification without drawing after it procreation as a necessary consequence." Acting on his own belief, he entered into a "complex marriage" (with full permission of Harriet Noyes and the lady's husband) with one Mary Craigin who, with her husband George, was a recently arrived convert.

"In a holy community," Noyes had written, "there is no more reason why sexual intercourse should be restrained by law than why eating and drinking should be, and there is as little occasion for shame in the one case as in the other." This was too much for Vermont to stand. Local clergymen were scandalized at the reports that the Putney group shared more than property. Newspapers vehemently denounced the "free lovers," citizens called indignation meetings, investigative committees called at the community, and church congregations passed resolutions. Noyes explained his theories carefully and fully to all who asked, but when local magistrates threatened to issue writs against him for adultery, he knew it was time to transfer his community elsewhere.

The site he selected for the new community was Oneida, New York. Because the area had been well evangelized by perfectionist preachers, Noyes expected to find greater tolerance than in Vermont. He bought twenty-three acres of land four miles from Oneida, and in 1847 a part of the Putney group moved to the site. They had only a log house, a hut or two, and a sawmill; the first few months were hard living. They constructed a sixty-foot frame barn four stories high to house the migrants and set about clearing and seeding the land. The women labored too, wearing shirts and trousers, finding them so practical that they adopted a modified form of the costume for constant wear.

Oneida's neighbors left the community alone after the first few wild rumors had been circulated, giving Noyes a chance to put his experiment on a stable footing. The members of the community worked hard, kept to themselves, and gained converts. In 1849 there were eighty-seven members at Oneida, with a few still left at Putney. Noyes lost a large share of the community's funds in a publishing venture (one of the few business mistakes he made) but by 1851 more than two hundred persons were in the group and it had a fairly substantial backlog of funds. Noyes had planned an agricultural community, much like dozens of others, but he had an open mind and a talent for business. By 1854 it was apparent from an analysis of the account books that farming alone would not carry his colony. Oneida needed a more diversified economy; it needed an industry. A few months later Fate sent him Sewell Newhouse.

Newhouse was a Vermont woodsman who had invented an improved steel trap. Though he had made a few such traps for the New England trade, he had never really gone into the market. Noyes immediately saw the possibilities of the Newhouse trap, and Oneida went into production. Within a year they had more orders than they could fill. Within two years the Hudson Bay Company sent a single order for more than their first year's entire production. Within five years Oneida traps were selling in Russia, Paraguay, and Australia; the community was manufacturing three hundred thousand traps each year in six sizes and employing forty outside laborers in addition to ninety community members. When someone pointed out that making traps was an odd way for a Christian community to support itself, Noyes replied that since God had cursed the earth with vermin, Oneida simply helped to cleanse it. If Oneida made the best traps in the world, as the case seemed to be, so much the better for the world and Oneida.

Traps put the community on a solid financial basis. Noyes kept it there, organizing its affairs in a manner that made most contemporary industrial firms look like child's play.

Oneida had twenty-one standing committees and forty-eight administrative departments, each with its own staff and subcommittees, covering every conceivable community activity from apple-growing to choral singing. There was even a committee on timepieces that granted possession of watches and clocks. Appointments to administrative posts were made by committee, with women given full equality. The department heads comprised a Business Board that met each week, discussed the week's business, and sent reports to each community member. Each department submitted monthly accounts to a bookkeeping staff (headed by a woman) whose system was so efficient that the exact financial situation of every department could be determined at the end of every day. A monthly inventory showed the location and condition of every article in the community; daily personnel records showed the activity of every person every day of the year. At the close of each year, the Business Board planned the community's activities for the next year, considered new projects, reviewed old ones, and heard suggestions. No plan was ever adopted except by unanimous consent.

Theoretically, Noyes was opposed to capitalism, the wage system, and private property; as a practical man of affairs he was not at all opposed to taking advantage of a free market and an industrial society. Oneida was blessed with some ingenious and skillful members, many of them Yankee craftsmen, and his committees therefore bubbled with ideas. In 1857, faced with a surplus of fruit, the women canned and sold it. Not long afterward Oneida canned fruit appeared in markets hundreds of miles away. A silversmith manufactured some spoons—and soon the community had a thriving silverware business. The Business Committee sent some young persons to a Connecticut factory to learn the textile industry. When they came back they showed the mechanics how to build the proper machines and Oneida developed a brisk trade in silk thread.

By the late fifties and early sixties the community had assets of nearly a half million and a net profit of between fifty and sixty thousand dollars a year, not counting the assets and profits of subsidiary communities at Putney, Vermont, and at Cambridge, Manlius, Newark, and Wallingford, New York. Oneida owned five hundred acres of land, several stores, a string of workshops, barns, and stables, a carpenter shop, a machine shop, a school, a chemical laboratory, and a photographic studio. During the sixties the community employed nearly two hundred and fifty outside workmen, and by the seventies most community members were foremen or superintendents in one or another of the multitude of businesses the community owned.

And with all its prosperity, life still seemed pleasant at Oneida. The employment committee, which assigned members to jobs, always attempted to recognize special skills and to consider individual preferences. To avoid monotony and regimentation, work assignments were changed frequently, for many at Oneida knew from experience the numbing deadness of nineteenth-century factory labor. Those who worked too hard were cautioned—for work must be pleasure, not toil. Those who were lazy were called into "mutual criticism" sessions—for each must do his share. "It is not impossible," Noyes said, "to be both happy and industrious," a combination the community tried hard to realize in its social and economic life.

"The Mansion," a huge brick structure begun in the sixties, housed nearly all the community members except a few who lived near the shops. It had central heating, seven kitchens, several meeting rooms and recreation rooms, a printing office, a good library, and parlors for visitors. The community also purchased two summer resorts on nearby lakes and owned a private hunting preserve. *The Circular,* which Noyes published and sent to "all applicants whether they pay for it or not," advertised the community so well that five thousand visitors a year came for a free meal and a guided tour. What they saw must have impressed them, for *The Circular* several times had to warn the public that Oneida had no space for new members.

Probably no contemporary community had a better-ordered or richer social life than Oneida's. It had dances, picnics, plays, and entertainments. It had a good community orchestra and an excellent choral group. "Self-improvement" classes were held in music, painting, reading, language study, and debating. The dreary mechanics of living were organized and simplified—by common kitchens and dining rooms, a community nursery, set hours for housework and no exceptions. Oneida had an absolute horror of monotony. The members changed jobs, changed the times of scheduled functions, and not only changed the time but the number of meals from as few as two to as many as eight per day. Living, thought Noyes, should be spontaneous, unpredictable, and exciting, even in ordinary things.

Visitors were particularly impressed, and sometimes shocked, by Oneida's women and children. Each woman was allotted thirty-three dollars per year for clothes, including hats and shoes. Each wore short hair, loose ankle-length trousers under a knee-length skirt, and a loose shirtwaist, thus enjoying freedom of movement while avoiding fashionable frippery. The costume may have been sensible, but as one visitor remarked, it was "totally and fatally lacking in grace and beauty." Children were placed in the Infant's Department at the age of three weeks and reared by the community. Until he was three, the child stayed at the nursery during the day and with his mother at night. From three to fifteen he lived at the Children's House. Parents were free to visit their children at any time, but, as Noyes believed it must, the community assumed full responsibility for the child at birth.

Oneida had perhaps the best schools in New York, for the community assigned certain of its young men and women to train themselves in the best outside teacher-training institutions. Every child learned a trade, and supervisors were constantly watching for exceptionally gifted pupils. Boys who showed talent were sent away to good universities and colleges to study, law, medicine, or engineering, to provide

153

the community with the professional skills it needed. Both girls and boys were sent out into factories to learn what the community needed to know—one young chemist came back with a new dye formula, another with new ideas in metallurgy, and another with a sketch of a device to test the tensile strength of cloth. Oneida's critics thought its family system cold and impersonal, devoid of the affection children needed for proper personal development. Yet, as Pierrepont Noyes described his own childhood, Oneida had plenty of family feeling, love, and parental affection. Whatever the criticism, the community seems to have turned out more than its share of well-educated, well-adjusted young men and women.

Complex marriage moved from Putney to Oneida without change. Every convert who entered the community accepted it, and the community for twenty-five years never challenged the system. Despite its implications, complex marriage in practice was neither promiscuous nor licentious, nor were there a great many capricious changes of partners. Members took their unusual connubial arrangements seriously, for as Noyes always reiterated, complex marriage was an integral part of their own evangelistic religious faith of perfection. "Revivals," he wrote, "because they are divine, require for their complement a divine organization of society." Revivalism "awakens religious love, religious love awakens the passions," and converts, finding themselves free from sin, "begin to look about for their mates and paradise."

To establish a complex marriage, the consent of both parties first had to be obtained "through the intervention of some third person or persons." A man or woman who felt "amativeness" toward another usually asked an older person to act as intermediary, who discussed the matter with each separately and then laid the matter before a board which approved or disapproved the union. Forcing one's attentions on another could be punished by expulsion; the only man ever expelled from Oneida was dismissed for this reason. (Charles Guiteau, who years later shot President Garfield, was not expelled but strongly encouraged to leave, which he did.) Once a complex marriage was established, propagation of children was controlled by another committee who, if the union seemed genetically and spiritually sound, gave permission for parenthood. There were jealousies and heartbreaks, of course, threshed out in mutual criticism sessions, and the rule against "exclusive attachments" was difficult at times for young people to understand. But the survivors of Oneida remembered complex marriages as an unusually pleasant and satisfying kind of relationship.

The marriage committee, until the late sixties, kept the number of births in the community small, from 1849 to 1867 an average of but two per year. In 1867 Noyes, who studied Darwin, knew Malthus, and read Francis Galton's *Hereditary Genius,* announced that indiscriminate procreation was criminally illogical and a threat to any orderly society. "We are too selfish and sensual and ignorant," he wrote, "to do for ourselves what we have done for animals." The answer, he said, was planned parenthood, an idea he had been working out for years. Oneida would have an experiment in "stirpiculture," or selective eugenics.

After the community discussed and approved the experiment, a committee headed by Noyes chose fifty-three young women and thirty-eight men (averaging thirteen years older than the women) who signed agreements to follow the community's orders. The experiment began in 1868 and continued until 1878. During the decade, fifty-eight children were born in Oneida, nine of them fathered by Noyes himself. The committee, before directing a mating, investigated the heredity of the prospective mother and father, matched physical characteristics, and checked health, disposition, and intelligence. Of the fifty-eight children, fifty-two were still alive in 1921, an unprecedented actuarial record of longevity and a tribute to the committee's care.

Curiously enough, neither complex marriage, nor stirpiculture, nor prosperity strained Oneida's closely-woven social fabric. Other colonies which attempted sexual experiments, or which became too wealthy, dissolved in jealousies, bickerings, and greed, but Oneida seemed successfully to defy human nature. The reason was mutual criticism, the device which more than anything else allowed Oneida to avoid the tensions and plottings that wrecked similar social experiments. It was Noyes' way of using the organized force of public opinion to keep the individual in harmony with the general wishes of the group, his way of handling the irritations and frustrations of regimented living. "Mutual Criticism," he said shrewdly, "subordinates the I-spirit to the We-spirit," an absolute necessity if any communal society were to exist peacefully. The sessions not only forced ill-will and complaints into the open, but served as a psychological release for those criticising as well as those criticised.

Mutual criticism could be an effective experience. "I was shaken from center to circumference," one man wrote after a session. "I was metaphorically stood upon my head and allowed to drain until all the self-righteousness had dripped out of me." As the community grew, cases were handled by a board which called before it at regular intervals those members whose deportment showed room for improvement. The members of the board stated the faults observed in the errant one, discussed them frankly, heard his reply, and offered advice, assistance, and warnings.

Any indication of ill-will, jealousy, or prejudice on the part of a board member was instantly quashed by the others; false humility, argumentativeness, or sullenness in the subject simply meant that he faced another inquisition. The whole affair proceeded on a high level of seriousness, not only because the members believed in it, but because a transcript of the entire hearing was published and posted. Some found the experience so salutary that they asked to appear before the board voluntarily—including one heroic man who requested that his wife and children be included among his inquisitors, a stiff test for Christian humility.

Noyes, who never believed in hiding Oneida's practices or beliefs, publicized them in *The Circular* and in the *Annual Report*, both of which carried full explanations of exactly what went on in the community. Nevertheless, Oneida met no organized opposition for nearly twenty-five years, though the colony itself was notorious throughout the nation for its experiments in "free love." In the mid-fifties, after some citizens complained to the county magistrates of "immoral practices" at Oneida, grand juries held hearings in both Madison and Oneida counties. Oneida's neighbors defended the colony manfully. The "free lovers" minded their own business, worked hard, ran a prosperous enterprise, and whatever they did in Mansion House bothered nobody. After citizens in nearby towns signed petitions declaring that the Oneidans were "persons of good moral character and we have no sympathy with the recent attempts to disturb them," the talk died down.

The fact that a hundred or so outside workers held jobs in the colony may well have had something to do with Oneida's defense. Then, too, the community's open-door policy and its obvious well-being disarmed visitors who came to criticize (as did the Reverend T. W. Higginson of Boston) and saw there "no signs of suffering or sin." The guides had a stock answer for ladies who asked, as they usually did, "But do the children know who their fathers are?" They always replied courteously, "Madam, they have no more proof than other children—only the testimony of their mothers."

The collapse of Oneida came from a variety of causes, some inside the colony, some outside. In 1874 Noyes made the mistake of admitting a group from an unsuccessful colony in Cleveland, Ohio, that soon proved to be a dissident element. Also, in the seventies, an internal threat appeared from another quarter which Noyes and the elders had never anticipated—the young men and women. The first generation at Oneida had been inspired with the fervor of the Perfectionist Forties. They had drunk of Finney's evangelism; some of them had heard the great man himself and had shaken his hand. To them, Oneida was and always would be a truly holy community, a grand design for Christian living, the closest thing to Heaven on earth yet conceived by man.

The second generation knew nothing of the enthusiasm in which Oneida was conceived. Its idealism came to them only at second hand. Some had been to war. Many had worked "outside" or had gone to Yale, Princeton, or Dartmouth. The postwar world they saw was a hard, cynical, materialistic world of a different kind than their parents' Golden Day, for the age of idealism was fading fast in the brassy clamor of Grant's great barbecue. And Noyes himself was growing old and deaf, losing contact with the community. The second generation simply did not know their leader except as a straight old man who gave out orders and appeared occasionally at meetings.

Young men bitterly resented the monopoly of leadership held by their elders. Young women dreaded the whole eugenic experiment. Neither the young men nor the young women wholly approved of complex marriage. Some thought it absolutely immoral and said so, and a few couples defied the committee, made "exclusive attachments," and produced unstirpicultural children. Beneath it all was the yearning of youth to be "normal." They did not want to be radicals, or pioneers, or "different." The unifying element of idealism in Oneida touched them only very lightly as time passed.

In 1872 Anthony Comstock began his crusade to make the nation vice-conscious. In 1873 Professor John W. Mears of nearby Hamilton College, following in Comstock's footsteps, opened fire on Oneida. Oneida had withstood criticism before, but Mears was vocal, tireless, and had the press behind him. The Methodist Association of Central New York endorsed an anti-Noyes petition. The Congregational Association of New York adopted an anti-Oneida resolution. The Baptists' State Convention appointed an investigating committee, and so did the Central New York Presbyterian Synod. This was extremely heavy ministerial artillery.

In 1876, with dissension within and attack from without threatening Oneida, Noyes admitted partial defeat and turned over community affairs to his son, Theodore Noyes, who was not only less able than his father but an agnostic to boot. Within three years the community was nearly at its end as an effective unit. Mears, after calling a conference of forty-seven clergymen, was about to move into the courts when old John Humphrey Noyes suddenly left with a few of his faithful for Niagara Falls, Canada, safe from extradition. Because it was clear that complex marriage lay at the root of both internal and external troubles, Noyes sent back a proposal in 1879 that it be abandoned in favor of either legal marriage or celibacy.

Very few chose celibacy. By the end of the year all complex marriages had been legalized by civil ceremony and the tremendous tangle of family relationships was nearly unravelled. The change was accomplished quietly and with order. Stirpicultural children took their stepfathers' names. Complex marriage relationships were gracefully dissolved in recognition of "exclusive attachments." For a few mothers no husbands were available, and some men could not marry the mothers of their children because the mothers married others. But what had begun in sincerity and idealism ended in dignity, even though Mears almost refused to believe it until he inspected the marriage licenses.

Next to go was the principle of community ownership. Some members saw a half-million-dollar corporation there for the taking, and many of the younger men had little sympathy for the "Bible communism" of their fathers. After much discussion, a committee appointed to study the problem recommended that the community re-form on a joint stock basis; it did, in January, 1881.

All community members received varying amounts of stock in Oneida Community Limited, free education for their children to age sixteen, and a two-hundred-dollar bonus for each child. The stock, valued at twenty-five dollars par, was parcelled out by a complicated system based on length of membership, work days, and various other factors. Two hundred twenty-five members received shares valued from four hundred and seventy-five dollars to thirteen thousand four hundred and seventy-five dollars, with the average amount approximately three thousand five hundred dollars. A few members who disliked the uneven distribution of stock brought suit and lost. A few who did not approve of abandoning communism left. Old Sewell Newhouse, whose traps started Oneida on the way to wealth, refused to sign anything unless he got the largest share, but eventually he, too, capitulated. Families moved out of Mansion House, bought homes of their own, and went into private employment or business. Long before April, 1886, when John Humphrey Noyes died in Canada, his "holy experiment" at Oneida had passed away.

Yet Oneida was probably the most successful, financially and ideologically, of the numerous American communal experiments. Certainly it was the least dreary, the best-regulated, and the least sanctimonious of the religious communities, though some were longer-lived. The vital factor in its success was John Humphrey Noyes, that odd combination of eccentric and businessman, of organizer and dreamer. His ideas on sex should not be allowed to overshadow his real achievements as a leader, for he did, after all, found and maintain an unusual experiment in communal living that lasted forty years. That he was able to do this is testimony to the streak of commonsense that, almost alone among contemporary cultists, he possessed—a Yankee practicality that kept him from being swept away, as others often were, by the winds of faddism.

Noyes was not exactly a compromiser, but he knew human nature and he knew how and when to adjust his ideas to it. He was convinced that he knew how to construct the perfect society, how to order men's lives so that each man lived in harmony with his fellow in God's brotherhood. He also realized that his Perfectionists had to live in an imperfect world, and he knew that his theories, if carried to extremes, led straight to chaos, licentiousness, and rebellion. Even perfect people still had to be responsible, orderly, and self-controlled. Oneida lived by this code.

Among the dozens of men who founded cults and colonies in the nineteenth century's burgeoning of idealism, John

Humphrey Noyes stands out as a leader of real ability, whatever his vagaries. Many of those who, like Noyes, tried to establish their heavens on earth, built a framework of delusion about themselves and fed on their own egos until they lost contact with reality. Noyes had his share of self-assurance, of course, but he also had a strong sense of responsibility and a deep humility concerning the task for which he believed he had been chosen. Instead of wrapping himself in a prophet's mantle, or losing himself in megalomania, Noyes imbued Oneida with a belief in human perfection, a spirit of friendliness, and a respect for one's fellows. The striking fact is that though Oneida failed, it did so without recriminations or regrets, or harsh memories of its leader. Because of him Oneida very nearly achieved what it hoped to be.

James Strang

★

KINGS HAVE NEVER done well in the United States. However, the United States places surprisingly few obstacles, either legal or constitutional, in the way of careful monarchs who do not overreach themselves. If a sufficient number of dedicated persons wish to declare themselves subject to a king, while retaining at least minimum allegiance to the government of the United States, the government wisely leaves them alone. No legal way exists to prevent the people from making fools of themselves, nor any legislation to eliminate human frailty, foolishness, and delusion. If, by playing on the natural weaknesses of man, one man can arrogate to himself the prerogatives of kingship, he can sometimes succeed, at least briefly—but it takes a brash, confident, powerful man, with more than his share of cynicism, to carry off. A few men have tried it. Very few have been successful. James Strang, until three bullets ended his reign, was one of these.

Jesse James Strang was born on March 21, 1813, in Scipio, New York. His background was in no way regal. His father was a farmer, not overly prosperous, who in 1816 moved his family farther west to Chautauqua county, New York, to take advantage of better land in a less populous area. Here Jesse grew up—frail, lonely, considered as little more than an idiot in school and a puzzle to his doting parents, who spoiled him.

Strang's childhood was not happy. His brief recollections, written during his middle years, reveal an introspective, moody youngster, withdrawn and difficult, with a strain of morbidity a little terrifying in a boy of ten. "Long weary days I sat upon the floor," he wrote, "thinking, thinking, thinking!" The things he thought about were "strange, un-infantile questions," his mind "wandering over fields that old men shrink from, seeking rest and finding ηone until the darkness gathered thick around and I burst into tears and cried aloud. . . ."

Young Strang worked about his father's farm and got the rudiments of an education from the poor rural schools. He read widely, gained in the local lyceums a reputation as a debater and speaker, and became a freethinker after digesting Volney and Paine, whose books at that time were favorite frontier reading. He had no close friends, and he did not like people. Somehow he felt the community was against him, that people thought him queer and gossiped about him. In the diary he kept from the age of twelve to eighteen he spoke darkly of "his enemies," of "those in life who had in-jured me," and of malice and revenge. The diary itself he kept partly in cipher, as if what the adolescent had to say was too secret to be known.

Yet young Strang had driving ambition. He taught school, studied law, and wondered whether he should enter business, join the army, go into politics, or edit "a literary and scientific journal." He confided to his journal, "I ought to have been a member of Assembly, or a Brigadier General before this time. . . . My head is eager and filled with projects." He wanted—and wanted very badly—position, power, and au-thority. In the long hours of thought that he distilled and poured into his diaries, he searched for the means of achieve-ment. He had neither education, nor talent, nor charm. He was not highly intelligent, but he was shrewd, shrewd enough to see that power could be less a matter of matching your strength against another's strength, than of matching your strength against others' weaknesses. Human nature was by no means flawless; the human heart was "a mere puff of air . . . , a pit of corruption . . . , changeable and polluted in the best of men." In this fact the clever man might find advantage. Pondering on life and experience, at nineteen he came to a conclusion. "In the last year," he wrote, "I have learned all that I profess to know. That is that I am eager and mankind are frail, and I do not half know that; nevertheless I shall act upon it for time to come for my own benefit." It was a long time, however, before he found his opportunity.

James Jesse Strang (he reversed the names about this time) was admitted to the bar in October, 1836, in Chautauqua county, but he had little real interest in law and rarely practiced it. Instead, he served as village postmaster, toured the temperance circuit as a lecturer (and a good one), and for two years edited a country newspaper. The Mormon movement was strong in upstate New York, where Joseph Smith had found the golden plates of Moroni in 1823, and where, in nearby Fayette, he had founded the growing Church of Jesus Christ of Latter Day Saints. Nominally a Baptist, though actually a freethinker, Strang could hardly have failed to be aware of the Mormons, particularly since Chautauqua county had contributed a sizable number of those Saints who followed Smith on the removal of his Church to Ohio and the West in the eighteen-thirties. Then, in 1836, Strang married Mary Perce, a Baptist clergyman's daughter whose sister had married a Mormon, Moses Smith. Smith, a devout and strong-minded man, had gone West with the Mormons to settle in Wisconsin; his letters home described attractively the excellent land and magnificent opportunities in the new Territory. In 1843, James and Mary Strang followed him.

Burlington, Wisconsin, where Strang decided to practice law, had a fairly large Mormon population. Less than a year after his arrival, Strang himself joined the Latter Day Saints. In early 1844 he went to Nauvoo, Illinois, the headquarters of the western Mormons, talked with Joseph and Hyrum Smith, the Mormon leaders, and was baptized by Joseph. No doubt exists that the Smiths were deeply impressed by their convert, nor any that Strang, the onetime freethinker, immediately found in the Mormon creed a certainty and solidity of faith he had never had before. The dynamism of Mormonism apparently provided for Strang something he had lacked, and what he searched for in the years of frustrated drifting—a framework of authority into which he could build his life.

Strang, during his Nauvoo visit, proposed to Joseph Smith that he be authorized to develop and settle a colony of Mormons near Burlington on the White River in Wisconsin. Smith made him an Elder of the Church, encouraged him to go to Wisconsin, send in a complete report of his plan and location, and begin work. Strang mailed his report in May, 1844, less than a month before Joseph the Prophet and his brother Hyrum died in Carthage, Illinois, at the hands of a mob. But on the day of his death Joseph Smith appeared in a vision to James Strang in Wisconsin, anointed his head with oil, and gave to him the leadership of all Mormon Saints on earth.

The death of the Smiths threw the Mormon organization into temporary confusion. Because visions were fairly common among the Saints, Strang's announcement of his visitation constituted credible evidence of his claim to the mantle of the fallen Prophet—particularly as neither Brigham Young, Sidney Rigdon, Lyman Wright, nor any other potential claimants among the Nauvoo faithful had, evidently, received any visions, or at least had failed to announce them before Strang's. Furthermore, Strang, in addition to his unwitnessed visitation from Smith, had a letter from Smith dated June 19, in which the Prophet appointed Strang as his successor (or seemed to) and authorized him to establish a new colony in Wisconsin called Voree, or "garden of peace," wherein all Mormons might find a resting place, peace, and security.

The letter from Smith to Strang was genuine, though a closer analysis of its contents by an emissary from Nauvoo failed to support completely Strang's sweeping claims of Smith-bestowed authority. The Council of Twelve Apostles at Nauvoo, where the struggle for place in the Mormon hierarchy was shaping, simply tried to brush Strang aside. But Strang refused to be brushed. At the beginning of 1845 he announced another revelation. God had announced to him, through a Messenger Angel, that He would give to Strang certain "plates of the ancient records" containing His instructions for the future of the Mormon Church. Because Joseph Smith had built the entire Mormon faith on records he had disinterred in upstate New York, Strang's revelation had solid Mormon precedent. What The Lord had withheld from Smith, He would give to Strang, for "Behold," the Angel told Strang, "the record which was sealed from my servant, Joseph, unto thee it is reserved." The actual location of the plates was not immediately revealed, however, and nine months elapsed before the Angel appeared again to Strang, with information that the plates were buried on a hill near Voree, beneath an oak tree. There Strang and a company of followers dug them up a few days later. No one could decipher the strange inscriptions, but within a week Strang called together the Voree settlers to listen to his translation. He had read them, he explained, with the aid of Urim and Thummim, two stones set in the rim of a bow, provided by the same angel who had once given them to Joseph Smith for his translation of the plates that comprised the Book of Mormon. No one, other than Strang, of course, had seen the magic bow, for it had been immediately restored to angelic custody.

The message of the plates was not very clear, except as Strang explained it. It was a record left by one Rajah Manchore of Vorito, ruler of an ancient godlike race, lost to history—but the Rajah's vanished people, levelled to dust, would one day, the plates predicted, rise again. The last sentence of the Rajah's message was not at all difficult to understand. "The forerunner men shall kill, but a mighty prophet there shall dwell. I will be his strength, and he shall bring forth my records." The forerunner was, of course, Joseph Smith; the mighty prophet who brought forth the records so conveniently deposited near Voree could only be

James Strang. Thus the Rajah Manchore of Vorito, unknown to history except for his single brief appearance in rural Wisconsin in 1845, added his evidence to Strang's claim of leadership.

The Twelve Apostles at Nauvoo were singularly unimpressed by the Voree plates—made by Strang himself, they implied, from an old brass kettle during that suspicious nine-month wait for angelic instructions. Yet, at the same time, the Nauvoo Apostles could not afford wholly to disregard Strang's vociferous arguments. Latecomer though he was to the struggle for power within Mormon inner councils, they recognized him as a dangerous contender for the post that Brigham Young had virtually clinched. The Mormons had great respect for the authority of visions and visitations; the letter from Smith, vaguely worded though it was, was nevertheless a letter from Smith; to dismiss the Voree plates as complete balderdash without by implication casting slurs on the Book of Mormon was difficult indeed. If the Angel had provided Urim and Thummim for Smith, why not for Strang, too? And Strang was an extraordinarily powerful, convincing speaker; he boasted that he had never been bested in open debate, and those who heard him testified to his sincerity and magnetism. He had a bitter, facile tongue, and more and more Mormons who heard him inveigh against the Nauvoo Apostles were converted to him. Strang sent agents out from Voree with his side of the argument, counselling in particular against Brigham Young's wild plan to "go into an unexplored wilderness among savages, and to seek a home in the wilds." "Let the oppressed flee for safety unto Voree," urged Strang, "and let the gathering of the people be there," as the martyred Smith had ordered.

Nevertheless, Strang lost. The majority of the western Mormons followed Young on the long trail west to Deseret. A few followed Rigdon eastward to Pennsylvania; a few others went with Wright to Texas. The Prophet James and his band stayed in Wisconsin. In April, 1846, the Mormons at Voree made the final break with the Brighamites, organized their own church, formally expelled Young and the Nauvoo Council, and recognized James Strang and only James Strang as the Prophet and Leader of the Primitive Church of the Latter Day Saints.

Strang was a good leader. Physically, he was not impressive—a small spare man with a heavy reddish beard, hatchet-like face, and a queerly high-domed forehead that was almost a deformity. But he made up in zeal and energy what he lacked in size, and he had real executive ability. He sent out agents to the Eastern Mormon colonies to gather recruits for Voree, and his group grew encouragingly. Some difficulties developed with Gentile neighbors, but nothing serious—most serious of all was the simple fact that Voree lacked land enough for a growing colony. Most of the farm land in the area was privately owned; the shrewd Wisconsin farmers drove hard bargains with Mormon buyers. Furthermore, few of Strang's colonists had enough capital to buy land which, on purchase, became community property under the Voree system of communal ownership. Strang needed space, and he also had dreams of empire, as grand as Brigham Young's. Some time in 1846 Strang heard of Big Beaver Island, some twenty miles off the coast of Michigan in Lake Michigan. A little correspondence established the fact that it was good land, and that the Federal government was about to throw open for settlement the island chain of which Beaver was a part.

In 1847 Strang and four Mormons from Voree visited Big Beaver. One of a chain of twelve islands, Big Beaver Island is about thirteen miles long and six miles wide, well-timbered, fertile, in the midst of the lake's best fishing area. On returning to Voree, Strang had another vision, in which an angel told him to move his colony to "a land amid wide waters and covered with large timber, with a deep broad bay on one side of it." Because this was a recognizable description of Big Beaver Island, the Voree community prepared to move.

Four Mormon families wintered on Beaver in 1847-1848, while Strang made preparations in Voree for the transfer of his entire colony. By the next winter twelve families were there, living in log shacks. When the Mormons came, the island contained a few Indians, a fishing colony, a small settlement of houses, a dock, and a store. Friction between Mormon and Gentile was small, though in 1848, when the public lands were thrown open for sale, a good many arguments occurred over claim-jumping. The Beaver fishermen, mostly Irish, a hard lot, occasionally roughed-up the new arrivals, but the situation on the island, until the Mormons began to arrive in strength, was fairly peaceful. Strang's people were quiet, clannish, and industrious. They minded their own business and the transient fishermen, after initial curiosity had worn off, usually left them alone.

After 1848 Mormons came to Beaver in a steady stream. Strang himself and his agents, working through the Mormon areas of the East, proselyted relentlessly for the Prophet's island haven, while on Beaver the Saints worked hard and well. They built a sawmill, made roads, built a boat, cut wood for sale to steamers, and began construction of a mighty log temple, eighty feet long. Following Mormon practice, they gave new names to their land of Zion. The highest point on the island, not much more than a hummock, became Mount Pisgah; the baptismal pond became Font Lake, and the new corduroy road became the King's Highway. The principal Mormon settlement on the bay Strang modestly named St. James. With the stability of his colony assured, Strang felt confident enough in 1849 to place the annual conference of his church on Beaver.

Strang had plenty of confidence. He possessed a flourishing colony, tightly organized and utterly devoted to him, situated on a remote island where outside influence was at a minimum and where his Gentile neighbors were a definite minority. In other words, he had in Lake Michigan what Brigham Young led his Mormons two thousand miles to find—and he had, as Young did not, easy access to the Mormon recruiting grounds of the East and Midwest. Strang also had more control over his colony than Young ever had over his in Utah. At the time of the removal from Voree, Strang changed the system of property ownership from a communal basis to one of "inheritances." The land, all of it, belonged to Strang, who had the right to allot portions to individual Saints to keep and bequeath at his pleasure.

The government of Beaver, following the pattern laid down by the Rajah's plates (later amplified in Strang's *Book of the Law of the Lord*) vested absolute authority in a king, a "prophet, seer, revelator, translator, and first president of the Church, governing by revelation or the word of God, and deriving his authority solely from God." This was James Strang. To assist him, Strang had two councillors, four assistants, a High Council of Twelve, an Apostolic Council of Twelve, and seventy minor assistants subject to the authority of the Apostles. None of them had any power except at Strang's will. Ten percent of all Mormon income went to Strang's treasury, the first fruits of each harvest, the firstling of every flock, herd, brood, or hatching. He controlled the treasury, the land, the roads, the proposed "army and navy." He made the law, interpreted it, and meted out justice; he created all offices and made all appointments to them. Few men in the history of the United States have succeeded in establishing so quickly so complete an authoritarianism. Strang's youthful discovery "that mankind are frail," and that an eager and clever man might trade upon human credibility and weakness, bore him fruit.

The fruits of authority were sweet to Strang. Virtually unlimited power had its advantages. Ever since his first baptism into Mormonism he had been a bitter opponent of polygamy. In the Voree *Herald* and in his new paper, the Beaver *Northern Islander,* he heaped abuse and scorn on the "Brighamite abomination" of plural marriage—until in 1847 or 1848, while he was on tour, he met Elvira Field, a nineteen-year-old Mormon schoolteacher in Southern Michigan. Then he changed his mind. Strang wanted Elvira, and wanted her badly. There was only one way he could get her, since divorce from Mary Strang was both undesirable and impossible. Accordingly, in 1849 George Adams, one of Strang's lieutenants, came to Elvira with an interesting suggestion. Strang, he reported, had received an angelic message approving the practice of polygamy. To set an example for his followers, Strang therefore offered Elvira the honor of becoming his first polygamous wife, and queen of Zion, before he revealed his new orders to the faithful. Oddly enough, Elvira unhesitatingly accepted what was probably one of the most transparent propositions in the history of American courtship. She went to Beaver with Adams, and the union was consummated a few days after the close of the summer church conference.

By an ancient theatrical device, Strang solved the problem of what to do with Elvira while the divine order concerning polygamy was not yet published to the Saints. He dressed her in boys' clothes and took her on his tour of the East, introducing her as a newly-found nephew, "Charley Douglas." Surprisingly, the device worked, though Elvira's youthful charms must have been difficult to hide in boys' clothes. In New York, Baltimore, Philadelphia, Washington, and other cities, Strang spent his days making converts to Primitive Mormonism and his nights with Elvira. In New York Strang had a bad moment when two Mormons, repeating some Beaver Island gossip, accused him of "adultery, fornication, and spiritual wifery." But they failed to penetrate Elvira's disguise; Strang brazened it out, demanded an investigation of his accusers, and cleared himself triumphantly. One of his accusers, L. D. Hickey, himself later took three wives.

In early 1850, after returning from his tour, Strang introduced Elvira to the Saints and announced the new policy of polygamy, eliciting some surprise but little protest. Mary Strang, apparently with strong suspicions of the validity of the angelic revelation, went home to Wisconsin. At the same time Strang announced that in July he would be crowned king, in obedience to the injunction laid down in chapter XX of the *Book of the Law of the Lord:* "God has chosen his servant James to be King; He hath made him his Apostle to all nations; He hath established Him a prophet above the Kings of the Earth; and appointed him King in Zion; by His voice did he call Him, and He sent his angels unto him to ordain him." The coronation was set for July 8, despite some disquieting news from the mainland about Gentile hostility to Strang and all he stood for.

The responsibility for difficulties between Gentile and Mormon in Michigan seems to have been about evenly divided. The argument over land titles began it, while the old families on the island—the Cables, McKinleys, Wrights, and Newtons—resented both the newcomers' selfrighteous smugness and their aggressiveness. The fishermen who summered on the island contributed their share to the troubles, and their free-and-easy living habits, despised by the abstinent, God-fearing Mormons, aroused nothing but contempt from the Strangites. Mormons complained that the Gentiles bothered Mormon girls, broke up meetings, administered beatings to some Mormon men, and threatened others, all of which was probably true.

As the number of Mormons increased, so did their power of retaliation. At the same time, the Gentiles complained of Mormon rudeness, theft, and harassment. Mormons considered Gentile society a morass of iniquity and never hesitated to say so. Strang's people considered themselves divinely chosen to possess Beaver Island, regardless of Gentile occupancy, for it was recorded in Strang's revelations that on Beaver "God shall establish his people . . . and the power of the Gentile shall not be upon them, and the arm of God shall be with them to support." As for theft, Gentile property was "unconsecrated." Whatever a Gentile owned could be "consecrated" to God's use by Mormon possession. Thus Gentile boats, nets, implements, or any property left unguarded was very likely to disappear into Zion. Constant pressure on some of the Gentile families drove them out, leaving their property open to "consecration," while Strang's Society of the Covenant, a picked group of tough Mormons, served as a private army to execute his orders.

As Strang heard it, the Gentiles planned to raid Beaver on Independence Day (appropriately), recover their lost property, capture Strang and his lieutenants, and drive out the Mormons once and for all. Organized by a half dozen disgruntled fishermen, the expedition was to have included several boatloads of armed men from as far away as Mackinac Island, who were to rendezvous at Whiskey Point on St. James Bay (a point *not* named by Strang) during the night of July 3. But the fishermen boasted a little too much. Word of the plan came to Strang, and his Mormons procured a small cannon by steamer from Chicago, stored powder and shot, armed themselves with rifles, and prepared for action. A boatload or so of raiders arrived on the evening of the third, correctly enough, and celebrated the Fourth far into the night. Late on the morning of the Fourth they woke with aching heads to the thunder of Strang's cannon firing "salutes" across the bay, using solid shot that skipped dangerously near their own boats. Furthermore, reinforcements expected by the invaders never showed up. Bowing to hangovers and superior armament, the attackers quietly left.

On July 8, 1850, Strang was crowned King James the Prophet at ceremonies in the log tabernacle. Dressed in a striking red robe, preceded by a procession of the Council and Elders, Strang placed on his own brow a metal crown, clustered with stars, symbolic of his divinely-ordered authority over Zion. The assembled Saints—more than four hundred of them—swore absolute allegiance to King James and unswerving obedience to God's law as revealed by him. After the coronation the faithful subjects assembled in the forest; there they sacrificed animals and made burnt offerings after the Biblical fashion, and indulged in jollity and dancing on the greensward. For the occasion Strang announced a new divine revelation—to him God had awarded supreme authority over all islands in the Great Lakes, that they might be apportioned by him among the Mormons.

After his coronation Strang embarked on a course that, he clearly hoped, would extend the boundaries of his kingdom far beyond Beaver Island. The seven remaining Gentile families were forced off the island, the fishing colonies were disbanded, and control of the rich fishing grounds gradually fell into Mormon hands. The Beaver Islands constituted Paine Township of Emmet County on the mainland but for judicial purposes they were attached to Mackinac County.

Mackinac Island, lying about fifty miles east of Beaver, was the commercial center of the upper Michigan area—or at least had been, until Strang's Mormon colony began to cut deeply into its trade. The Mormons were hard workers and good traders. Beaver had always been a refueling stop for woodburning steamers, and the Mormons, logging off the forested southern portion of the island, consequently developed a lively trade with the passing ships. Lumber from their sawmill and fish from their nets found a ready market in Chicago. The Chicago-Buffalo steamer made sixty stops a year at St. James, and numerous other boats docked there for fish, wood, and lumber. Strang's colony, the businessmen of Mackinac recognized, was a real challenge. The Mackinac Islanders, aware of Strang's imperialistic aims, harassed the Beaver Mormons in whatever fashion they could.

Complaints of Mormon theft, some true and some false, brought the Mackinac sheriff to Beaver regularly to carry Mormons off to jail for real or fancied offenses. The justice of the peace at Mackinac, one Charles O'Malley, caused particular trouble. O'Malley was a good hater—it was he who almost broke Henry Rowe Schoolcraft's heart by changing the Indian names of upper Michigan counties to Irish names, such as Clare, Roscommon, Antrim, and Emmet—and he made Strang's life miserable. Mormons were dragged into O'Malley's court on any pretext, there he imposed tremendous sentences that were always thrown out on appeal. O'Malley's legal ignorance and vindictiveness are illustrated by his attempt to sentence Strang to life imprisonment for contempt of court.

Strang's coronation and the Gentile-Mormon "war" in Michigan after 1850 attracted national attention. Polygamy lent itself admirably to juicy newspaper stories, cloak-and-dagger tales of Mormon raids and "piracy" made good copy, and the existence of a kingdom in Lake Michigan appealed to popular imagination. Strang's enemies made full use of their opportunities to spread stories. George Adams, an ex-actor and thorough rascal whom Strang expelled for bringing a prostitute to the island, joined the anti-Strang forces on the mainland and outdid himself with high-colored accounts of life on Beaver that the papers eagerly snapped up. Strang, it was said, had a printing press hidden in a cave on Mount Pisgah, turning out bales of counterfeit United States bills; his Mormons shot down Gentiles in cold blood, tore out their hearts, and spat on them; Mormons raided the mainland in fancifully named pirate boats with tan sails and murdered nonbelievers in their sleep.

Strang replied in kind, for he himself was an inveterate writer to newspapers, but he was more energetically engaged in consolidating his kingdom than in answering his critics. Though King James was a complete autocrat, his theory of kingship was sensibly adjustable. He claimed to be king of the Mormons only, assuming over them by divine right an authority that by contrast made Stuarts and Bourbons seem downright egalitarian. But he claimed no power over Gentiles and nonbelievers, recognizing the authority of the United States and the State of Michigan, and was happy to use the machinery of Federal and state law for his own purposes. Thus King Strang had his cake and its icing, too. Within his own colony he could enforce his rule by right of church law, which he alone made and interpreted. If necessary, he could deal with dissidents by civil law as well, for the sheriff, justices of the peace and all other local offices were soon under his control. Strang himself, in fact, was a justice of the peace and a township supervisor. Beyond his colony he could enforce his will on nonbelievers by employing all the machinery of county and township government. To Mormons, Strang was both church and state; rebels against his authority stood very little chance of winning an argument with him or of escaping punishment for disobeying him.

Constant complaints from northern Michigan, a stream

of newspaper stories and, quite possibly, a desire to make a reputation, led the United States District Attorney at Detroit, George C. Bates, to look into Strang's activities. To find charges on which to issue a warrant was not difficult. Bates did so, charging Strang and his associates with treason, counterfeiting, mail robbery, trespass, theft, and several other crimes. With forty armed men and the *U.S.S. Michigan* he went to Beaver, arrested Strang and thirty-one other Mormons, and brought them to Detroit for trial.

The trial itself was nearly a farce. Strang pleaded his own case, shrewdly emphasizing his and his colony's right to religious freedom and their constitutional rights to believe as and what they pleased. Unhappily for Bates, the Mormons won acquittal on every charge.

In 1850 King James decided to put the State of Michigan to work for him. The Beaver Mormons, voting in a solid bloc, simply took over the township government. In 1851 they elected him to the State Legislature as a Representative (Democratic) and he went to Lansing for two terms, escaping a warrant for his arrest on the way and barely evading deprival of his seat in a House investigation. But he stayed and went to work, conducting himself, said a Detroit newspaper, "with decorum and propriety."

King James was not a brilliant statesman, but he was industrious and tactful. He succeeded in detaching the Beaver Islands from both the Emmet and Mackinac districts, and in forming a new island county of Manitou, thus frustrating O'Malley and the Mackinac Irish Gentiles. Since by this time there were enough Mormons in sparsely populated Emmet County on the mainland to control it, Strang was left with two counties under his thumb. His district returned him to the Legislature in 1853, though he had done little of importance in his second term. He tried to introduce a bill to subdivide Michigan to provide a separate territory for Mormons, but got nowhere. He suggested to the Secretary of the Interior in Washington that he be appointed Governor of Utah Territory, so that he might uproot Brigham Young's colony and establish "true Mormonism" in the West. This proposal received short shrift. In 1855 he went back to Beaver Island.

In 1855 Strang was at the zenith of his power. He was absolute monarch of the Beaver chain and about twenty-six hundred Mormons. He controlled the political machinery of two counties; his treasury was fat with the revenue of the island's farms, forests, and fisheries; his colonies on the mainland were expanding and flourishing. John Forster, a young government surveyor working on the Great Lakes, spent some time on Beaver in early 1855, and reported "much evidence of thrift and industry," good roads, good houses, good crops, stores, docks, and huge stacks of firewood. The Mormons, though extremely suspicious of Federal men and exceedingly uncommunicative, seemed prosperous and happy. Strang, Forster found, was a pleasant and coöperative man, exuding power and confidence, though he told stories of polygamous life that one "did not expect to hear from a prophet." Forster visited Strang's home and was fascinated by the bedrooms of the plural wives. For Strang by this time had four wives. Such "evidences of domestic felicity," Forster wrote, "were pleasing to us bachelors."

In 1852 the king had taken to himself Betsy McNutt, and soon after he added two cousins, Phoebe and Sarah Wright. Elvira bore him four children, Betsy three, and the Wright girls one each. All four women lived together with Strang, apparently without friction, and all reported that the king at home was "a mild, kind man, though his word was law." As befitting a king, Strang had more, wives than any other Saints and perhaps, according to one of his sons, a concubine or two as well. Actually, polygamy was not popular on Beaver, for few Mormons could afford the luxuries of plurality of wives and eligible females were few. Probably no more than twenty Mormons had more than one wife, and only L. D. Hickey had three.

Yet all was not happy in Strang's realm. Some malcontents grumbled under his rule, a few escaped to the mainland, and some were expelled. Strang had no use for velvet gloves in dealing with his flock. A copy of his laws was required reading in every Mormon home. Deviations from his code were swiftly punished. He revived the use of the lash, following Biblical practice, and his sheriff and constables meted out beatings with Old Testament thoroughness. For "lying and talebearing" the prescribed punishment was thirty-nine lashes with birch rods; for more serious offenses the number was proportionately higher. Coffee, tea, and tobacco were expressly forbidden, male and female dress standardized, and social deportment strictly governed by iron rule. Women wore bloomers, and the wife who wore a dress exposed her husband to punishment. Strang himself might go to church barefooted, but men, women, and children dressed and comported themselves as he directed. Under the apparent unity and happiness on Beaver Island lay a sullen discontent, in some quarters at least.

Young Forster, in his surveying trips through the mainland near Beaver, remarked the presence of an amazing amount of "unremitting hostility and hatred" among Gentiles toward Strang's colony. While the Saints undoubtedly did "consecrate" untended Gentile property with impunity, the fault lay not wholly with the Mormons. The bitterness of the displaced fishermen over the loss of the rich fishing grounds of the island area, and the resentment of the Gentile settlers over the inexorable Mormon appropriation of farm land on the mainland, both were strong. The stories circulated by Strang's enemies of his "harrying raiders" and their "night piracy" were highly exaggerated; a good many of the fishermen considered the Mormons fair game, and the raiding that was done was about even on both sides. The "Battle of Pine River," in 1853, provided an example of how the stories grew. According to the Gentile version, Strang's armed pirates attacked the settlement at Pine River (now Charlevoix) searching for escaped Mormons and for something to steal, only to be driven off by brave and determined resistance. The fact was that Strang several times had warned the main-

land traders to stop selling "trade whiskey" (a searing con-
coction of alcohol, water, tobacco, and cayenne pepper) to
the Indians in the Pine River area, which was under Mormon
jurisdiction. Michigan law forbade the sale of liquor to
Indians, and the Mormons, who considered the red men their
especial wards, protested strenuously against what was common trading practice. The Pine River fishermen replied that
any Mormon officer who attempted to arrest them would be
shot on sight. Strang's sheriff, with an unarmed posse of
fourteen men and a warrant, was ambushed as his men
beached their boat. Six men were wounded, and the Mormons barely escaped greater casualties. The fishermen pursued the fleeing posse across twenty-six miles of open water
toward Beaver, slowly gaining, dropping rifle shots closer and
closer to the sheriff's boat. Only the providential arrival
of a Chicago-bound bark, which took the frantic Mormons
aboard, saved them from death. When the sheriff returned
to Pine River with an armed posse, the fishermen were gone.

That a conspiracy against Strang would develop either
within or without his colony as both his authority and the
number of his enemies, Mormon and Gentile, increased was
almost inevitable. The plot itself hatched in 1856 in the
brain of Dr. Hezekiah McCulloch, a Baltimore physician
who had joined the colony in its early stages as one of
Strang's trusted lieutenants. McCulloch had a fondness for
the bottle, a vice Strang detested, and the doctor, having
fallen from favor, brooded in his cups over his demotion.
Far too clever to plot alone, McCulloch enlisted three others
who also had suffered at the king's hands—Thomas Bedford,
Alexander Wentworth, and a "Dr. Atkyn," an itinerant
daguerreotyper whom Strang had banished from the colony
some months earlier. McCulloch smuggled in pistols from
the mainland for Bedford and Wentworth, who, with a
curious *sang-froid*, spent hours shooting at targets while
McCulloch waited for an opportunity. What went on in
Strang's mind is hard to fathom. Very few things on Beaver
escaped his notice; McCulloch's trips to the mainland there-

fore could hardly have remained secret. Strang even noted in *The Northern Islander* that "two doctors" and "some ignorant persons" were "on an errand of mischief," and he most certainly must have noted the presence of two malcontents openly perfecting their marksmanship with recently-acquired pistols. Overconfidence and carelessness, fatal flaws in an authoritarian ruler, did him in.

Eventually McCulloch had to make his own opportunity. On one of his trips to the mainland he made such violent complaints against Strang that the captain of the *U.S.S. Michigan,* charged with the enforcement of Federal law on the Lakes, stopped at Beaver in late June to investigate. It is doubtful that the captain was a party to the plot, as Mormons later claimed, though it is also doubtful that the captain could have failed to perceive that McCulloch most certainly was up to something. After anchoring in the bay, the captain sent a young officer to Strang's home to escort the king on board for questioning. Strang came willingly, and as he and his escort passed a woodpile on the dockside Bedford and Wentworth stepped from hiding and fired. One shot struck Strang in the head, another in the face below the right eye; as Strang sank bleeding to the ground, Bedford shot him in the back, and both men clubbed him with pistol butts. The killers ran aboard the ship, where McCulloch had already prudently concealed himself, while Saints carried their king to the nearest house. The ship's surgeon came ashore and did what he could.

The Mormon sheriff, late that night, sent a message to the *Michigan's* captain, asking custody of the killers, who, after all, had committed murder in plain view of numerous witnesses within his jurisdiction—to which the captain replied that he would deliver them to authorities on Mackinac. This he did. Bedford, Wentworth, and McCulloch met a wild ovation in O'Malley's land, served five minutes in jail, and were released. They were never tried.

Strang lingered for several days, in great pain though fully conscious. That his wounds were mortal he probably knew, and certainly his principal aides knew, for most of them quietly packed and left the island. Strang steadfastly refused to name a successor, though leadership was the one thing the confused islanders needed most. The *Michigan* came back from Mackinac, with McCulloch, Bedford, and Wentworth, demanded Strang "dead or alive," and sailed away when the Mormons gathered enough organization to resist. How the captain of the *Michigan* justified this return trip to Beaver is not known. Fearing another visit from the *Michigan,* the Mormons decided to carry Strang to Wisconsin. More than ten days after the shooting they put him aboard the *Louisville,* bound for Chicago, with two of his wives and several of the Elders. Soon after his arrival in Voree, on July 9, 1856, King Strang died, almost exactly six years after his coronation. All four of his plural wives were pregnant.

After Strang's departure, Beaver Island was in utter confusion. Leaderless, frightened Mormons left on every passing steamer, and in early July the sheriff of Mackinac notified the remaining families that the island must be vacated in ten days. The ubiquitous Dr. McCulloch and a mob from the mainland appeared to speed the evacuation, with McCulloch singling out for special attention those Mormons he particularly disliked. All horses, cows, sheep, boats, nets, provisions, and other property were to be left behind; armed men searched out Mormon farms and looted Mormon stores. It was an ugly, half-drunk mob, led by hard and angry men, and the record of its activities is not a pleasant one. Fortunately there was no gunfire, chiefly because the dispirited Mormons made no resistance. In a few days no Saints were left on Beaver Island.

Some of Strang's subjects went west to Brigham Young's thriving colony, some found quieter homes with Mormons in the East or in Illinois. Many simply scattered. The Gentiles came back to Beaver, reinforced by a flood of Irish immigrants, and within a few years only traces were left of the Kingdom of James the Prophet. The town of St. James remains, looking across the blue bay, though few who visit it know how it received its name.

The puzzle of Strang, too, remains. A man of ability, shrewdness and frightening drive, something vital seemed missing in him and in his leadership. Strang had daring and the ruthlessness to drive men before him, but he could never draw men with him toward something beyond him and themselves. His people obeyed him, but never liked him; without the avowal of God's authority behind him, it is doubtful they ever would have obeyed him at all. Strang's life was a paradoxical mixture of sincerity and cynicism. It is impossible to believe in his convenient angelic visitations, but it is equally impossible to doubt that he really believed in his co-partnership with God. This curious blend of cynical opportunism and deep sincerity provided the sources of his power over those whose cynicism alone, or whose sincerity alone, was less than his.

Somehow, nothing Strang did was in heroic terms that caught the imagination, or fired men with enthusiasm. The great vision of Zion that led Young and his Mormons in their tremendous trek across the great plains was never seen on Beaver. As megalomania crept into Strang's rule, Beaver Island became Strang's colony, not God's, and he pulled it down in death with him, almost deliberately. He left nothing except bitter memories—no church, no loyal band of followers, not even a Mormon legend of martyrdom—and at least one of his wives kept the secret of their parenthood from his children. The structure he built on human frailty had a weak foundation.

FAIRLY RESPECTABLE REBELS

★

Clement L. Vallandigham

Jacob Coxey

Clement L. Vallandigham

★

THE PROBLEM of how far a nation at war may (or should) go in infringing upon its own liberties is extremely delicate. Every war in which the United States had engaged has raised it, nor has the nation ever found a satisfactory answer to it. The Civil War, since it set Americans against Americans in a struggle over uniquely American issues, raised it in particularly intensified form on both sides of Mason's and Dixon's line.

There were many Northern men who voted against Lincoln and his party in 1860, men who believed neither in the Civil War nor the grounds on which it was fought. Slavery, they thought, was the South's business. It might be best, if the slave states found the union incompatible with their interests, to let the erring sisters depart. The South too had its dissenters, for the Confederacy was by no means solid in its support of Jefferson Davis and the Southern nationalists. Some Northerners believed in the South's right to secede and in its right to maintain its peculiar institution. Some Southerners were intensely Unionist and antislavery. Neither Davis nor Lincoln ever lacked for critics.

Abraham Lincoln's problem was the more difficult of the two. He was a partisan office holder, representing a coalition party that was an unsteady alliance of conservative, moderate, and extremist elements. After Bull Run introduced the North to the bloody realities of war, Lincoln had to keep some sort of unity among the disparate groups comprising his support through two years of military frustration, stalemate, and defeat. To do this he was given (sometimes he simply took) more authority than any Chief Executive had possessed up to his time. The fact that he refrained from misusing his tremendous wartime powers is tribute to his greatness—but nevertheless, intent on saving the Union, he used them at times in a fashion which led a number of Northern leaders (either for political advantage or from sincere conviction) to cry "Dictator" and "Tyrant."

There were others in the North, however, who were less respectful of civil liberties than Lincoln, and who under the grants of power issued to them by the President abused their authority in a manner often acutely embarrassing to him. His suspension of the *habeas corpus,* meant as an emergency measure, allowed some of his overzealous subordinates to imprison hundreds of suspected Southern sympathizers, some of them quite innocent, for long periods without trial. Under one Presidential proclamation, for example, more than thirteen thousand civilians were arrested, tried by court martial, and sentenced by military courts on charges ranging from simple theft to treason. Certain Confederate officials were equally guilty of infringing on the rights of Southern citizens. It was easy, North or South, to confuse disagreement with disloyalty, to muffle criticism with accusations of treason. There were men of sincerity in Union and Confederacy who preferred to lose the war rather than submit to what they considered to be the "arbitrary dictatorship of power-hungry politicians."

The sharpest thorn in Lincoln's side was an Ohio lawyer and editor named Clement Laird Vallandigham. Born near New Lisbon, Ohio, in 1820, Vallandigham inherited from his father (a rigidly Presbyterian minister) and his grandfather (a ringleader in the Whiskey Rebellion) a stubborn resistance to force and a dogged belief in the integrity of one's principles. He was educated at Jefferson College in Pennsylvania, taught school briefly, and entered law in Dayton, Ohio, in 1842.

A handsome man with an excellent voice and a commanding vocabulary, slightly purple as contemporary rhetorical standards demanded, he had a bright career in law ahead of him. His standards, in and out of court, were high. He was honest, sincere, and tremendously earnest, perhaps too inflexible in his thinking for his own good. Even as a college youth he showed a rigidity of conscience, a classmate said, that made him "self-willed, impatient of restraint, and reckless of opposition." At Jefferson, after becoming involved with the college president in an argument over a point of constitutional law, he withdrew from school when the president refused to capitulate. When the president apologized and offered him a diploma if he would only apply for it, young Vallandigham flatly refused. A teetotaller himself, he once drew a gun on a group of rollicking students who threatened to pour a drink down his throat—though later he left the temperance movement in protest against the use of legislative force in prohibiting the consumption of liquor. Such an inflexible adherence to principle must have made him a sobering influence on festive undergraduates.

Vallandigham was a good lawyer. Like most young lawyers of his time, he hoped to make a career for himself in politics, and in preparation drew up at twenty-three a set of rules for self-guidance, committing himself to "absolute honesty and strict construction of the Constitution." "I must pledge myself," he wrote firmly in his diary, "to pursue the dictates of my judgment and my conscience, regardless of consequences to party or self . . . , to make peace with all nations, and pursue it, persuaded that a pacific policy is the true wisdom of a State and war its folly." Thus morally armored, he joined the Democratic party. In 1845 Vallandigham was elected to the Ohio legislature, the youngest member of the House, already with a reputation as a good speaker and an iron-willed young man. Two years later he left the law to become editor of the Dayton *Empire*, a Democratic newspaper, though he served another two terms in the legislature.

Abolitionism worried Vallandigham more than any other political issue of the forties. Since Ohio was a hotbed of antislavery activity and the home of the powerful Ohio and

Western antislavery societies, he observed the beginnings of the abolitionist movement at first hand. Cincinnati, not far away, was a particularly troublesome spot—James Birney's newspaper had been wrecked there, the well-publicized "Lane Rebels" had left there for Oberlin, and the city had experienced one rather serious race riot. Agitation of the slavery question, as Vallandigham saw it agitated in Ohio, he considered potentially dangerous to "the stability of the Union and the peace and harmony of its different sections." This was the prevailing doctrine of Northern Democrats, and Vallandigham, like his party's leaders, condemned the Wilmot Proviso, favored the Mexican War, and praised the Compromise of 1850. He was not pro-slavery, he explained in the *Empire,* but pro-Union and pro-Constitution; Garrison, whose Boston paper carried "No Union with Slaveholders" on its masthead, would eventually smash both if his followers were allowed to flourish and multiply. Slavery was an evil, he agreed, but one from which the South, gradually and in its own way, would rid itself. The abolitionists were trying to force the South to abolish it, and he was against force.

By 1852 Vallandigham was a power in Ohio Democratic circles. He ran for Congress that year from Ohio's third district, lost, and lost again in 1854. In 1856, after he had apparently lost, he contested the election, claiming that his opponent's winning margin was made up of falsely sworn Negro votes. The litigation stretched out for nearly a year and a half, but he finally won the seat in the House of Representatives. Only a few months later he successfully defended it in the Congressional elections of 1858 and returned to Washington.

Clement Vallandigham, when he entered the House, was an anti-abolitionist, Unionist, Peace Democrat. Congressional tempers were short in the 1858 session, debates were hot, and the question of slavery and its extension overshadowed everything else. Like other Northern Democrats, Vallandigham believed that the slavery issue was a powder-barrel with a slow-burning fuse. Unlike Stephen A. Douglas, who "did not care whether slavery were voted up or down," Vallandigham recognized the explosive nature of the slavery question and blamed its agitation directly on the New England abolitionists. "The abolition hordes of the North," he firmly believed, would eventually "rend the Union apart [and] the Union is of more value than many Negroes." Abolition was not a political question, it did not belong in politics, and he wanted it kept out of politics. It had split the Eastern Democrats wide open, he pointed out, and had captured the Republicans. Western Democrats alone stood for Union and unity, and unless they took a firm stand in Congress, the nation would be irrevocably divided. In 1858 and 1859 he spoke frequently in the House, warning of "a most imminent danger of a speedy disruption of the union of these states," begging for less sectional bickering and greater tolerance. If there was a Democratic leader in the West who ranked next to Douglas in the tense years from 1858 to Sumter, it was clearly Clement Vallandigham.

As the South moved toward secession Vallandigham's popularity in the House and in Ohio waned. He kept pleading for compromise, and compromise talk was not popular, nor were men who spoke as bluntly as he. But he was convinced he was right, a conviction made even stronger by John Brown's raid at Harper's Ferry in 1859. Vallandigham, on his way home to Ohio by train from Washington, arrived in Harper's Ferry only a few hours after Brown's capture. He hurried from the train to talk to the fanatic old man, who lay on the floor of the arsenal, his head still bleeding from a sabre cut. His interview with Brown confirmed all of his fears. Harper's Ferry showed him abolition in action—war, death, hatred, disunion. He resolved on the spot that he would have none of it.

Vallandigham ran for Congress in 1860 and won on a platform opposing "Northern sectionalism and fanaticism." The abolitionists, he claimed, were determined to split the nation apart and very probably in so doing would provoke a civil war. He himself supported Stephen A. Douglas for President (though he had reservations about Douglas' "popular sovereignty" theory) and in the campaign he attacked Lincoln as "a revolutionary, disorganizing, subversive man" who would most assuredly bring the nation to dissolution by capitulating to the abolitionists in his party. In Congress, as he saw the Southern states secede one by one in the closing days of the year, he continued to plead for conciliation, voting for all the desperate compromise measures submitted in late 1860 and early 1861. "My object—my sole motive,—" he explained, "is to maintain the Union . . . The Union can be preserved only by maintaining the Constitution and constitutional rights, and above all, the perfect equality of every state and section of this Confederacy." There must be another way to solve the problem, he argued, than by war.

In early 1861 Vallandigham proposed three Constitutional amendments that embodied his solutions to the twin issues of slavery and secession. So long as slavery remained the primary issue in national politics, he reasoned, it was impossible to maintain a national political union of free and slave states. Let Congress, therefore, recognize the fact that slavery was a *sectional* problem by deliberately dividing the nation into four sections (North, South, West, and Pacific) not on the issue of slavery, but on broader issues of economic, social, and cultural interests. With the establishment of proper Constitutional safeguards and necessary checks on executive and congressional power, the sections would balance each other by compromise and adjustment. The nation would be a *union* of four separate sections, all under the same Constitution, each with adequate representation in the national governing body but with autonomy to handle its own sectional problems without interference or coercion. No section would be powerful enough to oppress others; each would be powerful enough to protect itself. Vallandigham's proposed amendments revealed a shrewd, if fundamentally unworkable, answer to the problem, posed by Lincoln, of maintaining a national union among sectional interests. The house, he believed, *could* exist half-slave and half-free under such a system. It need not fall, nor need it cease to be divided if the warring sections resolved their differences by properly readjusting their relationships within the Union. "Votes, checks, balances, concurrent majorities—these are the true conservators of free government," he wrote. "Let us maintain the Union by dividing or arranging the States into sections *within the Union, under the Constitution*." But events rushed on, far beyond compromises such as Vallandigham's. Sumter came, Lincoln's call for troops, and the tents of army camps mushroomed along the Potomac.

Vallandigham was not a tactful man, and his language took on a sharper edge in the House debates after Sumter. In the extraordinary session of Congress called in July, 1861, he heard the Speaker of the House, in a blood-thirsty address, pledge a cheering Congress to maintain the Union "though the waters of the Mississippi should be crimsoned with human gore." The nation, Vallandigham thought, must have gone insane. The craze for war swept the country as it did Congress, while he watched sick at heart. Lincoln's policy, he warned, "would plunge the nation headlong into war," a useless, pointless war. And he could already see how war, even in its early stages, nibbled away at the traditional rights and liberties of Americans—how preparations for war gave "fools and autocrats" an opportunity to oppress and tyrannize. Lincoln's suspension of the *habeas corpus*, his authoritarian methods of censorship, his violations of due process, "Every principal act of the Administration has been a glaring usurpation of powers," said Vallandigham, "and a palpable and dangerous violation of that Constitution which this Civil War is professedly waged to support!" Lincoln and his party, he was convinced, had provoked a state of emergency in order to establish a dictatorship. If war were necessary, he told the House, he would support it—but it was not, and he raised his voice against the "blind voting of millions of men and money" in "aggressive and invasive warfare." As a result the Ohio troops stationed near Washington nearly mobbed him when he visited their camp.

Vallandigham was not alone among Congressional Democrats in his opposition to "Mr. Lincoln's war," but his powerful speeches made him, in 1861, the leader of the anti-war forces in Congress, which included honest pacifists and middle-of-the-road Republicans as well. In Illinois, Lincoln's home state, mass meetings called for a convention "to settle the terms of peace, which should have in view the restoration of the Union as it was"—just as meetings in parts of the South called on Davis to negotiate for terms. Some of the opposition in the North was organized, pro-Confederate, and probably treasonable. On the other hand, "Peace Democrats" such as Vallandigham opposed the war in perfectly legal fashion and from sincere convictions. As citizens they were pledged to support the government in its effort to preserve its safety and authority; at the same time they believed that neither was actually threatened, that the war was "for the purpose of conquest or subjugation of the Southern states" and not for what Lincoln and his party said it was. But where was the line to be drawn? At what point did criticism of the Administration provide aid and comfort to the enemy, and become treason? How loyal must a "loyal opposition" be in wartime?

Vallandigham received threats in the mails and insults in Congress. Some Congressmen suggested publicly that he ought to be investigated, and some accused him privately of outright disloyalty. "It is common rumor," remarked Hickman of Pennsylvania in the House, "that the gentleman from Ohio is, at least, open to grave suspicion if not to direct implication." Petitions came from Ohio for his expulsion from Congress, but they were tabled while Vallandigham kept up his attacks. "My opinions are immovable," he said. "Fire cannot melt them out of me." His speeches, and he gave many of them in Ohio as well as in the House, were neither tactful nor temperate. He was heard to refer to "King Lincoln," to "Lincoln the tyrant," and at the Ohio Democratic convention he wrote and sponsored a resolution condemning Lincoln's "tyrannical infractions of the rights and liberties of American citizens."

"I am for the suppressing of all rebellions," Vallandigham

told a mass meeting in Dayton, "the Secession Rebellion South and the Abolitionist Rebellion North," explaining that he favored any movement for truce or peace which involved restoration of the Union on any reasonable terms. He spoke convincingly and well—and he had an effect. Crowds grew larger, ladies sent him bouquets, gentlemen gave him gifts of gold-headed canes, and newspapers (Democratic ones at least) gave his speeches full coverage. By the time of the Congressional elections of 1862 Clement Vallandigham was perhaps the greatest single political threat in the West to Abraham Lincoln, the Republican party, and the successful prosecution of the war.

The Ohio Democrats enthusiastically endorsed him for another term in Congress. The Ohio Republicans recognized that his return to Washington, which seemed quite likely, would be a strong rebuke to the Lincoln administration and a powerful stimulus to the peace movement. The Ohio Legislature, under Republican control, therefore gerrymandered Vallandigham's Third District and added to it the strongly abolitionist county of Warren, which Vallandigham was bound to lose. He was beaten before he began. He campaigned vigorously but the Republican votes from Warren were too many to overcome, though his margin of loss was not humiliating. He did return to Washington, of course, but as a lame duck.

From January to March, 1863, Vallandigham spent his last days in Congress in violent attacks on the Administration and the war. The war, he said, was an utter failure. What had twenty months of fighting accomplished but bloodshed? Had any seceded States returned to the Union? Had any slaves been freed? Instead, Lincoln had created in twenty months "one of the worst despotisms in history." Opposition had been "silenced by the fierce clamor of disloyalty;" precious liberties had been lost; civil rights had been smothered in Lincoln's demand for "abject submission" to authority. An end to a purposeless war, and to the tyranny of Republican rule, could come only through an immediate negotiated peace.

The Conscription Bill of February, 1863, elicited an especially bitter speech from the Ohioan. There were Republicans, as well as Democrats, who opposed shifting control of the draft from the states to the Federal government, and there were a number of hot speeches in the House, of which Vallandigham's was probably the hottest. To him the draft bill was but another link in "a chain forged about civil liberties . . . , a bill further to abrogate the Constitution [and] to erect a stupendous superstructure of despotism . . . , a confession that the people of the country are against this war." Further, he pointed out, the bill placed power in the military to investigate "treasonable practices," a perfect example of what the Administration was really up to.

The Conscription Bill passed, nevertheless, in March of 1863, shortly before the close of the session. The arguments in Congress, spearheaded by Vallandigham, most assuredly damaged its subsequent operation. Army desertions had been a problem ever since Bull Run, and resistance to the new draft law in certain areas (such as the Pennsylvania coal towns and the Eastern cities) several times broke out in open riot. The Peace Democrats and pro-Southern sympathizers, by this time lumped together under the label of "Copperheads," counselled resistance to conscription openly and covertly. Secret political societies, such as the Knights of the Golden Circle and the Order of American Knights (both strong in the West) discouraged enlistments, encouraged desertions, sent arms South, and occasionally engaged in actual spying. Vallandigham, who opposed secret societies on principle, refused to join any of the Copperhead organizations, but at the same time his speeches undoubtedly gave them encouragement and support. In a very real way, Clement Vallandigham was a threat to the Federal war effort.

At the end of the Congressional session in March, 1863, Vallandigham left Washington for Ohio by way of Albany, where he conferred with New York's Governor Horatio Seymour, the leader of the Eastern Democrats. On the way he spoke in Philadelphia and in New York, declaring to cheering crowds that if the war was continued "You will not have one remnant of civil liberty left among yourselves." Meanwhile the war, from the Administration's point of view, was not going well at all. Peace talk was growing in the East as well as in the West, and Vallandigham's accusations of "failure" and "tyranny" seemed to be finding support in a good many quarters. If Vallandigham and Seymour could find a formula by which Peace and War Democrats in East and West could be united, the Republican administration might be in deep trouble.

At about the time that Vallandigham arrived home in Dayton, General Ambrose E. Burnside, the new Commander of the Department of Ohio, arrived at his headquarters in Cincinnati. Burnside, a little man with imposing side-whiskers, a liking for theatrics, and a great deal of self-importance, had just been relieved of command of the Army of the Potomac after his bloody botch of Fredericksburg. His new post gave him a much-needed chance to redeem himself. A New England Democrat and a soldier, Burnside had little liking for "peace men;" furthermore, Ohio, Indiana, and Illinois, all under his jurisdiction, were trouble spots where the Copperheads were strongest. With warnings from Secretary of War Stanton fresh in his mind, Burnside set about to make the Department of Ohio safe from Vallandigham.

The General began at once to emit a stream of orders, some of which he possessed a right to issue under military powers, some of which he did not. Order Number 9 forbade citizens to criticize the military policies of the Administration; Order Number 15 forbade civilians to possess or bear arms. Order Number 38 was the most astonishing of all, since in effect it forbade citizens to harbor improper opinions. The order read in part, "Treason, expressed or implied, will not be tolerated. . . . The habit of declaring sympathy for the enemy will not be allowed," and anyone found expressing such sympathy would "be at once arrested . . . or sent beyond our lines into the lines of their friends." Burnside did not believe in defining his terms. What he meant by "implied" treason or "declarations of sympathy" he left for military courts to determine.

In April, 1863, shortly after the appearance of Order 38, Vallandigham spoke in Columbus, flaying Lincoln, the Republicans, and especially those "ambitious military gentlemen" who issued orders. For the rest of the month he continued his attacks at dozens of meetings through the smaller Ohio cities, virtually challenging Burnside to arrest him. As Vallandigham's crowds swelled, and as the Ohio papers reported his tour in greater detail, Burnside's anxiety increased. It became almost a personal contest between the Democrat and the General, and Vallandigham's habit of publicly tearing a copy of Order 38 into bits and spitting on it was hardly calculated to increase Burnside's authority in Ohio. Involved was not only the General's prestige, but that of the whole Lincoln Administration and the military policy that Burnside represented in the West.

On May 1, 1863, Vallandigham spoke at an open-air meeting of Democrats in Mount Vernon. The crowd was large, enthusiastic, and many of them wore "copperhead buttons" made from pennies. While Vallandigham repeated his usual charges against Lincoln and Burnside, Captain H. R. Hill of the 105th Ohio Volunteers, dressed in civilian clothes, stood by the corner of the platform and industriously took notes. Farther back in the crowd, Captain John Means of the 105th listened to the comments around him and noted crowd reactions. That night they reported to Burnside in Cincinnati.

On May 2, early in the morning, a special train left Cincinnati with a company of Ohio troops. They arrived late that night in Dayton, and at midnight marched to Vallandigham's home. The editor and his wife were in bed, but Vallandigham, awakened by hammering at his door, saw the soldiers drawn up in order on his front lawn. Anticipating some such emergency, he had arranged with his friends to fire a pistol shot as a signal for help, and when the troops heard the shot they broke down the door and burst into the house. Vallandigham dressed at gunpoint, was hustled to the train, and his friends arrived to find his frightened family huddled in the kitchen. The next day he was lodged in Kemper Barracks in Cincinnati, a military prisoner.

News of Vallandigham's arrest spread swiftly. In Dayton, before party leaders could establish control, angry Democrats set fire to the offices of the local Republican paper and threatened to march on Cincinnati. Burnside moved very quickly. He had already appointed a commission to try Vallandigham, its personnel chosen shrewdly to forestall Democratic accusations of foul play. Two of its members were Colonel James Van Buren (of the ex-President's family) and Captain James Cutts (brother to Stephen Douglas' second wife), both of impeccable Democratic lineage. Vallandigham appeared before this commission on May 6, 1863, only four days after his arrest.

The charge, as it was read to the defendant, accused one Clement Vallandigham of "publicly expressing, in violation of General Order 38, sympathy for those in arms against the Government of the United States, and declaring disloyal sentiments and opinions, with the object and purpose of weakening the power of the Government in its efforts to suppress an unlawful rebellion." Specifically, the Army claimed that Vallandigham on May 1 had uttered eleven disloyal statements, among them that "this was a wicked, cruel, and unnecessary war," that it was "a war waged not for the preservation of the Union," that the "men in power are attempting to establish a despotism," and that Order 38 was "a base usurpation of military authority."

Vallandigham refused to plead Guilty or Not Guilty, since he argued that the commission had no right whatever to try him, a civilian, for a violation of a military order. He was, he maintained, subject only to judicial courts, entitled to a public trial by an impartial jury of the State of Ohio by virtue of rights granted to him by the Constitutions of Ohio and of the United States. Brigadier General Potter, chairman of the commission, ordered that a plea of Not Guilty be entered for him and asked the prosecution to call its first witness. Captain Hill had voluminous notes, from which he recited almost verbatim more than a third of Vallandigham's Mount Vernon speech, swearing that he had heard the speaker use all the phrases attributed to him.

Captain Means added a few more. He had heard the phrases "King Lincoln" and "military despot;" furthermore, Vallandigham had said that "he was a free man and claimed the right to criticize and discuss . . . the war for the freedom of the blacks and the enslavement of the whites."

Vallandigham himself cross-examined Hill, though he explained that his decision to do so did not mean that he recognized the commmission's right to try him. That he had made the statements attributed to him by Hill he did not deny—but that they were disloyal he refused to concede. Under questioning, Hill admitted that Vallandigham had emphasized his opposition to secession in the Mount Vernon speech, and that he had several times expressed his support of the United States government. Vallandigham next called his friend S. S. Cox, a prominent Ohio Democrat, to the stand. Cox testified that he had heard no "odious epithets" at Mount Vernon, nor did he think that the speech itself "encouraged resistance to law and order." Vallandigham's remarks on the war were not attacks on the war itself, but on "its perversion from its original purpose," a sentiment with which he heartily agreed. There being no more witnesses, the commission recessed.

The Ohio Democrats had not been idle since Vallandigham's arrest. He smuggled a message out of Kemper Barracks, which they printed and broadcast through the state, pointing out that he was "in a military bastile" simply because he was a Democrat, "for no other offense than my political opinions." At the same time his friends asked Judge Leavitt of United States Circuit Court to issue a writ of *habeas corpus* in order to test the legality of Lincoln's suspension of this Constitutional right. There was a good case for the writ, but Burnside sent a General to the hearing and the Judge prudently denied the request.

On May 15 the commission met to give its verdict. Clement Vallandigham was found guilty on two counts and not guilty on a third—to have convicted him of calling Lincoln a "despot" would have smacked too much of partisan politics.

He was sentenced to "close confinement in some Fortress of the United States . . . , to be kept there during the continuation of the war." On May 16 Burnside chose Fort Warren, in Boston Harbor, as Vallandigham's place of incarceration, in the midst of a roar of protest from Democrats throughout the North. In New York City a crowd estimated at twenty-five thousand heard a series of speakers flail Burnside, Lincoln, and the Republican administration. In Albany, a huge mass meeting resolved that if the sentence were upheld, "Our liberties are overthrown, and our constitutional guarantees broken down," sentiments that were echoed from meetings in Philadelphia, Chicago, Cleveland, and Cincinnati itself.

As Commander-in-Chief of the Federal forces, Abraham Lincoln found the problem of Vallandigham resting squarely on the White House doorstep. Deeply immersed in much more pressing problems of war, Lincoln did not hear of Vallandigham's trial until May 16 or 17. The sentence placed Lincoln in the acutely embarrassing position of having to uphold or deny an extremely stupid act of a subordinate. If Burnside's action stood, it meant the alienation of a powerful segment of Democratic opinion—and 1864 was an election year. If Burnside's action were vetoed, it meant encouraging the Copperheads, angering the Radical Republicans in Congress, and undercutting the authority of the military. The Vallandigham affair was already receiving a bad press, for even some staunch Republican papers expressed doubts about the legality of his arrest and trial.

On May 19 Lincoln brought the problem to his Cabinet. All "regretted the necessity of arresting Vallandigham," he wrote Burnside, "some perhaps doubting there was a real necessity for it; but being done, all were for seeing you through with it." Burnside offered to resign, but Lincoln, with one of his strokes of political genius, found a way out. In Order 38 he noted the phrase, "sent beyond our lines to the lines of their friends." Why not commute the sentence to exile to the South? This upheld the authority of the military orders, recognized the legality of the commission, and had the additional advantage of making Vallandigham look a trifle silly. So on May 19 Burnside received orders from the War Department to send Vallandigham "beyond our military lines," and if he returned, to arrest and imprison him for the duration of the war.

The order surprised Vallandigham and the Democrats. He was still a martyr, perhaps, but much less a martyr as an exile in the South than as a prisoner in Fort Warren. "If he likes the Rebels so much, let him join his friends," the papers remarked, and heads nodded in agreement all over the North. Thus by one stroke Lincoln obfuscated the real issues involved in the Vallandigham' affair and blunted the Democratic argument. Vallandigham had never claimed that the Southern cause was just; he had never supported secession; he had never expressed sympathy for slavery; he had never opposed what he believed the "real aims" of the war should be. The vital issues of free speech, civil liberties, trial by jury, and Constitutional rights that his case raised were simply lost in the confusion created by Lincoln's astuteness.

Ambrose Burnside gratefully seized the chance to get rid of his celebrated prisoner. The War Department telegram arrived in Cincinnati on the afternoon of May 19, and the General had Vallandigham on the gunboat *Exchange* within four hours. There was some uncertainty about exactly where to send him, but on May 22 the boat left for Louisville, where a cavalry guard met Vallandigham and took him to Murfreesboro, General Rosecrans' headquarters in the field. The Federal officers and men, Vallandigham reported, were quite polite to him—"He don't look like no traitor," he heard one trooper remark—and one or two staff officers discussed politics with him. He offered to explain his views on the war to the troops themselves, an offer hastily declined by Rosecrans, who was uncertain of what the effect might be on draftees tired of camp life and marching.

How to dispose of Vallandigham was something of a puzzle. Rosecrans knew of no military precedent for the exile of a United States citizen who had not been convicted of anything beyond "disloyal sentiments," nor was he certain of the protocol involved in such a transfer. Like Burnside, he too was anxious to get Vallandigham off his hands. Therefore at two o'clock on the morning of May 26 he sent his guest with a cavalry guard down the Shelbyville Pike toward the Confederate lines. At dawn Vallandigham had breakfast at a farmhouse while the Federal officers, under a flag of truce, approached the nearest Confederate outpost. The outpost was manned by an Alabama line regiment, and the Alabamians were not sure what to do. In the traditional manner of armies, the privates called the lieutenant, who called the colonel. The colonel could remember nothing in his military training about accepting exiles. Should Vallandigham, a civilian, be accepted as a prisoner? What were the legal implications of accepting him as a prisoner, or under any conditions? The colonel decided to play safe. He refused to recognize the flag of truce, but he did agree to receive Vallandigham as he would "any other citizen"—though he wisely did not specify of what nation. The Federal officers therefore left Vallandigham a hundred yards or so from the Confederate lines and rode away.

Vallandigham walked over to a Rebel rifle pit and announced to a puzzled Alabama private that he was "a citizen of Ohio and of the United States . . . , within your lines by force and against my will." The Confederates chatted with him while the colonel sent a hasty message to General Bragg, sixteen miles away, asking for instructions. Three hours later a messenger returned with orders to bring the new arrival to headquarters, so Vallandigham, riding in an ambulance with cavalry escort, left for Shelbyville. Here, he recorded, he was received "in a kind and courteous manner," quartered at the house of a Mrs. Eakin in "a spacious and pleasant room" under the charge of General Hardee.

Vallandigham stayed in Shelbyville nearly a week while Bragg and Davis exchanged telegrams. The Confederate government was not particularly happy about his presence, for Vallandigham had no sympathy for secession and was perfectly willing to say so. Furthermore, Vallandigham the Peace Democrat, stirring up opposition to the war in Ohio, had some value to the Confederacy. Vallandigham the exile in Dixie had none at all. "Send him back by all means" advised the Chattanooga *Rebel.* "Vallandigham is not our friend, nor an alien enemy of the North; he has never declared for us!" The Mobile *Register* would have preferred Stevens or Sumner ("They at least curse the Union and so do we") to Vallandigham the Unionist. For that matter, Vallandigham too wanted to leave the South as soon as possible. The Confederate Alien Enemies Act of 1861 provided a solution. The authorities asked him if he were a loyal citizen of the United States. He replied that he was, thereby making himself an enemy alien, subject under the law to immediate deportation—theoretically, at least, to the country of his origin. But since he was barred from the United States under penalty of imprisonment, Canada, which received Confederates sympathetically, seemed to be the answer. In early June Davis wired orders that Vallandigham should be sent on parole to Richmond and then to Wilmington, North Carolina. The blockade-runner *Cornubia* took him to Halifax in early July, 1863, and he took up residence in Quebec City.

In June, 1863, while Vallandigham was still in Kentucky, the Ohio Democratic State Convention met in Columbus. It was a remarkable convention, attended by more than ten thousand Democrats, the majority of whom were not delegates. "Crowds on street corners," reported the Cincinnati *Gazette,* "cheered for Vallandigham . . . , boys peddled photographs of the exile, and everywhere cheering and flags and shouts of 'Hurrah for Vallandigham!' " The nomination of "that incorruptible statesman and fearless patriot" for Governor of Ohio was a foregone conclusion. With Vallandigham the Democratic party in Ohio knew it had the best political issue since Jackson's war with the Bank. The exiled Ohioan accepted the nomination from Canada and the campaign was on. There have been few stranger political campaigns in political history. Vallandigham moved from Quebec to Niagara Falls, and then to Windsor, across the river from Detroit, where he issued a stream of messages, broadsides, and speeches for Ohio consumption. Newspaper correspondents crossed the border to interview him; a delegation of students from the University of Michigan visited him; Democratic clubs called on him with flowers and resolutions. All the while a Federal gunboat patrolled the Detroit River opposite his house and Detroit crawled with Army agents and plainclothes detectives.

The Ohio Republicans nominated John Brough, a War Democrat, editor of the Cincinnati *Enquirer,* a good campaigner and an intelligent man. At the same time they knew that Vallandigham had strong support among independent voters, that his exile added appeal to his candidacy, and that his constant pokes at Lincoln and the war were hurting the Administration's cause in Ohio. But the Republicans had luck on their side. Smashing Union victories at Vicksburg and Gettysburg in July spiked the Democratic claim that the war was a failure. Late the same month the Confederacy stupidly sent General John Morgan into Indiana and Ohio on a raid that angered even the Copperheads. Morgan's men took horses and burned barns without regard for the owners' political sympathies, effectively refuting Democratic claims that the South fought only a defensive war to guard its rights. Furthermore, the Republicans controlled the soldiers' vote.

In Ohio, Brough led Vallandigham two hundred and forty-seven thousand to one hundred and eighty-five thousand. The Ohio soldiers in the Army of the Ohio, trapped ignominiously in Chattanooga, voted for Brough forty-three thousand to twenty-five hundred. At that Vallandigham pulled the largest Democratic vote recorded up to that time in Ohio—while Brough polled sixty-eight thousand more votes than the Republican vote of 1862, giving rise to Democratic speculation as to their origin.

To this point in his career, Vallandigham had committed no act that could reasonably be labelled as treasonable. He had, of course, severely criticized the government and the

Army in wartime, and he had (though without malicious intent) interfered at second-hand with the war effort in his persistent (and occasionally intemperate) exercise of his right of free speech. Not even Burnside, who certainly would have done so had he felt he could, had accused him of outright treason. But others were less circumspect than Vallandigham. The Copperhead political societies, the Knights of the Golden Circle and the Order of American Knights, both encouraged draft-dodging, gave aid to the South, planned revolts, and did actual spying—all them clearly treasonable activities. Vallandigham, until 1864, would have nothing to do with secret societies on principle, yet, when the Order of American Knights changed its name early that year and reorganized as the Sons of Liberty, he accepted the post of Supreme Commander.

There were probably three reasons for his decision. First, his exile and political defeat left him embittered, ready to strike back in any way he could at the government that had banished and humiliated him. Second, the longer his enforced absence from Ohio, the less his political influence, and the Knights provided him with a means (though not a good one) to keep his name in politics. Third, and perhaps most important, he sincerely believed that the war could and should be stopped, and that the Sons of Liberty, imperfect as it was, might be a tool to accomplish that end. In accepting the post, however, he stipulated that the ritual of the order must be rewritten, chiefly in language adapted from Jefferson and the eighteenth century liberals (including the password of "Calhoun" pronounced backwards) and that the organization (or so his brother later claimed) avoid any military action against the United States government.

There were wheels within wheels in the Sons of Liberty. Whether Vallandigham knew or approved, the order had already organized a military department, armed some of its members, and planned an armed revolt against the Federal government in the Western states. Though its councils were heavily infiltrated with Federal agents, still it claimed sufficient membership to make it a threat to the stability of the government in the West. The Confederacy was interested in the order too; the tide of war was turning against the South, and some Confederates hoped that the conflict might be stopped by provoking some cataclysmic event in the North. A Confederate commission came to Canada to see Vallandigham, who initiated at least one member into the Sons. Years later Confederate agents claimed that Vallandigham agreed to a plan whereby the order would precipitate a revolt, liberate Confederate prisoners held in Western prisons, seize the state government of Ohio and other states to the West, secede from the Union, and create a separate Northwest Confederacy. If Vallandigham did (and he denied it) this was treason. The weight of the evidence seems to lie with the Confederate agents. The South did contribute a half million dollars to the Sons of Liberty for arms and transportation, and it is undeniably true that certain leaders of the order were deep in the plot; Federal intelligence knew all the details and reported on it week by week. Nothing ever came of the revolt, for the Sons of Liberty were too badly organized to be capable of carrying out any such intricate plan. Furthermore, the Democrats had hopes of beating Lincoln at the polls in 1864 and a peaceful victory was far preferable to an armed uprising.

On June 15, 1864, Vallandigham stuffed a pillow under his waistcoat, glued on a false mustache, and took the boat from Windsor to Detroit. When he appeared suddenly on June 17 at the district Democratic convention in Hamilton, Ohio, a delegate wrote, "He touched off cheering such as has never before been heard on this continent." Abraham Lincoln was probably not surprised. Prominent Democrats had already put out feelers asking for commutation of his sentence, and it was obvious that if Vallandigham wanted to maintain any influence in Ohio politics he had to return. Lincoln did absolutely nothing about it. There would be no second martyrdom. The returned exile toured Ohio and the East denouncing Lincoln and the war, but the sting had gone out of his speeches. Nobody bothered him; nobody arrested him. It was not very effective to call Lincoln a tyrant under these conditions, and the string of Union victories simply did not support his claim that the war was a failure.

Vallandigham went to the Democratic presidential convention in Chicago as a delegate from his Ohio district. Named to the Committee on Resolutions, he helped to confuse further an already confused convention. The Committee on Resolutions, charged with drafting a platform, was evenly divided between Peace Democrats and Union (or War) Democrats, led by Samuel Tilden of New York. After a long argument in committee, Vallandigham's faction won. The platform, as it was reported out, declared that "the experiment of war to restore the Union was a failure"—that "justice, humanity, and the public welfare demand that immediate effort be made for a cessation of hostilities . . ." Curiously enough, the Union Democrats put up no fight on the floor and the platform passed.

But Vallandigham's victory suddenly recoiled on the Peace Democrats. The convention nominated General George B. McClellan, "Little Mac" of military fame, who accepted the nomination and immediately repudiated the platform. There could be no peace without Union, said McClellan, "the Union is the one condition of peace—we ask no more." So the Democrats ran McClellan on Vallandigham's platform— which declared the war a failure while Sherman marched through Georgia and Grant welded an iron circle about Richmond. Lincoln's intuition was right. The Democrats, with Vallandigham's help, had hanged themselves, and Vallandigham looked foolish again.

Appommatox finished Vallandigham as a politician. He went back to Dayton to his newspaper and his law practice, still popular among Democrats but without much influence in the party. At the news of Lee's surrender a mob gathered at his house, but he appeared at the door with a brace of pistols and dispersed the crowd with a shot in the air. He was never bothered again. His editorials in the *Empire* praised Lincoln for his fairness to the defeated South, and the news of the President's assassination shocked him as it did others. He did not like Andrew Johnson, nor did Johnson like him, but the *Empire* backed the President in his battles with the Radicals, whom Vallandigham hated more than he did Johnson. In 1868 he tried to win the Democratic nomination for the Senate and lost. The next year he won the nomination for the House, but lost the election and retired from politics for good.

In early 1871 a man was killed in a shooting affray in a Hamilton saloon. The accused was one Thomas McGeehan, an Irish tough with a bad reputation, who hired Vallandigham to defend him. Vallandigham believed McGeehan innocent, and succeeded in moving the trial to neutral territory in Lebanon, Ohio. McGeehan's story was that the dead man had shot himself while attempting to draw a gun, so Vallandigham procured a Smith and Wesson .32 to re-enact the fight. He experimented with the gun in his hotel room, satisfied himself that McGeehan's story could be true, and laid the pistol (with two shots left) on the table. When two friends entered the room Vallandigham said, "I'll show you how it happened," picked up the pistol, and shot himself in the stomach.

He lingered several days in great pain, dying on June 16, 1871. General McCook, his boyhood friend and a Civil War hero in his own right, said at the funeral, "He died with his armor on, and it clanged as he fell." McGeehan, who said nothing, got a hung jury and later an acquittal. Clement Vallandigham never knew he had won the case. All he received from fate was a sort of ironic immortality as the exiled traitor of Edward Everett Hale's famous story, "The Man Without a Country."

Whether or not Clement Vallandigham merited a better fate is an open question. He was a man of undoubted sincerity, of genuinely high principles, dedicated to an honorable cause. Yet his field of vision was limited and his mind narrow in a way which Lincoln's was not. Vallandigham could not see beyond the confines of his own rigidity, could not perceive the broader implications of the war he opposed so bitterly and the events he did his best to forestall. He was, in effect, trapped by his own principles. His memory might have been greener had he not—in a manner completely foreign to his instincts—toyed with treason. His lapse from honor, however brief and understandable, is hard for posterity to forgive, for by it he threw away the chance to become a symbol of independence and integrity. Possibly, by forgetting him, history has been as kind to him as he deserved.

Jacob Coxey

★

IT BEGAN IN 1891 on a bad road in Ohio. The depression of 1893 was still nearly two years away, but even then prices were sliding, wages slipping, foreclosures mounting, and business failing. The nation was about to elect Grover Cleveland President, though the Populists were organizing and were to have a million votes behind them by election time. There were unrest on the farms (cotton at eight cents, corn at five cents a bushel) and stirring in the cities, where the unemployed waited in long lines for free bread and soup. Tramps in bands of fifty or more rode the flat cars and freights—so many of them that the trainmen did not bother trying to keep them off. The national economy was fast running down.

In 1891 Jacob Sechler Coxey drove his blooded horses and his buggy over a muddy, rutted road near Massillon, Ohio, trying unsuccessfully to avoid mudholes as deep as the hubs. He owned a sandstone quarry which supplied sand to nearby glass and pottery works, ran a scrap-iron business in Massillon, and owned several good farms—enough to make him well-to-do, nearly rich. He also bred fine racing horses, and the Coxey colors were known on tracks from coast to coast. Though he knew times were beginning to be hard (he had to discharge forty of his quarrymen) his businesses did very well.

But Jacob Coxey was a crusader, and had been one all of his life. Born in Pennsylvania in 1854, he quit school at fifteen to work in the rolling mills beside his father, a convinced Democrat, who encouraged his boy to read. Young

209

Coxey was interested in economics; he read pamphlets on his lunch hour and devoured books at night. When he was twenty he joined the Greenback Party and argued politics, paper money, credit, and interest rates with fellow workers interminably. At twenty-five he started a scrap-iron business, prospered, and moved to Ohio. At thirty-seven, worth a quarter of a million dollars, he was still fascinated by currency problems, still a Greenbacker, thoroughly convinced that nobody had yet found the answer to the problem, as Henry George had phrased it, of "poverty in the midst of progress."

Though Coxey was a convinced paper-money man, he recognized that the Greenbacker plan of simply printing more and more money would never solve all the complicated economic problems that plagued the nation in 1891. Wealth and security were to be had in the United States; he had sufficient of both, obtained by hard work and skillful business management. Yet there were thousands of men out of work, men as honest and deserving as he, men simply down on their luck in this land of opportunity and plenty. Men out of work bought nothing, and factories that sold nothing put more men out of work. The muddy Ohio road gave him an answer in a sudden flash of inspiration. The nation needed good roads, thousands of miles of them. Why not put all these men to work building roads?

Coxey drove home and put all his ideas together. Unemployment was a national problem; so were good roads. Therefore whatever was done must be done on a national scale. The Federal government, he reasoned, could finance a national road program by issuing five hundred million dollars in Treasury notes, of which each state would receive a pro-rata share. The state could then hire unemployed men to build roads at a minimum wage of a dollar and a half for an eight-hour day. The plan was simple, direct, and had three distinct advantages. First, it prôvided roads. Second, it gave employment and pumped new buying power into a sick economy. Third, and not least important, it established a national minimum wage-and-hour standard in the labor market; no man would work ten hours for a dollar in a sweat-shop if he could get a dollar and a half for eight hours of work on the roads. The result was the formation of the Jacob Sechler Coxey Good Roads Association, launched in 1891 with pamphlets, broadsides, and letters to editors and Congressmen.

The Good Roads Association attracted a little attention, but not much, for too many other economic panaceas were competing for public support. Some of Coxey's correspondents pointed out that his Good Roads plan helped the farmer and migrant worker, but that it did little for the urban unemployed, who were both unlikely and unable to travel long distances to work on the roads. Coxey saw the point, and evolved a second plan. The Federal government, he explained, could issue bonds to any state, territory, county, city, township, or municipality up to one-half the valuation of its real estate. These bonds could be used as security for a loan in the form of Treasury notes, printed in denominations of one dollar to twenty dollars, which would then be used to pay workmen at the usual minimum rates for civic improvement—streets, schools, parks, buildings, anything the municipality needed. The loan would be repaid without interest from money raised by local taxation over a twenty-five-year period, at the end of which the bonds would be returned and Treasury notes to that amount taken out of circulation. Thus Non-Interest-Bearing Bonds joined Good Roads.

As times grew steadily worse, Coxey's double-barrelled plan attracted interest. An energetic speaker and indefatigable writer-to-editors, he neglected his businesses to travel to conventions, organize clubs, and write pamphlets. He was not a good organizer; he had no flair for public relations; he was superb in street-corner discussion, but less convincing in print. Coxey needed a publicity agent—someone who could think up new and startling ways of getting Coxey's ideas into the news. In the summer of 1893, while he was attending a convention in Chicago, Coxey found the man he wanted at the World's Fair—Carl Browne, who was working the Midway as a spieler and chalk-talk artist.

Browne, born in 1849, had had an unusually checkered career as cartoonist, painter, rancher, editor, carnival barker, labor organizer, and agitator for radical causes. He had already made a reputation in Chicago as a soapbox orator (selling Kickapoo Indian Blood Remedy between speeches against the plutocrats) and the Chicago police were watching him. He also was something of a character. He wore long hair, Buffalo-Bill style, a white Western sombrero, high boots, a long buckskin coat, and a string of beads instead of a collar. As he did not believe in bathing, he was known locally as "Old Greasy." He also had a religion of his own, based on some peculiar theories of reincarnation, which he preached when he was not attacking the rich or selling patent medicines. According to Browne, not only souls but actual portions of the body might be reincarnated. One might have in him, therefore, actual bits of Plato, Caesar, Louis the Fourteenth, or Washington—an interesting thought for his street-corner audiences to ponder.

Coxey and Browne hit it off at once. Coxey asked Browne to spend the winter with him as his guest in Massillon, and Browne, who was about to be ejected from Chicago by the police, gladly accepted. What Coxey, a scholarly and dignified man, saw in the loud and arrogant Browne is difficult to understand, but Browne had a brash confidence that Coxey lacked and the two got on famously together. Browne knew little or nothing about economics or currency, but he did know how to attract attention. The two agreed that because Coxey's ideas needed national publicity, the customary pamphlets and speeches would plainly never be enough. A Populist Senator could be depended upon to introduce Coxey's bills into Congress; there they would die in committee unless Congress could somehow be forced to act upon them. One day, as Coxey and Browne rode from the quarries into Massillon, Coxey had another inspiration. Why not organize all the unemployed and march on Washington, thus dramatizing the Coxey bills and the crisis they were designed to remedy? Call it, he said, "a petition in boots."

The idea of marching on Washington was not particularly new, but as the nation sank deeper into the trough of depression, many persons were ready to march on the capital for any reason at all. There were two millions unemployed. Farmers burned corn for fuel; cotton stood at five cents. A wave of strikes washed at the cities. The bitter Homestead Strike in Pennsylvania shocked the nation as nothing in years had done. The Cleveland administration, which believed that the best way to cure a depression was to pretend that it didn't exist, did nothing while forty to sixty thousand unemployed floated restlessly about the country, simply drifting. Charity organizations in New York City gave away a million loaves of bread. Chicago had seven thousand families on relief. Six hundred banks failed that year; seventy-four railroads went into receivership; businesses collapsed by dozens. The nation was both frightened and angry, and Coxey's proposed march reminded some of another march, from Paris to Versailles.

Coxey and Browne in January, 1894, made their announcement of a march on Washington, with bulletins and press releases explaining organization, aims, and probable itinerary. Browne thought the march should originate in Chicago, but Coxey, who paid the bills, reserved the honor for Massillon and announced it would start for the national capital on Easter Sunday, March 24. Browne handled the publicity and organized the affair on a semi-military basis. The marchers were to be recruited in groups of five, each commanded by a "Group Marshal." Groups were to be combined into "Communes" of fifty to one hundred, Communes into "Regiments" of two hundred to a thousand, with two "Regiments" forming a "Canton." Browne designed flags, badges, titles, and gave the army a name, "The Army of the Commonweal," injecting his own religious notions into the venture. According to his theories (which Coxey never took very seriously) "General" Coxey was the re-incarnated Cerebrum of Christ while he,

"General" Browne, modestly chose to be the Cerebellum of Christ. Carried away somewhat by his enthusiasm, Browne trimmed his beard to resemble Christ's and painted a banner for the army with a picture of Christ that strongly resembled Browne.

Browne, in his publicity, emphasized the fact that he and Coxey wanted to attract only "respectable unemployed, no anarchists, thieves, boodlers, or bankers." The Coxey bills, introduced into Congress in early March by Senator Peffer of Kansas, in Browne's words represented "the principles of Christianity applied to affairs on this earth," while their enactment into law would "usher in the Kingdom of Heaven with peace and plenty in place of panic and poverty." The response to the announcement was encouraging. Letters poured in, some from cranks, but many from genuinely interested correspondents. Coxey reported that he received nearly a bushel of letters a day, containing contributions ranging from two-cent stamps to dollar bills—a check for a thousand dollars turned out to be a fake. The newspapers began to run stories on Coxey's Army, some against, some watchful, a few for. Browne claimed that he expected ten thousand men in Massillon by Easter—and the thought of ten thousand unemployed men descending on Washington in the depths of a depression was enough to make Congress tremble. Special District Attorney Pugh of the District of Columbia told reporters that District Police would jail Coxey, Browne, and as many of his men as possible if they ever arrived in Washington; the New York *Times* commented that if the police persecuted Coxey's Army, "the people of the United States will rejoice in the persecution." The United Press reported from the capital, "Nothing is heard here but ridicule in regard to the Coxey movement."

Coxey bought a circus tent to house the men who began to drift into Massillon in February. They had to eat, so he bought three commissary wagons and footed the food bills. By mid-March there were present perhaps a hundred and fifty men—some professional tramps, some curious visitors—

but at least a hundred unemployed workmen or "industrials" whose intentions were serious. The usual queer characters also were attracted to Massillon by the unorthodox nature of the project and, of course, by Browne himself: Dr. Cyclone Kirtland, a Pittsburgh astrologer, who came to give daily reports on the situation of the stars; Douglas McCallum, a Chicago radical, who wore a top hat and cutaway and was the author of an odd pamphlet called *Dogs and Fleas;* Honore Jaxon, a huge French-Canadian who wore moccasins and carried an axe, and had been with Louis Riel in the Riel Rebellion; "Oklahoma Sam" Pfrimmer, a real cowboy; a "mysterious rich man" who refused to give his name (he turned out to be a medicine-show barker) ; and a half-breed Indian food faddist who intended to make the march on a diet of oatmeal and water. The Massillon crowd also included a few Secret Service agents and forty-three reporters, of whom sixteen lasted out the trip. Because Browne, who hated newspapermen, called them "argus-eyed Demons of Hell," the reporters organized an A.E.D.H. Club and wore appropriately-lettered badges.

The Army of the Commonweal lent itself admirably to comic newspaper stories but, as one reporter wrote, it was not wholly amusing. "The rank and file," he noted, "is made up of regular workmen, earnest in a dumb, helpless sort of way." Beneath the newspaper joshings lay a real uneasiness— times were very bad, and while Coxey's plan might seem ridiculous, the time was ripe for somebody to do something. City labor groups, though unenthusiastic about Coxey's bills, nevertheless gave his army sympathy if not official support, and Senator Allen of Nebraska announced that he thought a Senate committee ought to meet Coxey half-way and at least discuss his ideas with him. The papers carried reports of other "armies" forming in New England, in California, and in the Pacific Northwest. What Coxey had started, said the Populist leader James Weaver, was "a protest against wrongs that have become quite universal and intolerable to the vast excluded multitudes." Secretary of Agriculture Mor-

ton replied that the Coxeyites were "worthless drifters as
homeless and taxless as the aborigines" who spent their money
on tobacco, whiskey, and cards, but others in Washington
were less inclined to whistle in the dark.

Easter Sunday, March 24, 1894, was cold in Massillon.
About a hundred men, not counting reporters, gathered at
dawn; before noon the march to Washington began. The
procession:

> A Negro carrying the flag of the Army of
> the Commonweal
> General Browne, riding Coxey's seven-thou-
> sand-dollar stallion
> Mounted Aides, including Coxey's son Jesse
> wearing a blue coat and gray trousers to
> represent the union of North and South.
> Windy Oliver, the Army's official trum-
> peter, playing calls
> General Coxey, riding in a buggy drawn by
> Acolyte, his forty-thousand-dollar pacer
> The second Mrs. Coxey, riding in a phaeton
> with little Legal Tender Coxey, their in-
> fant son
> A seven-piece band
> A Negro carrying a banner inscribed "Death
> to Interest Bearing Bonds!"
> Marching Industrials and disguised Secret
> Service Agents
> Commissary Wagons
> Reporters.

Coxey had hoped to have his sixteen-year-old daughter by
his divorced first wife lead the procession as the Goddess of
Peace, but her mother refused permission.

The army did not move fast. The day was cold and snowy,
and reporters, complaining of the food and weather, began
to drop out. In three days the column was in Alliance, Ohio;

there the students at Mount Union College cut classes to cheer the marchers. In four days they were in Salem, Ohio, where charitable Quakers replenished the commissary wagons. Columbiana, Ohio, provided a thousand loaves of bread. Surprisingly, the army began to pick up recruits, until it numbered almost two hundred when it crossed the Pennsylvania line. At New Beaver, Pennsylvania, more than a hundred striking pottery workers joined up. By April 3, the marchers approached the outskirts of Pittsburgh, and crowds gathered along the roads to cheer them on.

The Army of the Commonweal had good organization and good discipline. No beer or whiskey was allowed in camp. Coxey boasted that though they marched by hundreds of hencoops, "You cannot find so much as a chicken feather among my men." Nevertheless, farmers on the way stood guard with shotguns, and sheriffs and deputies met the column at county lines to escort it to the next county. The march usually began at ten in the morning and ended at four in the afternoon; then the circus tent was pitched and the men made ready for the night. Some men carried their own tents; others slept in the open. In bad weather city officials often provided the marchers with lodging in jails or city halls, while the city, churches, and relief organizations donated food, the quality of which varied with the generosity of the community—usually bread, potatoes, onions and, occasionally, tough beef. In the evening the army held a public meeting with sermons, songs, and speeches by Coxey or Browne (who also did cartoons), closing with a collection. The men sold pamphlets and souvenirs until curfew at ten, when sentries were posted and the camp closed. On Sundays the army halted for religious services to which visitors were invited to hear Browne preach sermons that mixed reincarnation, politics, theology, and finance in about equal proportions.

Coxey had his first troubles in Allegheny City, where memories of the Homestead Strike were still fresh. Police raided the camp at night, hauled off thirty men, jailed them for vagrancy, then let them go the following day. From

Allegheny to Homestead, deep in Carnegie Steel territory, police followed the column by day and surrounded the camp at night, especially after a hundred striking coke-oven workers came to join the march. However, the worst trouble was the cold, wet weather that turned roads into quagmires, ankle deep in mud—proof of the need for good roads, said Coxey. By the time the army reached Uniontown, ready to cross the mountains, defections had reduced its ranks to three hundred. The trip from Uniontown to Cumberland, Maryland, took six days and cost another hundred men who dropped out. The two hundred survivors received certificates of merit signed by Browne.

At Cumberland the army transferred to scows and followed the Chesapeake and Ohio canal to Williamsport, with Coxey footing the bills. Maryland's reception was not cordial. At Hagerstown and Frederick, townspeople hooted the marchers, and at Frederick someone who sneaked whiskey into the camp caused a drunken brawl. On April 28 the army camped at Rockville, Maryland; a new, seventy-man contingent arrived from Philadelphia, led by Christopher Columbus Jones, resplendent in a striped coat and tall silk hat. On April 29 the column made camp on the outskirts of Washington in Brightwood Park. A crowd of nearly ten thousand persons came to watch.

Washington was nervous. In the metropolitan newspapers Coxey's march had received full coverage, much of which was lurid and inaccurate. Furthermore, reports reached the nation's capital city that more "armies," led by Kelly and Fry, were on the way from California, as well as one from Chicago under a Dr. Randall. Other armies, it was rumored, were forming in Montana, Washington, Oregon, Missouri, and Colorado, and all were going to converge on the capital. District officials swore in two hundred special police, alerted the National Guard, and kept fifteen hundred regular troops on duty. Still, there was no trouble. General Coxey rode into Washington on April 30th to obtain a permit for a parade from the District Police Superintendent, who warned him that the Capitol grounds were barred to parades, meetings, speeches, and demonstrations. Coxey replied that, as a law-abiding man, he hoped to respect the law; his men would enter the Capitol grounds as private citizens, not as a parade, and would re-form after he had made his speech. But to speak from the Capitol steps was also illegal, said the superintendent of police. No, said Coxey, this he had a constitutional right to do, and he intended to exercise it.

May 1 was a fine clear day. The Army of the Commonweal, numbering about four hundred and fifty persons, went into parade formation at dawn, while two hundred mounted police waited at the Capitol. The march began at ten. It was led by the Commonweal Band, blasting away at *Marching Through Georgia*, and *See The Conquering Hero Comes!* It moved down Fourteenth Street Road to Mount Pleasant, then along Fourteenth Street to Pennsylvania Avenue, which was lined with more than ten thousand curious spectators. Pennsylvania Avenue was blocked at the end of a solid phalanx of police; not quite certain where to go next, the column stopped at Second and B Streets. Coxey, Browne, and Jones walked straight toward the Capitol, vaulted a low stone wall, and disappeared into the shrubbery, pursued by police. Browne and Jones were captured, but Coxey made it to the Capitol steps, where Captain Kelly of the District Police waited with two mounted policemen. Coxey tipped his hat to the captain and drew a manuscript from his pocket.

"You cannot read a speech here," said Kelly.

"Then I wish to enter a protest," replied Coxey.

"You can't do that, either," Kelly said, but Coxey started to read from his manuscript. The mounted police collared him before he finished his first sentence. Meanwhile another police squad came up with the captives, Browne and Jones, and began to push its way through the crowd. Unfortunately, the crowd began to jeer. The policemen lost their heads, used their clubs, and before they got their prisoners through the crowd had ridden down or clubbed fifty persons. Coxey was released that day. Browne and Jones, considerably battered, were released on bail the following morning. The army, after waiting passively for an hour, marched back to camp.

Coxey, Browne, and Jones were charged with violation of the Capitol Grounds Act, for they invaded the Capitol lawn and "did then and there step upon certain plants, shrubs, and turf." They were sentenced to pay five dollars fine each and to serve twenty days in jail. A few days later two men in Colorado sent a package of grass seed to Congress, with instructions to sow it on the Capitol lawn.

Coxey served out his time and went back to Ohio to campaign as the Populist candidate for Congress from the Massillon district. His two bills died swiftly in Senate committee. Browne moved the army from Rockville to Hyattsville, then to Bladensburg; marchers straggled in from various other armies. The marchers caused no trouble; their camp attracted thousand of visitors at an admission fee of two cents each. About four hundred men were in camp, according to the correspondent of the *Review of Reviews*—"for the most part a very decent class of workingman, with not a sick man in camp and not a particle of evidence of grief or distress or crushed spirits among them." They played baseball, planted flower beds, and fished, evidently settling down for a long stay.

The way Coxey was dealt with in Washington excited a great deal of comment, pro and con. Populists pointed out that a "petition in boots" was a perfectly legal manner of calling attention to grievances, "one not to be met with armed force." Coxey's Army had come to influence legislation, true—but so had the wealthy railroad and trust lobbyists who lived at the Willard. How did Congressmen receive *them?* On the other hand, Major General O. O. Howard believed the whole thing "socialistic and anarchistic." Remember, Howard wrote darkly, how the French Revolution began! A New England paper feared that Coxey would start "a craze for assassination, and every half-cracked man in the country will think he is doing his country a blessing by assassinating a lawmaker or a capitalist." Commissioner Byrnes of the New

York Police Department thought that, if anything, the Washington police had been too careful—Coxey was, after all, "the most dangerous man this country has seen since the Civil War." Dr. Alvah Doty of the New York Health Department approached the issue from a different angle. Coxey's Army, in his opinion, was "an un-American and unsanitary horde of carriers and propagators of contagious diseases." It was significant, he pointed out, that "an epidemic of smallpox has appeared in many of our large cities about simultaneously with the breaking out of Coxeyism"—though Coxey's Army had been nowhere near any of the cities involved, and the newspapers noted no unusual number of smallpox cases.

Standard procedure in much of the press was to portray Coxey's Army as composed either of comic vaudeville tramps with patched pants, or as dangerous, quasi-criminal anarchists. There was very little truth in either accusation. An alert sociologist who interviewed two hundred and ninety men in one camp near Washington found "only five or six who appeared to be of questionable character." One-half of the men interviewed were American born; of the remainder, the majority were English or Scottish born. The average age was thirty-one, the average years of schooling seven. Three-quarters of the men were skilled workmen, representing seventy trades, and the majority were not members of any union. Of those who expressed partisan political preferences, eighty-eight were Democrats; thirty-nine, Republicans; and ten, Populists. W. T. Stead, the British journalist, who visited another camp, found most of the men sober, quiet, and sincere. One or two were "hard cases," he agreed, but the army was chiefly what Coxey said it was—an aggregation of honest unemployed industrials.

A great deal of the bad publicity attached to Coxey's Army came from the activities of the Western armies, with which he had no connection. The West Coast was extremely hard hit by the depression and, even before Coxey's announcement of January, 1894, sporadic attempts had been made to organize the unemployed in California. The news from Massillon simply speeded up the process and gave it direction. Lewis Fry, a Civil War veteran from Indiana, began organizing an army in February, 1894, and by March he had a group of six hundred or more men ready to start for Washington. Charles Kelly, an itinerant printer from New England, led about three hundred and fifty men from San Francisco. Neither Fry nor Kelly knew or corresponded with Coxey; they were, they said, sympathetic with Coxeyism, but Coxey was not their leader, nor were they interested in good roads or non-interest-bearing bonds. Kelly's and Fry's platform—no immigration for ten years, exclusion of aliens from property ownership, governmentally-created jobs for the unemployed—reflected California's particular problems as well as its anti-Oriental bias.

Coxey's march was a clever idea, but the Westerners faced three thousand miles of trudging. Fry's Los Angeles group, which left in mid-March, piled on freight trains while the crews looked the other way. Texan cities, fearful of an "invasion of tramps," gave the men food and hurriedly shipped them on, sometimes paying the railroads to expedite their departure. By April 3 Fry was in St. Louis. Merchants there paid the marchers' ferry fares to Illinois. In East St. Louis, Illinois, the railroads refused to provide free transportation, the city refused to provide fare or food, and the police threatened to jail every man in twenty-four hours. Fry's men walked from East St. Louis to Vandalia; two hundred dropped out on the way there, but a contingent of two hundred "replacements" arrived by train from Little Rock. At Vandalia another hundred and fifty men, tired of walking, left Fry's foot-sloggers under the leadership of "General" Galvin. Galvin's group caught trains across Indiana into Ohio, where Governor McKinley called out four companies of infantry and an artillery battery to escort the marchers through his state to Wheeling. On May 1st, when Coxey's parade started for the Capitol, Galvin's men were nearing Pittsburgh. About three hundred of them arrived in Washington on May 30, and encamped on the Virginia side of the city.

Fry's own detachment had a difficult trip. Because he

threatened city authorities that he would surrender his army to the police as vagrants (meaning that the city would have to provide lodging and food for them) most towns were more than eager to move them on. Terre Haute gave all members of the army free vaccinations. Indianapolis, after five days, took up a public subscription to pay their way to Cincinnati; there they took barges to Parkersburg. Half of Fry's band melted away between Parkersburg and Washington, slightly more than two hundred reaching Washington with him June 26th.

Kelly's army of three hundred and fifty left San Francisco on April 3, with the city paying ferry passage to Oakland where five hundred more men waited to join. Oakland authorities offered to provide boxcar transportation of the men to Sacramento, but Kelly refused it. He led men, he retorted, not cattle, and his men deserved better accommodations than boxcars. Twelve hundred deputies, police, and firemen surrounded Kelly's camp on the 15th, arrested Kelly and his lieutenants, and held them until they agreed to accept the offer. At Sacramento, where three hundred more men joined up, the city hastily arranged to ship them all to Ogden, Utah, on the Southern Pacific.

The prospective appearance of a thousand unemployed men in Utah put Governor West into a panic. After wiring the Southern Pacific that it was against the law to bring unemployed persons into Utah, he boarded a train for Ogden with several militia companies, a Gatling gun, and two thousand loaves of bread. The Southern Pacific brought Kelly's men to Ogden nevertheless, for there was nowhere else to take them. Governor West immediately demanded that the railroad return them to California. The Southern Pacific refused. The Union Pacific refused to take them farther into Utah unless all men paid full fare. Kelly refused to move his army until some one provided transportation. Because no jails in Utah could hold a thousand men, Governor West clearly could not arrest them.

Governor Waite of Colorado, himself a Populist, resolved

the dilemma by wiring permission to Kelly to enter his state if his army were allowed to cross Utah, so Kelly and his men started out on foot. The walk was long, the Union Pacific trains ran tantalizingly close by, and there were railroaders with Kelly. To "borrow" a U. P. train standing on a siding was easy; before the railroad knew it, it was done. Fortunately, the railroad decided to ignore the matter and Kelly's stolen train steamed across the plains to Omaha.

Governor Jackson of Iowa called out the National Guard before Kelly crossed the Missouri to Council Bluffs, Iowa. The Rock Island and the Northwestern, refusing to be bluffed into compliance as the Western roads had been, demanded militia protection from the "invaders," while Judge Hubbard, the railroads' counsel, issued blasts against "Kelly's tramps" (among them was young Jack London) and demanded that the State of Iowa "rebuke and throttle this new form of Anarchy." Governor Jackson, who sympathized with the marchers, tried to get free trains for them but the railroads were adamant. Kelly's men, now nearly fourteen hundred strong, set out on foot for Des Moines and made it, after a hard march, on May 1st. Then they built one hundred and four boats, floated down the Des Moines River to St. Louis, and started up the Ohio, to meet nothing but trouble. Most of the river towns refused to let the floating army land, donated a little food, and hurried it on. Discouraged men left the march by dozens, so that when Kelly reached Washington in early July, he had no more than a hundred or so with him.

Beside those of Kelly, Fry, and Coxey, perhaps a half dozen other "armies" formed, some of which never arrived in Washington. Dr. J. H. Randall's Chicago contingent, which left the city May 1, appeared with sixty out of its original four hundred and fifty. Sullivan's second Chicago army was even smaller. Three New England groups, totalling fewer than a hundred men, made the journey. "Jumbo" Cantwell's group from Oregon and Washington broke up in Indiana. Of Vinette's Californians, few ever got to Washington.

Grayson's Colorado division disappeared somewhere in Iowa. Sanders' Coloradans stole several trains and ended up in Kansas jails. Hogan's Montana miners brushed with police and never got beyond St. Joseph, Missouri; Hogan was arraigned in Federal court for train theft. Because the newspapers tended to label almost any group of drifters or hoboes an "army," it is difficult to establish exactly how many "legitimate" groups of marchers there actually were. *The Independent*, in May of 1894, claimed there were forty "armies" on the march with perhaps fifteen thousand members, undoubtedly an exaggerated estimate. The more conservative Stead estimated seven or eight armies totalling six thousand men, of whom no more than three thousand or so were on the road at any one time.

Coxey failed in his bid for Congress, but he had no thought of giving up. Having spent most of his modest fortune on his great idea, he set about making another fortune, not quite so large as the first, which he dribbled away, bit by bit, in his crusade. A perennial candidate for Congress, he never won office, and when Bryan and the Democrats absorbed the Populists in 1896 Coxey fought the Great Commoner tooth and nail. Coxey also ran a few times for Governor of Ohio, and between elections spent his time in Washington arguing with Congressmen. Presidents learned to expect his visits— he called on every President from McKinley through Franklin D. Roosevelt with advice on financial matters.

In 1914, with business again lagging and unemployment rising, Coxey added a new twist to his program—government-owned railroads, lower freight rates, and Federal loans to individual persons for home construction, farm improvement, and small business investment. Letters to Wilson got him nowhere, so he planned another march on Washington, confidently predicting at least a million-man army. On April 16, his sixtieth birthday, he left Massillon with fifty or so men, of whom a few were still with him when he arrived at the Capitol in May. He spoke briefly from the Capitol steps, this time with permission, and returned to Massillon to campaign for the office of governor of Ohio on the Socialist ticket. He campaigned again for a Senate nomination in 1916, and in 1922, at sixty-eight, planned a third march that never came off. He had a long argument in the press with Secretary of the Treasury Mellon, and very nearly converted Henry Ford. In 1924 he ran for President on the Farmer-Labor ticket, polling fewer than ten thousand votes. Undaunted, he filed in 1926 and 1928 as an independent candidate for Congress. In 1928, as the nation slid downward toward the big crash, Coxey planned a fourth march and persuaded a Pennsylvania congressman to introduce his bill again (as Peffer had done thirty-four years before) but it died in committee.

Jacob Coxey was not quite sure how many times he ran for office, but he was fairly certain that he was a gubernatorial candidate three times, a congressional candidate five or six times, a presidential candidate twice, the last time in 1936, when he was nominated by the Farmer-Labor party but withdrew to campaign for Lemke's Union party. The only office to which he was ever elected was that of Mayor of Massillon, a post he occupied from 1931 to 1933. Though he was nominally a Republican, his platform was still the familiar one of 1894. The city, he contended, could work its way out of the depression by issuing bonds for two hundred thousand dollars, in amounts of twenty-five cents to ten dollars and carrying one-tenth of one percent interest, to finance city improvements. City workers could be paid in these bonds, which thus could work and put new currency in circulation; furthermore, Coxey favored a plan whereby idle men could borrow from the city on promise to pay when they found work. He lost out in the next election, however, and again in 1943, when he ran as a Democrat.

The city may have had better mayors, but never one livelier. Policemen who picked up a vagrant drunk became accustomed to having the mayor, after giving the culprit a lecture on temperance and industry, send him in a taxi to a rooming house, with a grubstake out of the mayor's own pocket. Unlike any other mayor in the United States, Coxey manufactured a medicine called Coxey-Lax ("an efficient tone-up for the system"), an antiseptic lotion for sinus infections and hemorrhoids, and insoles of copper and zinc which, when worn in the shoes, "allowed free flow of the earth's magnetic currents through the body, cured rheumatism, and drew acid out of the system."

Coxey spent his later years running a rooming house, writing letters to the newspapers, reading books on currency, and tapping out letters on an ancient portable, tuning his financial policies to the changing times. He attended conventions and conferences when his health and his funds permitted, and always sent copies of his non-interest-bearing bond plan to the platform committees of Republican and Democratic conventions. In 1932 he called on Franklin D. Roosevelt to explain Coxeyism, believing ever afterward that F.D.R. took scraps of his plans and pieced them into the New Deal. After all, Coxey contended, what were W.P.A., P.W.A., and the rest but rather maladroit adaptations of what he himself had advocated in 1894, 1914, and 1928? "I said the same things," he commented dryly, "and they put me in jail for it." In April, 1944, in observance of the fiftieth anniversary of his original march, he went to Washington to speak from the Capitol steps to about two hundred puzzled spectators. "They had police there, too," he told the newspapers, "but I walked on the grass." It took a trip to the history books by most of the reporters to find out who he was.

World War II gave the General a chance to talk about non-interest-bearing bonds again. He had seen three wars, had childhood memories of another; he had lived through three major depressions; poverty and war were to him cause and effect, effect and cause. "No one is ever going to fight," he said, "if he is contented and happy." Undeterred by fifty years of trying to show men how to be contented and happy, he saw in the creation of the United Nations a magnificent opportunity to put the whole free world on a solid Coxeyite basis.

Briefly, as Coxey explained his new post-World War II

plan, legal tender should be "internationalized," with notes secured by non-interest-bearing twenty-seven-year bonds issued by the debtor nations. These notes would be issued in an amount equal to the nation's postwar indebtedness, or equal to the amount it needed for peacetime reconstruction. Money would be printed with American dollars on one side and the equivalent in monetary units of the debtor nation on the other. The debtor nation would then issue bonds equal to the amount of its loan, calling for amortization payments of two percent of the face value for the first four years and four percent for the next twenty-three years. Goods produced by the debtor nation and exported to the United States would be paid for in "double-faced currency" and the amounts applied to the amortization payments. Thus, Coxey wrote in his paper, *The Big Idea,* the world could "avoid future wars over debt and poverty and reduce taxes by twenty-two percent." All nations willing to sign the U. N. Charter would be eligible, though Britain, a nation of experienced financiers, was, in Coxey's belief, the logical nation to begin. All it would take, he said, was an Act of Parliament authorizing a bond issue of forty-three billion, six hundred million dollars, and an Act of Congress lending Britain five billion dollars. Lesser men might have lacked confidence in their abilities of persuasion, but Coxey did not; he decided to work on Congress before petitioning Parliament for a hearing. He sent copies of his plan to the Senate Banking and Currency Committee and to the House Banking Committee. In 1946, after fifty-two years, he was granted a hearing in the Senate.

Coxey appeared before the Senate committee on March 20. It was perhaps his thirty-fifth trip to Washington (he was uncertain himself) and he was ninety-two years old. Senator Barkley, the committee chairman, apologized for calling him a half hour late, but Coxey remarked, "It doesn't matter. I waited a year to see Warren Harding." General Coxey explained his plan, talking on and on into the lunch hour while Barkley, with Kentucky courtesy, let him talk. And as he talked of men long dead and political battles long forgotten, the years rolled back a half-century to the turbulent nineties, to the ominous march of hungry men led by the gentle old man quietly telling his story in the conference room. Jacob Coxey, who had once made Wall Street tremble, finally had his say. It was a slow progress, he said when he came home to Massillon, but still progress, and he was willing to wait a little while longer for victory.

Not much time was left. In 1947 he fell and suffered a broken pelvis, and in 1949 he weathered an attack of virus pneumonia. Nevertheless, he kept on working, hoping, he said, "to educate the people so that they may instruct their Senators and Congressmen in the Big Idea." At times, he admitted, he felt discouraged, feeling that perhaps men preferred lies to truth, but he had gone too far to concede defeat. He could not believe that his life's work was pointless. Men could live in peace and plenty; he must show them how. It was his personal battle, and he could not give it up. In early 1951, at the age of ninety-seven, he remarked wistfully that if his health would only permit he'd like to try another march on Washington. But on May 18, 1951, Jacob Coxey died quietly at his Massillon home, surrounded by his pamphlets, a half-completed letter on his desk.

With Coxey died the great nineteenth-century American radical tradition of Ignatius Donnelly, of James Weaver, of Pitchfork Ben Tillman, Sockless Jerry Simpson, and the remainder of the hell-raising school of American politics. It had its share of crackpots and fanatics, but it was, for all that, a lively, native, bumptious American thing that meant a man could think what he wished, say what he pleased, and stand up to be counted. Coxey, like his generation of radicals, was a doggedly purposeful man, willing to be laughed at, but he was earnest, selfless, utterly devoted to his cause.

With his anachronistic stiff collar suggesting an illustration out of Dickens and his private bug buzzing in his brain, Jacob Coxey became a sort of comic figure in his own lifetime. It was easy to find him amusing. The phrase "Coxey's Army" generated smiles for two generations, and historians (when they mentioned him at all) tended to classify him among the crackpots and reformers. Yet there was in the man something that commanded respect, a sincerity and dignity that made the title of "General," once bestowed in amusement, appropriate and fitting. He died fighting the same battle, he firmly believed, that his idols Jefferson and Jackson had fought before him, for mankind's security, contentment, and plenty. "Nobody is going to be discontented or unhappy," he wrote in 1946, "when I win." He did not win, but General Coxey never surrendered.

FREEDOM ROAD

★

Nat Turner

Elijah Lovejoy

Nat Turner

★

NEITHER THE INSTITUTION of slavery nor its abolition became an important issue in the United States until the third decade of the nineteenth century. Dissatisfaction with the system had been expressed since early colonial days, but not until after the Revolution, after the enunciation of eighteenth-century ideals of liberty and equality, did Americans give serious thought to the slavery question. Jefferson himself, after all, inserted a stricture against it in the first draft of the Declaration of Independence. Washington, it was believed, expressed doubts about it. To the generation that founded a new nation on the belief that all men possessed a natural right to life, liberty, and the pursuit of happiness, the existence within it of slavery seemed to deny its basic principles.

Northerners and Southerners generally agreed that the system of slavery was bad, and that something should be done about it. After the turn of the century sentiment against slavery increased, encouraged by church groups and organized antislavery societies. The twin problems of how and when to do something received thorough discussion, particularly in the South. There were various schemes—gradual emancipation, establishing colonies in the West, paying slaves wages so they could buy their freedom, and others—none of which satisfied slaveholders or antislavery societies. The American Colonization Society, formed in 1817 to collect funds for the transportation of Negroes back to Africa, found after years of trying that its venture was too expensive to be practical. Nevertheless, through the eighteen-twenties, North and South alike tried to find some solution to the slavery problem.

By the eighteen-fifties, all this had changed. Southern leaders proclaimed the virtues of slavery as the best, perhaps the only foundation for a truly free society. Southerners who expressed sympathy for Northern or antislavery views were sharply warned. Antislavery societies that once drew their main support from Southerners disappeared below Mason's and Dixon's line. Antislavery Northerners travelling in the South were watched, jailed, sometimes beaten. Books were censored, mails inspected, strangers questioned and searched. The South was pro-slave, incontrovertibly and aggressively so, ready to call slavery a "positive good" and to fight a war over it. There were many reasons for this shift in the attitude of the South. One of them was a short, pious Negro named Nat Turner.

Nat was born on October 2, 1800, in the slave quarters of Benjamin Turner, a well-to-do planter of Southampton County, Virginia. Nat was not a strong or healthy boy, and it was assumed that he would never be particularly valuable as a slave. His mother, a recent arrival from Africa and still half-savage, was convinced that her son was destined for great things—he had a birthmark, he could remember events (or so she claimed) that happened before he was born, and he sometimes sat still and quiet, as if hearing faraway sounds. From the day of his birth Nat Turner was accepted as different.

It was true that Nat, even as a child, was not like the other Negro children. A moody, quiet boy, he preferred to keep to himself, displaying none of the friendly gregariousness characteristic of the slave quarters. Most of all he seemed to be curious about everything. He probed into machinery to see what made it work, constructed models of strange inventions, asked questions about everything he saw—about why the sun shone, or the stars moved, and other things that the Negroes did not know. He tried to make paper, gunpowder, and chemical potions, running wildly complicated experiments to see what things were made of.

Somehow Nat taught himself to read, a tremendous accomplishment for a slave. He never remembered how he did it, except that one day all the letters suddenly fell into place in his mind. There was not much for a Negro to read except the Bible, so Nat pored over it for hours, mixing what he found there with the African lore he learned from his mother and the highly emotional evangelism he heard from the Negro preachers. By the time he was sixteen, he had a considerable reputation as a sage among Southampton Negroes, who often asked his advice in making plans to steal, run away, or otherwise deceive their masters.

Nat, his grandmother remarked, "had too much sense to be of much use to anybody as a slave." She was quite right, for he was not rugged enough to make a good field hand and he had a bad habit of disappearing into the woods for weeks at a time. Turner never accounted him as valuable property, and when he died Nat's ownership passed to Turner's brother, who sold him to Thomas Moore. Moore died and left him to his son Putnam. Moore's widow married Joseph Travis, who kept Nat (though Putnam Moore owned him) and got as much work out of him as he could. Travis was an easy master, allowing Nat to do much as he pleased since he was not a troublemaker. He never stole, rarely drank, bothered no one, and kept to himself. Because he could read and knew the Bible he was in demand as a preacher, though he was never licensed.

When he was about twenty-five, Nat began to hear voices, first at night, later in broad daylight. The thunder spoke to him, promising to reveal "all the knowledge of the world," the revolutions of the planets, and the secrets of life. All around him he began to see strange signs. The veins of leaves appeared to be hieroglyphs in an unknown language; he found drops of blood in an ear of field corn and peculiar human forms drawn in the sand. Looking up at the sky one night, he "saw the forms of men in different attitudes, and there were lights in the sky, to which the children of darkness gave other names than what they really were, for they were the lights of the Saviour's hands, stretched forth from east to west." He was not sure what the voices said, or what the signs meant, but he was convinced that God was trying to get a message through to him in some way he could not yet translate.

A few months later he had a vision that he understood. Working in the fields one day he heard a voice from the sun telling him he had been chosen for a great mission, for "the time was fast approaching when the first should be last and the last first." There would be signs, the voice said, that "would make known to me when I should commence the great work, and until the first sign appeared I should conceal it from the knowledge of men." Nat obeyed, and waited for the sign, but it was not until 1828 that the voice spoke again, ordering him to be baptized so that he could carry out his duties as God's anointed agent. Since Negroes were forbidden the rites of white churches, he was doused in a creek by a jackleg preacher; at the precise moment of his immersion a thundercrack split the sky, pierced by a voice telling him that he "must fight against the serpent." It took two more years for the precise nature of his fight to be explained to him.

In the spring of 1830 Nat ran away from Travis and hid somewhere in the woods for nearly three weeks. Living in solitude on only what food other slaves smuggled to him, he had a series of visions that clarified everything. "I saw white spirits and black spirits," he said later,

> "engaged in battle, and the sun was darkened, the thunder rolled in the heavens, and blood flowed in streams, and I heard a voice saying, "Such is your luck, such you are called to see, and let it come roughly or smoothly, you must surely bear it."

Nat's mission was to lead a slave rebellion.

It is not surprising that Nat's messages came to this conclusion. Thoughts of freedom were never far from the surface of a slave's mind since the day the first Dutch ship discharged its load of Africans in America in 1619. There had been slave revolts before, a long history of them dating back to

the early eighteenth century. Thirty years before Nat's vision
one Gabriel Prosser tried to form a slave army to take Richmond, claiming that "we had as much right to fight for our
liberty as any man." Prosser's plot was nipped in time, and
thirty-five Negroes hanged for it. Only eight years before,
in Charleston, North Carolina, thirty-seven Negroes were
hanged as accomplices of Gabriel Vesey, a free black who
also attempted to organize a revolt. Few Southerners had
forgotten the great and bloody slave insurrection in Santo
Domingo, where hundreds of whites died at the hands of
slaves in 1791. Nothing struck terror into the South more
swiftly than the prospect of a slave revolt, and Southampton
County, with ninety-five hundred Negroes and sixty-five hundred whites, was no different than any other Southern community. People lived with it, rarely mentioned it, and barred
their doors at night. There was a great deal more to the ante-
bellum South than magnolia-scented mansions, ladies in crino-
line, courtly gentlemen, and the tinkling banjoes of happy
darkies.

Nat returned to the Travis farm and reported his vision
to several other slaves. Within a few days Negroes for miles
around knew of Nat's plot, but in the deep-seated slave tradition of silence, no Negro said a word to a white man. Nat
found two or three slaves interested in following his voices,
and after consulting the omens, chose July 4, 1830, as the
day when the great uprising should begin. On July 4 he was
ill, a clear indication that he had made the wrong choice.
Nearly seven months passed before he received another sign.
On February 12, 1831, a solar eclipse "darkened the sun"
exactly as his vision had foretold, but he heard no voices with
instructions. Still he waited, until on August 13 he received
the sign he needed. On that date atmospheric conditions were
such that the sun rose with a greenish tint (a phenomenon
noted as far away as New York City), changing to blue, then
white in the afternoon, with a black spot on the sun's surface
visible to the naked eye. "As the black spot passed over the
sun," Nat decided, "so shall the blacks pass over the earth."

August 13 was a Saturday. What he did during the next

week no one knows, but on the evening of Sunday, August 21, Nat and four slaves (Sam Francis, Hark Travis, Henry Porter, and Nelson Williams) met in the woods with a bottle of brandy and a stolen pig. They drank the brandy, roasted the pig, and planned the revolt. Around midnight they were joined by another slave, Will Francis. Nat and Hark proposed that the killing begin with their own master, Joseph Travis, after which they would travel swiftly from farm to farm, gather the slaves, and kill whites without mercy until Southampton County belonged to the black man.

Nat was not a cruel man, but his voices had informed him long ago that killing was God's will. The six slaves set out for the Travis farm about one o'clock in the morning of August 22, joined by another slave named Austin on the way. A search of the Travis barn turned up some hatchets, an axe, and a ladder. Neither Travis nor his wife heard them place the ladder against the house, nor Nat climb through a second story window, tiptoe down the stairs and unbar the door for the six waiting Negroes. Nat, armed with a hatchet, led the slaves up the stairs to the master's bedroom. It was dark and he could not see well. His first blow struck Travis a glancing blow on the face. When Travis staggered up, Will split his skull with an axe. At almost the same moment Travis' wife and two older boys died under the hatchets of Hark and Sam.

Nat and his group spent little time at Travis'. Taking four muskets and some powder and shot, they started for the farm of Salathiel Francis, owner of Sam and Will. At two forty-five a.m. they hammered at Francis' door. When he opened it, Will killed him with his axe. Then they killed the rest of the family. They passed up Mrs. Harris' house, a half-mile down the road, for some inexplicable reason, arriving at Reese's farm about three thirty. Here they left three dead. By four a.m. they were at Wiley Francis', but Francis, already informed of his brother Salathiel's death by a loyal slave, drove them off with gunfire. Nat and his men made no attempt to storm the house and went on.

The next stop was Mrs. Turner's, two miles to the northeast. As yet there was no general alarm, though slaves from the Travis and Salathiel Francis farms had spread the news to a few of the families in the vicinity, some of whom, accustomed as most white people were to wild Negro rumors, were only half-convinced. The message spread swiftly on the slave grapevine system, however, and on the road to Turner's Negroes drifted in to join Nat, one by one, until there were about fifteen in his band. Mrs. Turner had not been warned. She died, her sister died, and her overseer, aroused from his sleep, rushed out of his room to meet Will's deadly axe. After leaving Turner's the group divided, half-a-dozen or so following Nat toward Whitehead's, the rest taking a different route to Bryant's farm. At Bryant's no one escaped. At Whitehead's all died except young Harriet, whom a loyal slave hid under a bed. At William Williams' farm Mrs. Williams, up and dressed, saw the slaves approaching and hid in the bushes, where someone found her, marched her into the house, and shot her across her husband's body.

By early morning of Monday, August 22, there were more than forty Negroes, in groups of six to twelve each, ranging through the countryside. Trajan Doyle was killed on his way to the mill with a load of grain. Henry Harris' family, warned by a mulatto girl, escaped to the woods; the Richard Porter family owed their lives to the same girl. Mrs. John Williams and her child, coming to visit Mrs. Nathaniel Francis, both met death on the road. Of Peter Edwards' slaves only old Jeff gave his master warning; the other five Negroes joined Nat, and a neighbor shot them when they returned the next day. Captain Barrow, who heard from one of his slaves that "the British were coming," waited for his wife to dress. She took too long, and the invaders cut his throat while his wife escaped out the back door. Mr. Bittle, warned by his Negroes, kicked off his shoes and won a footrace to the swamp, where Nat's group lost him. George Vaughan, riding on his way to a fox hunt, was himself run to earth and decapitated.

By eight o'clock in the morning the majority of the house-holders in the area, realizing that something was happening, were up and armed. These houses the slaves passed at the first show of resistance; they had only a few guns and wanted easier prey. One or two bands tried to storm the farmhouses, losing a few dead in the process, and at least one group of insurrectionists lost heart and went home. Some farmers simply refused to believe the news. These men and their families died swiftly. Many Negroes fled to the woods until it was over, acting on the time-honored slave principle that it was best to stay away from trouble. Some slaves warned their masters, some did not. More than a few stayed to defend their owners, fighting beside them with forks and guns. But a shockingly large number joined Nat.

Nat's rebellion came as a complete surprise. Whether Nat was aware of it or not, on August 21 many Southampton farmers were at a huge camp-meeting in Gates County, North Carolina, thirty miles away. Since such revivals might last two or three days, Nat had planned better than he knew. At about nine o'clock of Monday morning, August 22, a rider on an exhausted horse dashed in with the news. The camp-meeting dissolved in panic, wagons and buggies careening off for home, the horses lashed by frantic, swearing men. In Southampton, at about the same time, the militia officers began trying to gather men, a difficult job since communication among the scattered farms was slow, and some of the militiamen were already dead.

At noon of August 22 at least one militia company was organized and on the roads looking for Nat's slaves, but since the insurrectionists had split up, reports of them appeared from several places at once. The reports had to be coördinated, outlying farms warned, white men armed, women and children collected in some safe place, and pursuit of the rebels organized. The false rumors of a British invasion, current until mid-morning, hampered the militia's work, nor was it at all clear for several hours how widely the revolt had spread. Despite the fear and confusion, Southampton began to recover rather swiftly from the initial shock. Groups of women and children were herded into defensible farmhouses; others were sent under guard to Jerusalem, the county seat. Militia officers set up a command post, organized road patrols, and sent couriers to nearby towns. By late afternoon the report reached Richmond that eight hundred armed slaves had killed a hundred whites, sacked five towns, and were spreading a path of destruction across southern Virginia.

Nat's forces by afternoon numbered about sixty, partially mounted on stolen horses, armed with hatchets, axes, razors, scythes, forks, and a few guns. Though militia sighted the insurgents from time to time, the Negroes melted into the woods and swamps at the first shot, to re-form somewhere else. By this time Nat, knowing he had lost the advantage of surprise, realized that his forces were neither large enough nor sufficiently well-armed to continue operations in the area for much longer. Possibly because the name called up Biblical associations, or possibly because he could think of nothing else to do, he decided to aim at Jerusalem, where he might find arms and reinforcements. The back road to Jerusalem, less likely to be patrolled, lay across the Nottaway River, a narrow stream bridged near Parker's farm. Unfortunately for Nat a body of eighteen militia, searching the back roads, caught up with him in a field near the bridge and opened fire. The Negroes fired back, but their muskets were poor, their aim bad, and lacking buckshot, some had loaded with gravel. The Battle of Parker's Field lasted no more than ten minutes before the Negroes broke and ran for the swamp. Nat could collect only a dozen or so by evening.

The slaves stayed in the swamp until dawn of Tuesday, August 23rd, when they emerged to look for food. Dr. Samuel Blount, who lived near the swamp, was not one to scoff at rumors. Three of his neighbors had brought their families to his house the day before, and the men and older boys, when they saw the Negroes enter the yard, opened fire and killed two of them. Hark, badly wounded, dragged himself into the brush while the rest fled back to the swamp. At ten o'clock that morning a company of Greenville militia ran into the slaves on the Jerusalem road and killed three more, among them Will the axe-man. The rest of the day, while troops scoured the country side, Nat and his men hid. That evening they scattered. Nat remained alone in the swamp.

On Monday morning Governor Floyd of Virginia notified Washington of a state of emergency in Virginia and ordered troops to Southampton with all possible speed. All through the night militia companies left Richmond, Petersburg, Smithfield, Norfolk, Suffolk, and towns in North Carolina, marching toward Southampton. Norfolk Navy Yard offered arms for a thousand men and sent a company of Marines; Fortress Monroe sent three companies of Army regulars and artillery. Since Floyd thought there might be at least a thousand blacks on the loose, by Tuesday noon there were three thousand men on the way to Southampton County, and General Epes, commander of the military district, found himself inundated with regular troops, militia, vigilantes, deputies, and plain armed citizens. On Wednesday morning he reported to the Governor that the emergency was over; all slaves were under control, all leaders dead or captured except Nat Turner. There were fifty-five white dead—thirteen men, eighteen women, and twenty-four children.

The killing was not yet over. The Virginia and Carolina militiamen, who feared a slave revolt more than anything else in the world, were determined that it should never happen again. Since no one knew exactly how many slaves had been involved in the rebellion, those who had simply disappeared during the trouble were suspect with the rest. Slaves were hunted down like animals, guilty or innocent, questioned, beaten, or shot; according to a Richmond paper, "the roads were strewn with the carcasses of Negroes." The Murfreesboro militia, which captured a group of wandering Negroes near Cross Keys, cut off their heads and stuck them on poles by the roadside. One militia captain carried a Negro head impaled on his sword as his company marched through Vicksville. Another militia company, finding a Negro drunk in a ditch, debated what to do with him. "Not wishing to be burdened with a prisoner," a Virginia historian delicately wrote, "and to give him the benefit of the doubt, they cut his heel-strings" to keep him from running away. The next militiamen to find him stood him against a tree and shot him. Slaves who could not account for themselves, or those who were frightened into silence, were killed to make sure no guilty black was missed. General Epes tried to stop the killings, (so did Southampton residents, for slaves were valuable property) but not until the twenty-seventh, when the militia started home, was it safe for a slave to leave his master's farmyard. There is no accurate record of the number of Negroes who died during the week of August 21. One Richmond editor estimated forty; an Alabama paper reported a hundred and fifty. Whatever the number, it is true that, as a contemporary account put it, "a number of innocent blacks were shot down."

Nat Turner hid for six weeks, though it is virtually certain that a number of slaves probably knew where he was. He remained in the swamp near Parker's for forty-eight hours, emerging on the night of the twenty-fifth. At the deserted Travis farm, the only home he knew, he found food, ate, and wandered over to the Francis farm, where he dug a hole under a pile of fence rails. Here he stayed, coming out at night to pick up corn in the farmyards and scraps of food put out for him by the slaves. Several times he decided to give himself up, he said later, and once he knocked on Nathaniel Francis' door, planning to surrender, but lost his nerve and fled. Meanwhile armed men searched every foot of woods for miles around, for no family felt safe with Nat still loose. Reports of him came in from all over Virginia, from North Carolina, even from Georgia and Alabama. In mid-September a group of Negroes out hunting flushed Nat out of his cave. Though they all swore secrecy, one told his master, but Nat had already dug a new hole a mile away when the posse came. After that he kept on the move, rarely spending more than one or two days in the same spot. On

October 27 Nathaniel Francis saw him in a field, fired, and missed. On October 30 Benjamin Phipps, who was out after quail, found Nat's cave and captured him.

Nat made no resistance. Phipps took him to the Edwards' farm, where the news of his capture was signalled across the county by gunshots. More than a hundred men collected at the farm, most of whom wanted him hanged on the spot. But Judge Parker prevailed, and the crowd settled for a whipping. Then his guards tied him to a horse and set out for Cross Keys, stopping at house after house on the way so that each farmer could whip him again. That night, alive but terribly lashed, Nat stayed at the Westbrook farm. On October 31 he arrived at Jerusalem, where Hark, Nelson, and Sam were already in jail. Two justices of the peace examined him for an hour and a half and returned him to his cell to await trial.

Nat and his allies were not lynched because there were too many questions people wanted answered. Only a public trial could answer what everyone wanted to know—why and how had it happened? What led presumably happy, docile Negroes to embark on the most barbaric spree of murder in the history of the South? Some slaves turned suddenly and savagely on their masters; others, nearly as culpable, simply said nothing and did nothing to save them. Ugly things came to light as men compared stories. One sixteen-year-old girl, a pet house-slave, showed the raiders where her mistress was hidden and watched them kill her. A strapping, friendly young Negro admitted he knew of the revolt on Sunday, saw Turner's men approaching Monday morning, and failed to give an alarm. Another slave seized his master's arm and held him while the marauders broke the door down. Negroes like these, and many of Nat's sixty, were trusted, well-treated slaves. There were no large plantations in Southampton; few white men owned more than a dozen Negroes, most of whom they knew as well as they knew their own families. Yet the slaves had turned on their masters, killed fifty-five white people, and spread death and terror across an entire county. Why did it happen?

The trials failed to give an answer. Fifty-three Negroes, including one woman and five free blacks, were tried for insurrection. The five free Negroes were tried in Superior Circuit Court, and on September 8, 1831, the trials of the forty-eight others began in Southampton County Court. Three local lawyers were appointed as counsel for the slaves, each of whom entered a plea of Not Guilty. Prosecutor Mereweather Broadnax found the going hard. It was almost impossible to obtain a straight story from any of the slaves, and both prosecution and defense threaded their way through hours of vague, evasive, contradictory testimony by frightened Negroes, trying to find out exactly what had happened.

The identity of those slaves in Nat's group was relatively easy to determine, since various white men had seen them several times. Those who had joined other bands, which might or might not have killed any whites, were much more difficult to name. Approximately sixty slaves had rebelled. Fifty-three were on trial, but were they the right fifty-three? Of those slaves who had disappeared on Monday and Tuesday, all, or some, or none might have been involved—there was no way to find out. And to find out whether or not a slave had known of the revolt and had *not* warned his master was impossible; furthermore, it was not at all clear that failure to act was a crime. The prosecution, the judge, and the jury did the best they could with the evidence, though Southampton County was convinced that there were more guilty Negroes than were on trial. Of the forty-eight slaves tried in County Court, seventeen were sentenced to death, twelve were sentenced to transportation to Africa, and the rest were discharged, either through lack of evidence or on their master's testimony. Of the five free Negroes, four were convicted. None of the slaves or freedmen could provide any rational explanation, at least one understandable to a white man, of why they had done what they had done.

Nat Turner was tried last, on November 5, three days after he made a complete confession to one of his lawyers, Thomas Gray. He pleaded Not Guilty, he said, "because he did not feel guilty," though he readily admitted planning the revolt, leading it, and murdering Peggy Whitehead. Brodnax questioned him closely for hours, but Nat steadily maintained that he had acted on God's orders—Brodnax could get nothing else. There was no doubt of his sanity, the judge ruled, for "his testimony was clear and intelligent."

Nor was there any doubt of his guilt. The death sentence was automatic, and on November 11, 1831, Nat and the last three of the convicted Negroes were hanged. Hanging day, Nat predicted, would be filled with darkness (a sign of God's anger) and though a violent thunderstorm an hour before his hanging frightened Negroes and superstitious whites, the trap dropped on schedule. The bodies of all the executed Negroes were buried in unconsecrated ground, without benefit of clergy—except Nat's, which was given to local physicians for dissection. They skinned it, reduced it to a skeleton, and put the skull on exhibition. For some years a few men in Southampton displayed purses made of Nat's tanned skin as warnings to fractious Negroes.

The accepted conclusion in the South was that Nat was an unbalanced religious fanatic, yet his hanging solved none of the problems that his revolt raised. Were there other religious fanatics among the South's slaves, other undiscovered Nats? Nat could read—was this a factor to be considered? Nat's masters had all been tolerant men, and Nat himself admitted he held no grudges—was it meaningful, as some believed, that Nat "had been allowed too many privileges in his youth?" And then there was the most frightening question of all—was Nat Turner's revolt merely one part of a great design for wholesale insurrection, murder, and pillage throughout the South? Was Nat the leader, or only a subordinate, in a greater plot?

Repercussions of the Southampton affair rocked the South for months after Nat's death. "It is like a smothered volcano," one woman wrote. "We know not where or when the flame will burst forth." No one could be quite sure that this sullen field hand, or that faithful old retainer, might not be another

"Crazy Nat." This Negro prayer meeting might hide a conspiracy; those slaves, presumably hunting coon in the woods, might really be plotting their master's murder. Southern towns doubled their night-time patrols and rang a curfew bell at nine in the evening. (Some still had a curfew for Negroes seventy years later.) The Negro who went abroad after dark or before dawn ran the risk of a severe whipping or perhaps death, for patrollers were likely to shoot before asking questions. Farmers in sparsely settled areas moved their wives and children into guarded farmhouses; very few slept without barred doors, locked windows, or guns at their sides; some built hideouts in the woods and stocked them with food. For many years the "Black Terror" of slave revolt, as a Southern legislator called it, "ate at the vitals of the South." Wherever there were slaves, there was fear.

Looking for plots, the South of course found them everywhere. The more they looked, the more evidence imaginative Southerners discovered of a vast slave conspiracy stretching throughout the South. The Reverend Lorenzo Dow spoke for many when he concluded that "the Negro plot of General Nat extended from the State of Delaware to the Gulf of Mexico." Newspapers reported dozens of slave arrests and confessions, or accounts of Negro "conspirators" shot while trying to escape, and a Southern correspondent wrote to *Niles' Register* that "there is much *fear* and *feeling* here, with the white inhabitants in a constant excitement."

Though Nat himself categorically denied that his plot extended beyond Southampton County, few really believed him. Intense excitement spread over Virginia and North Carolina as proof piled up of a far more extensive conspiracy than anyone had suspected. Sixty-three slaves were jailed in eastern Virginia, several shot, and at least two hanged. Reports that two or three thousand Negroes were hiding in the great Dismal Swamp, which stretches from Southampton County into North Carolina, kept the militia of both states mobilized for weeks. "The people of Duplin County," one North Carolinian wrote his Governor, "have examined ten or fifteen negroes and found two guilty and have put them to *death*, there never was such excitement in Sampson and Duplin before!" A company of artillery was dispatched to Newbern during the Southampton trials to guard the city from a rumored attack by Nat's confederates, and in Virginia and North Carolina the arrests, whippings, hangings, and lynchings lasted well into November of 1831. Alabama feared a combined revolt of Negroes and Indians; in Georgia, Tennessee, and Mississippi the authorities claimed to have discovered conspiracies probably linked to Nat Turner's.

The majority of Southern states quickly passed new laws to control the Negro, or enforced the old ones more strictly. Negro preachers were arrested, Negro religious services suspended or allowed only in the presence of white men, and Negro meetings of any kind were forbidden. The old prohibitions against teaching Negroes to read or to assemble "for the purpose of mental instruction," honored more in the breach than in the observance, came back into force. Free Negroes lost many of their legal privileges—for if Nat Turner had been allowed too much freedom, one way to forestall potential Nats was to tighten control. No free Negro could possess any weapons. Assault by a Negro on a white person was punishable by death. No Negro, free or slave, should "undertake to preach, exhort, or conduct, or hold any assembly or meeting, for religious or other purposes, either in the daytime or night," on pain of thirty-nine lashes. At the same time antislavery opinion began to disappear from the South. Within twenty years the white man who believed the system was wrong, or had its faults, or ought to be modified—and said so—most certainly endangered his own freedom and perhaps his life. To preserve its unique institution, the South deliberately infringed upon its own rights more than it knew. To protect slavery, the Southern white man in a sense made himself its slave.

The constant stream of rumors, both true and false, was the worst part of it. There were major scares in the South in 1835, 1836, 1845, 1849, 1855 and 1856, as well as lesser frights in intervening years. Wilmington, North Carolina, at one time called out militia and placed the town under martial law to prepare for a revolt. Raleigh called out its militia after it heard that Wilmington had been sacked and burned by a slave army; by the time the story reached Virginia it included uprisings in Maryland and Delaware. There was no revolt in Wilmington, or anything resembling one, but six slaves were hanged nevertheless for planning a conspiracy. A report from Nashville, Tennessee, in 1836, that included detailed reports of burning houses, fleeing masters, and rebelling slaves, stirred the upper South for weeks until it was proved completely false. The *Times* of Columbus, Georgia, reported an insurrection of seven hundred Alabama slaves in 1849 that proved to be an absolute hoax. Mississippi authorities uncovered a conspiracy involving two hundred slaves in 1854, though it took some whippings to obtain confessions.

Some of the rumors had some truth in them. Among the hundreds of reports of slave plots to which veiled allusions were made in the Southern press, sixteen seem to have been authentic, and on a scale large enough to be dangerous. However, it is almost impossible to establish how many slave plots were actually uncovered, or how many of the "conspiracies" had any basis in fact. Southern newspapers, admitting that "it was a delicate subject to touch," refrained from publishing accounts of suspected plots, lest the infection spread. Such news was suppressed or referred to only by indirection, for, as one lady wrote, "The negroes hear what is published if they do not read it, and such examples produce disastrous consequences." Admittedly incomplete statistics show approximately seventy Negroes convicted and executed in various parts of the South from 1831 to 1861 for complicity in real or fancied plots. From the day of the Southampton revolt until the Civil War the rumors never stopped.

Cooler heads, of course, agreed that the widespread fear of slave revolt was largely groundless. The Tennessee Methodist Convention of 1836 thought that a serious revolt was highly unlikely, while the Missouri *Democrat* blamed the scare on politicians who agitated the issue until the public was over-conscious of it. Yet the fear of slave rebellion after Nat Turner's Southampton revolt became an important factor in conditioning Southern pro-slavery thought. There were those in North and South who pointed out that perhaps the institution of slavery itself was at fault, that the subjection of one mass of people to another bred revolt by the very nature of the relationship. But to ask the slaveholding South to accept this was asking far too much. For one thing, it was hard to fit the Black Terror of revolt into the picture drawn by pro-slavery writers of a patriarchal Dixie paradise of kind masters and contented Negroes. And for another, if slavery were wrong, the underpinning of Southern political, social, and economic life collapsed. It could not be so. Slavery was right, necessary, Christian, a "blessing both to master and slave," a "positive good" to Negro, white, South, nation, and world. To explain the Nat Turners of slavery, it was imperative to find some other reason. They found the reason in the North.

William Lloyd Garrison, an obscure reform editor in Boston, Massachusetts, published the first issue of his paper, *The Liberator,* in January, 1831. He believed in the immediate emancipation of all slaves, and he said so in violent, occasionally insulting language. Not many read his paper. He had no Southern subscribers, though he did send exchange copies to Southern editors, following contemporary journalistic practice. To the Southerners who read it, *The Liberator* represented the very worst aspects of Northern abolitionist thought, and Garrison's intemperate prose lent itself admirably to juicy quotation. Consequently the South received from its own press the impression that Garrison represented Northern opinion concerning slavery. Since it was inconceivable that a slave revolt might be self-generating, or its causes inherent in the system itself, the rest of the explanation was easy.

Within a few months after the Southampton insurrection it was generally believed in the South that Northern abolitionists were responsible for it. There were "white men behind the scenes," Lorenzo Dow said darkly, "for no Negro was capable of organizing this." Governor Floyd of Virginia gave the theory official sanction by announcing that Nat's raid was "undoubtedly designed and matured by unrestrained fanatics in some of the neighboring states." Since the most unrestrained fanatic at hand was William Lloyd Garrison, the connection was simple. There was no doubt at all, wrote a North Carolina editor, that Nat Turner was egged on by "an incendiary paper, *The Liberator*, published by a white man in Boston or Philadelphia with the avowed purpose of exciting rebellion in the South." One by one Southern newspapers picked up the charge until the South was filled with clamor against Garrison and rewards for his capture. The legislature of Georgia in 1831 offered five thousand dollars for the trial and conviction of Garrison, whereas some years later Louisiana was willing to go as high as fifty thousand dollars for the president of New York City's American Antislavery Society.

The fact that Garrison was a nonresistant pacifist, opposed to violence in any form, escaped everyone. Nevertheless, to many in the South, Garrison and the abolitionists came to represent the North, a North that tolerated or encouraged slave revolts, a North that in attacking slavery endangered the safety of every Southern white man, woman, and child. From the North came "those vile emissaries of abolition, working like moles underground, who have been breathing the poison of insubordination into our slaves." From the North came "emancipation talk" that "addled slaves' brains," talk about freeing the Negro from those very laws and controls that kept him from murdering his masters. In the North, a Baltimore editor believed, "preachers prayed and their women longed for a general insurrection of slaves . . . with the murder and destruction of all around them." And if the Negro were freed as the North hoped, a Louisianan warned his compatriots, the ex-slave would be free to kill and plunder on a scale never dreamed of—"Your lands will be covered with ruins and your altar stones with blood and desolation." Born in fear and nurtured in prejudice, the idea that slavery meant safety, and free black men meant death, grew in the South until temperate or reasoned discussion became virtually impossible. John Brown's raid at Harper's Ferry verified what the South had said and thought for thirty years.

Nat Turner's place in the history of the controversy over slavery is at first glance small and unimportant. He never freed a single slave. The only result of his ill-starred rebellion was severity, repression, and a worsening of the Negro's lot. After Nat's revolt the lynching rate rose sharply, while the lynching party and the vigilance committee became virtually institutionalized in the South.

Yet poor, crazed Nat Turner crystallized a mixture of fear, suspicion, and insecurity that had been brewing in the South for generations. He eventually cost the South millions in hard cash, in the increased cost of patrols, police, militia mobilization, lost time, and uncertainty. He gave the abolition movement, already growing swiftly in the North, invaluable ammunition against slavery, just as he provided pro-slavery leaders with the all-compelling argument from public and personal safety. No one among the abolitionists approved Nat's methods—but the fact of his rebellion pointed up one of the inherent flaws of the slavery system and shattered the carefully-fostered dream of an Athenian-Dixie democracy. Until the Civil War, the shadow of Nat Turner always hung over and behind the slavery argument.

Nat was an unbalanced fanatic, but it was only logical that slavery would produce him. Even from the scanty evidence it is apparent that he had an unusual mind, one that could find no way of breaking out of the rigid limits imposed on it by slavery. Thomas Gray, who talked with Nat for hours in his cell, was struck by his "uncommon intelligence," concluding that "for natural intelligence and quickness of apprehension he is surpassed by few men I have ever seen." Yet whatever potential Nat possessed was twisted and perverted into mania and murder by the slave system, the real cause of Nat Turner's revolt and the plain truth that the South could not accept. Under slavery the Negro was hopelessly condemned to eternal ignorance; to admit anything else or to have allowed anything else would have destroyed the basic myth on which slavery rested.

The South could not explain Nat Turner. It could only hang him, which answered none of its questions and settled nothing. There might be more Nats, and more killing, so long as a million black men remained in chains. "We may shut our eyes and avert our faces, if we please," a South Carolinian wrote despairingly in 1838, "but there it is, the dark and growing evil at our doors. Oh my God—I don't know, but something must be done!"

Elijah Lovejoy

★

THE PASSIONS AROUSED by the controversy over slavery were not confined solely to the South. There no doubt were nearly as many men above the Ohio River who owned no slaves and who believed in the inevitable rightness of the system as there were who owned slaves and lived below it. The tiny group of men in New England and New York who cried that slavery was evil and should be abolished were regarded at first as certainly not respectable and possibly dangerous men. For one thing, moderate-thinking men in the North thought the slavery issue far too explosive to be handled by irresponsible radicals, for involved in it were the peaceful existence of the Union and the matter of some millions of dollars in trade between North and South. That slavery was hardly a system suitable to a free republic few Northerners were prepared to deny; on the other hand, if slavery were assumed to be a regional, not a national problem, no one in the North really had a right to meddle in the affairs of sovereign sister states.

But while the average Northerner might condemn the abolitionist radical for what he thought and said (and particularly for the ungentlemanly way in which he said it) he believed implicitly in the abolitionist's right to think and speak, for he and the abolitionist held that right in common as part of their traditional heritage of American civil liberties. When the abolitionist was prevented from exercising that right by force or subterfuge, the slavery controversy took on a much broader meaning than simply a controversy over the rights of slaves in a distant South. The abolitionist, tarred and feathered and ridden on a rail, instantly found allies among those who disagreed with his unpopular opinions but rigidly sustained his freedom to have them. In the space of less than a decade after Garrison's *Liberator* rang the alarm in 1831, the issue of slavery became inextricably bound up with the issue of liberty—that of the white man as well as that of the black. The net effect of attempts in the North and South to suppress abolitionism was to gain for it a body of supporters who thought less of the wrongs of the slave system than of the civil rights of the white man. The abolitionist movement thrived on persecution. Thus William Ellery Channing, the Boston divine, wrote in 1836 that "One kidnapped, murdered abolitionist would do more for the violent destruction of slavery than a thousand societies." Channing had only a year to wait.

Elijah Lovejoy was born in Kennebec County, Maine, in 1802. His father, a Presbyterian minister, was a godly man who instilled much of his own piety into his children. Elijah, who stood in the middle of the succession of eight Lovejoy sons and daughters, was a bright lad, quiet and pleasant, the one chosen by his father as most likely to follow him into the ministry. The Lovejoys were able to give all their children a good education, and Elijah graduated with honors from Waterville College in Maine with the class of 1826. He did not, to his father's disappointment, feel an urgent call to the pulpit. Instead he drifted West, like dozens of other young New Englanders, to look for his fortune in a new country.

Young Elijah ended his trip in St. Louis, a raw, bustling city growing swiftly in population and importance because of its position astride the trade routes of the expanding West. He planned at first to find a position teaching school, but since St. Louis needed newspapermen more than it needed schoolteachers, he hired out to the St. Louis *Times* as a reporter. He liked newspaper work and did well at it, so well that within a few months the publishers of the *Times* appointed him editor. Western journalism in the eighteen-twenties was likely to be financially shaky, and an editor's responsibilities, though the title sounded impressive, covered everything from setting type to soliciting advertising. Five years of it, Lovejoy felt, was enough. His father and brothers, still hopeful of making a minister of him, urged him to reconsider, and in 1832 he returned East to Princeton Theological Seminary.

Elijah spent a year at Princeton and received his license to preach. He had made many friends in St. Louis, among them a number of Presbyterians who felt a strong need for a religious newspaper in that godless city of riverboatmen, traders, and drifters. During his stay at Princeton they corresponded with him, encouraging him to return to St. Louis to establish a Presbyterian weekly. By the time of his graduation from Princeton they had raised twelve hundred dollars to buy him a press and had a sufficient number of subscription pledges to guarantee him a salary of five hundred dollars a year, so Lovejoy accepted and went. In November, 1833, he issued the first number of the St. Louis *Observer*, whose "leading object," he told his subscribers, "will be to diffuse information of the religious operations of the day among Christians and other citizens of the West."

There were a number of similar papers in the West, small, struggling religious journals edited on pittances by dedicated young men. Lovejoy's *Observer* was neither better nor worse than the rest. He faithfully recorded events of interest to Presbyterians, reprinted columns from Eastern papers, editorialized against the Catholics, and warned the unwary of the city's temptations, which were many. He did some preaching among the smaller settlements of eastern Missouri, helped to organize evangelistic revivals, attended meetings of the synod, and in general made himself a young man of good reputation and influence. He also married and began a family, though five hundred dollars a year was barely enough to rent a small house and buy food.

During his year at Princeton the controversy over slavery stirred up sharp argument in church circles in New England

and New York. In its early phase, the abolitionist movement in the East was primarily religious in its motivations—Garrison himself was a Baptist, nearly all his lieutenants were ministers or licensed preachers of various denominations, and the new antislavery societies drew the majority of their members from Baptist, Methodist, Congregational, or Presbyterian congregations. To Garrison and others the case for the abolition of slavery rested almost wholly on moral and religious grounds. If slavery did not "harmonize to the law of God," they reasoned, then slave-holding was "a moral crime" and neither those who held slaves nor those who approved of slavery belonged in a Christian church. Slavery might be legal, it might be constitutionally defensible, it might be economically feasible, but it was a sin, and no true Christian could compromise with sin. To the Garrisonian group, then, there could be but one conclusion—abolish slavery at once. All other solutions — gradual emancipation, manumission, colonization, and so on—the abolitionists considered to be nearly as sinful as slavery itself, and like slavery, to be fought as Christians fought other sins, by exhortation, argument, and conversion.

Lovejoy, who read Garrison's *Liberator*, found the Bostonian's arguments extremely convincing. In Missouri, a slave state, he saw the system in operation and did not like it. In 1834 occasional editorials on slavery began to appear in the *Observer*, rational, temperate, and mildly written, for as Lovejoy explained, his "object as a Christian was peace and concert in action with every good man in every good work." Though some of his own Presbyterian subscribers held slaves and the American Colonization Society (which hated Garrisonians and abolitionists) was strong in Missouri, there were no significant protests.

However, Lovejoy's conscience refused to allow him to do things by halves. The more he thought about it, and the more he wrote of it, the more he became convinced that of all the religious issues of the day slavery was the most important. As the months passed his comments in the *Oberver* took on a sharper edge, until a few subscribers, in 1834, took the matter up in stockholders' meeting. They subscribed, they supposed, to a religious weekly; what they received each week looked more and more like a Western edition of the *Liberator*. Though Lovejoy explained that slavery was a *religious* question, and that frank discussion of it belonged in a religious paper, the board of publishers thought it wise to insert in the *Observer* a notice that a number of protests led them to feel that perhaps the journal "ought to suspend all controversy upon the exciting subject of slavery." The whole matter, the publishers promised, would be discussed with Editor Lovejoy so that "the future course of the paper could be finally arranged in such a manner as, we doubt not, will be consonant with the wishes of the proprietors."

Lovejoy would have none of it. After his conference with the publishers ended in disagreement, he continued his attacks on slavery and his espousal of abolition with greater fervor than before. It was clear to some of his readers that he had been badly infected with Garrisonism; none of them wanted in St. Louis the violent controversies over abolition that had erupted in Boston. Still, Lovejoy's critics recognized the delicacy of the situation. Elijah Lovejoy was an honest Christian, thoroughly sincere in his beliefs. He was a good editor, and though the publishers disagreed with his attitude toward slavery they were determined to respect his editorial right to think and write as he believed. A month after the first announcement, the publishers inserted a second notice, asking all those "opposed to the mad schemes of the Abolitionists" to "stand patiently by" while matters were arranged with Lovejoy. So the board met again, asking him to "pass over in silence everything connected with the subject of Slavery and announce in the paper your intention to do so." Lovejoy flatly refused.

The *Observer* attracted the attention of many more than merely Lovejoy's Presbyterian subscribers. Missouri considered slavery to be a social and economic question as well as a moral one, and the issue was rapidly becoming a touchy one in the Southwest, as it already was in the East. A good many St. Louisans believed that if Mr. Lovejoy presumed to edit a religious paper, he had best confine himself to issues of a purely religious nature. The city's civic leaders wanted no Garrisonism in Missouri, for the state's commercial and emotional ties with the South were far too strong. In late 1835, therefore, several prominent citizens called for an open mass meeting to discuss not only the problem created by the *Observer,* but the broader problem of abolitionism in Missouri.

The meeting was attended by perhaps a hundred people, who agreed after a reasonable discussion that since slavery was "too nearly allied to the vital interest of the slaveholding states to admit of public disputation," Mr. Lovejoy's paper represented "a dangerous influence in the community" because his abolition sentiments were "seditious, calculated to incite insurrection and anarchy, and ultimately a disseverance of our prosperous union." As for Editor Lovejoy, while the meeting recognized his right to free speech and a free press, that right did not "imply a moral right to freely discuss the matter of slavery, either orally or through the press." It would be advisable, the meeting resolved, to appoint several vigilance committees "to look up all persons suspected of Abolitionism" and to discourage them.

This was plain, almost threatening language. Copies of the resolutions were sent to Lovejoy, who replied with an eloquent editorial phrased in equally plain terms. First of all, he reminded his critics that the Constitution of the United States and the Constitution of Missouri gave him an unalienable right to free speech—"and whether I exercise that right or not is for me, and not for the mob, to decide." Second, he was utterly convinced that slavery was immoral, sinful and unChristian, and as a man of God he could do nothing other than fight against it with all his being. "I do therefore," he concluded

> as an American citizen and Christian patriot, and in the name of law, liberty, and RELIGION, solemnly protest against all these attempts to frown down the

liberty of the press and forbid the free expression of opinion. Under a deep sense of obligation to my country, the church, and my God, I declare it to be my fixed purpose to submit to no such dictation. And I am prepared to abide the consequences. *I have appealed to the constitution and the laws of my country; if they fail to protect me, I APPEAL TO GOD, and with Him I cheerfully rest my case."*

"I suspect," he wrote to his brother after the editorial appeared, "that I shall be *lynched,* or tarred and feathered, or maybe *hung up.* Pray for me, that I may pass through this fiery trial without denying my Lord and Master."

After his reply a number of threats came to the *Observer* offices and a few men spoke roughly to him on the street. Once by accident he escaped a crowd which had decided after several hours in a saloon that the "damned abolitionist" ought to be run out of town. Feelings against him, his friends warned, ran high. In January, 1836, after someone circulated a handbill promising that the *Observer* had not long to live, his publishers, fearing a mob attack on the offices, remonstrated with Lovejoy either to temper his language or drop his editorial crusade entirely. Lovejoy's reply was to begin organizing church antislavery societies in the small parishes outside the city.

The climax came in July, 1836, over a series of editorials in the *Observer* that ironically did not directly concern slavery at all. In April of 1835 a Pittsburgh mulatto sailor named McIntosh had trouble with the St. Louis police. When a deputy sheriff and a constable went aboard the riverboat *Flora* to arrest him, McIntosh resisted, and in the fight that followed he wounded the constable and killed the deputy. Though McIntosh was caught within a few hours and lodged in the city jail to await trial, the next night a mob stormed the jail and captured him, meeting no resistance from his jailers. Then they chained him to a tree and burned him to death, slowly and horribly, after which some of the mob threw stones at the charred body, placing bets on who might be the first to smash the skull.

Elijah Lovejoy, breaking the unwritten rule that governed Southern journalism, printed the story of the lynching in all its gory detail. In July, 1836, he compounded his offense by his reports on the trial of the lynch leaders, who were tried before a judge with the unfortunate name of Lawless. All the defendants were discharged after Lawless, in his charge to the jury, directed a Not Guilty verdict on the ground that since McIntosh's death was not the act of "numberable and ascertainable persons, but of congregated thousands, the case then transcends our jurisdiction—it is beyond the reach of human law." Lovejoy's editorials, which foamed with bitterness against Missouri justice and the slave system that perverted it, confirmed St. Louis in its opinion that the editor was not a desirable citizen. It was not improbable, remarked another St. Louis paper, that Editor Lovejoy himself might soon feel the fury of the mob unless he left town.

Lovejoy was quite aware that his days in St. Louis were numbered. In the same issue that carried the last of his comments on the McIntosh case, he announced the removal of the *Observer* to Alton, Illinois, across the Mississippi, listing three reasons for his decision. First, the *Observer* was five hundred dollars in debt and losing subscribers fast; obviously his paper did not belong in St. Louis. Second, he had been promised the support of a group of Alton antislavery men, who had for some months urged him to transfer the paper to that city. Then too, he admitted frankly, he feared for the safety of his wife and children—as for himself, he feared nothing, but the danger of a mob attack on his home was a consideration he could not overlook. As if in reply, a mob descended on the *Observer* offices the night after his announcement, destroyed the furniture, smashed the press, and destroyed the type. Lovejoy himself was fortunately absent at a church meeting, or he might have met his martyrdom in St. Louis.

Elijah Lovejoy left St. Louis in late July of 1836, but before he moved he ordered a new press to be delivered to him at Alton. There were many Alton citizens who were not pleased at his appearance in their city, for Southern Illinois was Southern in sympathy and Lovejoy's reputation preceded him. Opinion about his decision to set up his paper in Alton was sharply divided. According to the Reverend Edward Beecher, one of the staunch abolitionists who invited him to Alton, the town had a strong minority of pro-slavery men, a strong minority of anti-slavery men, and a large body of citizens who while neither for or against slavery were still much concerned about the propriety of introducing a highly controversial issue into an otherwise orderly and peaceable community. A delegation of citizens called upon Lovejoy shortly after his arrival, hoping to discuss with him what his plans for Alton's new paper might involve.

Lovejoy was quite frank with them. He was a licensed preacher and a religious editor. He intended to publish a religious paper, not an abolitionist journal, and he did not intend to create ill-feeling or disorder in Alton—but, he concluded, he "reserved the right to speak, write, and publish whatever I please on any subject, being amenable to the laws of my country for the same." His answer may have satisfied the committee, but not all Alton's citizens. When his new press arrived by steamer in early August, a half-dozen men broke open the crate as it lay on the dock, smashed the press with sledgehammers, and threw the pieces in the river.

Lovejoy's supporters immediately collected money for a new press, and when it arrived three weeks later they met the steamer at the dock and carried the press safely to the *Observer's* offices. The first issue of the Alton version of Lovejoy's paper appeared in mid-September. As the weeks passed, it seemed to be, much as Lovejoy had promised, primarily a religious journal, but its columns carried a fairly high percentage of abolitionist doctrine and perhaps two out of three of his editorials dealt with slavery in one fashion or another. Though there were murmurings about it in Alton, still the list of subscribers climbed by 1837 to nearly two thousand, scattered through nearby Missouri and Southern Illinois.

FREEDOM ROAD: *Elijah Lovejoy*

It was perhaps not so much the *Observer* as Lovejoy himself who created friction in Alton. He was a literate and convincing speaker, much in demand in country pulpits, but the theme of his sermons and talks seemed always to be abolition in the Garrisonian manner. In 1837 he precipitated a violent argument over slavery in the Presbyterian General Assembly, leaving ruffled tempers among some of Alton's own ministers. Then too, he began to organize antislavery societies among smaller church groups, and most serious of all, he was instrumental in founding the Illinois State Antislavery Society, which was affiliated with the American Antislavery Society in New York, and thus with the notorious Tappan brothers, Theodore Weld, and Garrison. In a sense, some Alton citizens believed, he had violated his pledge. Why could not Alton, the St. Louis papers asked, "put a stop to the efforts of such fanatics or expel them from the community?"

The citizens of Alton did not want their city to become the abolitionist capital of Illinois. In July, 1837, handbills announced a meeting of interested citizens at the Market House "to suppress abolitionism in our town and to take into consideration the course pursued by the Reverend E. P. Lovejoy in the dissemination of the highly odious doctrines of modern abolitionism." The matter was a serious one, and Alton treated it seriously. The Market House meeting was chaired by a prominent local physician, attended by the town's most influential men, and handled in a well-organized and dignified manner. After long discussion, the assembly resolved

> *That Mr. Lovejoy had pledged himself not to agitate the slavery question, but had violated his pledge.*
> *That in agitating the slavery question, he acted contrary to the will and disposition of the majority of the citizens of Alton.*
> *That a committee be appointed to confer with Mr. Lovejoy, and ascertain from him whether he intends in the future to disseminate through the columns of the Observer the doctrines of abolitionism.*

Though the committee never called on Lovejoy, the chairman of the meeting sent him a copy of the resolutions, which he published in the *Observer* with his reply. If he accepted any of the resolutions, he explained, it meant virtually conceding that his freedom of speech and press was subject to extra-legal control, which he was not willing to do. As for his future policy, he assured the committee that he would continue "to discuss the overwhelmingly important subject of slavery with the freedom of a republican and the meekness of a Christian." But he most certainly would continue to discuss it.

On the evening of August 21, Lovejoy finished putting his next issue to bed and left his office to perform a marriage at a house on the outskirts of town. At about nine o'clock his assistant, completing the press run, heard noises outside, followed by the crashing of window glass. A swift look out the shattered window showed him perhaps thirty men approaching in the darkness. The assistant quickly escaped through the back door, and within fifteen minutes the *Observer* offices were thoroughly wrecked, the press smashed, the furniture ripped to kindling. One of Lovejoy's friends, hearing the commotion, ran to notify Mayor John Krum and the police but neither appeared. Then, after wrecking the office, the crowd departed in search of Lovejoy.

Someone in the mob knew where he was, and as the editor was on his way home after the marriage he met the crowd in the street. They recognized him at once and surrounded him, shouting, "Rail him!," "Tar and feather him!," "Run the damned abolitionist out of town!" Lovejoy, reporting the affair to his brother later, wrote, "I then said to them, 'You have no right to detain me; I have never injured you.' They began to curse and swear at me, and I said, 'I am in your hands and you can do with me what God permits you to do.'" Apparently such calm resignation had its effect, for "after consulting a few moments, then they told me to go home."

There would be no *Observer*, of course, until Lovejoy bought another press. His friends again pledged contributions and Lovejoy paid for the printing of a request for funds that he distributed in Alton and neighboring towns. He needed a new press, he said, not to publish abolitionist propaganda, but rather "to determine whether the liberty of speech and of the press is to be enjoyed in Illinois or not." "The question of the supremacy of the law of our state," he continued

> is one of deep interest to us all, and we do not feel at liberty to yield to the violence of a mob. We therefore are determined to sustain the laws, and guard the freedom of the press without reference to the fact whether we agree or differ with doctrines of it. We deprecate violence but we are determined to yield to nothing but Law.

Contributions came in swiftly, including a good many from citizens who had little sympathy for abolition but strong beliefs in civil rights—as one Alton lawyer expressed it, he "would rather give Lovejoy a hundred dollars for a new press than five dollars for a subscription." It took him less than a month to collect enough to order another press, his third, from Cincinnati.

The press arrived in Alton by steamer late on September 21, 1837. Since Lovejoy was attending a presbytery meeting, three of his friends took it to the warehouse of Gerry and Walker, notifying Mayor Krum of its arrival and requesting police protection for it. Krum responded by sending a constable to guard the warehouse; curiously enough, the constable's shift ended at midnight and no one was assigned to the warehouse from midnight to morning. Five minutes after the constable went off duty a dozen men entered the warehouse, rolled the press down to the river, and threw it in. Since they made a fair amount of noise in the process, a crowd gathered to watch. Mayor Krum, awakened by the commotion, hastily dressed and went to investigate. Since he had been charged with the protection of Lovejoy's property, and since the men were obviously engaged in destroying it, Krum ordered them to desist and disperse. They were, Krum said, "most quiet and gentlemanly about it"—they promised that they would gladly do so as soon as they were finished.

Thus Lovejoy's third press disappeared into the Mississippi. The next morning he started his appeal for another. Subscriptions came in a little more slowly this time, for even his friends were beginning to doubt that the *Observer* would ever succeed in publishing another issue. It was common talk in Alton that Lovejoy's presses would be tossed in the river as fast as he could order them, and furthermore, tempers were turning ugly. Men stopped Lovejoy and his friends on the street to threaten them; once, walking home in the dark, he had a narrow escape from a thrown brick. Someone started a rumor that he had encouraged a Negro to rape a white woman in Mississippi, and occasional drunks stopped before his house to shout curses and throw stones.

Though Lovejoy received plenty of warning, none of the threats materialized until October. Following his custom of preaching guest sermons for fellow ministers in outlying small towns, Lovejoy accepted an invitation to St. Charles, some miles from Alton, and took his wife (who was seven months pregnant) and small son along. Since the sermon lasted late, they decided to stay overnight at the home of the Reverend William Campbell. At eleven o'clock that night, Mrs. Lovejoy heard a knock at the door and opened it. It was dark, and she could see but one man, who politely asked to see the Reverend Lovejoy. When Lovejoy came to the door several men jumped from the bushes and tried to pull him outside. Mrs. Lovejoy, however, slapped one of the men, grasped her husband's arm, and pulled him back into the house and slammed the door. Within a few minutes the men rushed the door and tried to push in, but the Reverend Campbell, who had arrived by this time, had it locked. The men remained in the yard shouting curses at Lovejoy until finally one of them put a note under the door ordering him to get out of town by ten the next day. Lovejoy hastily scribbled a note to the effect that he intended to leave on the nine o'clock stage. This satisfied the mob, who left, but two hours later they were back, throwing stones and shouting threats. One of the Reverend Campbell's parishioners, who had come to help, broke the crowd up by promising to stand everyone to free drinks at the local saloon. Fearful for his wife's safety, Lovejoy borrowed horses and left with his family before dawn.

Lovejoy ordered his fourth press in October, 1837. On November third another mass meeting was called at the Market House "to take into consideration the present excited state of public sentiment in this city." There were a number of worried men in Alton; after all, there had been two mobs, dozens of threats, and a great deal of threatening talk. Faced with Lovejoy's stubborn resistance on the one side and with increasing resentment from certain elements among the townspeople, no one knew exactly what to do. The men who called the meeting invited Lovejoy to attend, and V. F. Linder, Attorney General of Illinois, whose home was in Alton, agreed to serve as its chairman. Lovejoy spoke, defending his constitutional right to speak and print as he saw fit. Others spoke, pleading for temperance, good-will, and calmness. Linder, who as a state official felt a double responsibility, admitted Lovejoy's constitutional right but contended that it was his civic duty to refrain from exercising it, since to do so at the moment "would be destructive of the peace of the citizens of Alton." No man had the *moral* right to endanger the peace and safety of others, as further agitation of the slavery question, Linder concluded, most certainly would.

Not so, replied Lovejoy. The continued existence of slavery threatened not only Alton, but the nation itself. Failure to crusade against it was in itself a sin, and so long as he possessed the constitutional right of free speech he intended to use it. Nevertheless, the meeting agreed with Linder. "It is deemed a matter indispensable to the peace and harmony of the community," the meeting resolved, "that the labors and influence of the Editor of the *Observer* be no longer identified with any newspaper establishment in this city." Rising to his feet, Lovejoy made his answer. "I have concluded," he said,

> after consultation with my friends and earnestly asking counsel of God, to remain at Alton and here to insist on protection of the exercise of my rights. The contest has come here, and here it must be finished. Before God and you all, I here pledge myself to continue it, until death; and if I fall, my grave shall be made in Alton.

After the Market House meeting, the impending arrival of the new press provided the focal point for discussion pro and con Lovejoy. Exactly when it would come no one knew, but all of Alton knew that when it did arrive there was certain to be trouble. Winthrop Gilman, one of Lovejoy's strongest supporters, called on Mayor Krum for advice. How far could they go in safeguarding Lovejoy's property? Could his friends expect protection from the authorities, more than had been provided for the second and third presses? There was no doubt whatever, in Krum's opinion, that Lovejoy had a legal right to defend his property and he, Krum, would see to it that the Alton police this time provided an adequate guard. Since the antislavery men in Alton had experience with Krum's promises, Gilman wanted a little more assurance. He and other Lovejoy men, he informed the Mayor, preferred to take no chances; they would all be armed, and if Krum would swear them in as special militia, they could do legally what they intended to do if it were necessary. Krum did not approve, and after talking further with Gilman, agreed to go with him to Samuel Roff's store, where five other antislavery men were gathered.

John Krum was caught in a dilemma. He knew perfectly well that when Lovejoy's press arrived an attempt would be made to destroy it, while at the same time he knew that Lovejoy had a perfect right to defend his property. The men at the store argued with him for some time over the feasibility of appointing them as deputies or militia, but Krum knew too the danger of giving authority to men with guns in a town seething with animosities. When the press arrived, he advised them, move it to a safe place quietly and quickly— and if they felt they had to have guns, keep them out of sight.

On Sunday, November 5, Lovejoy received word that his press had been landed in St. Louis, where a steamer would pick it up for delivery at the Alton dock at about three o'clock Tuesday morning. On Monday Gilman and William Chappell again called on Mayor Krum, told him the news and again asked for reassurances. Krum transmitted their request to the City Council, hurriedly called together for the occasion, but the Council tabled it and went home. The Mayor, apparently washing his hands of the whole affair, did not even bother to notify the police.

Lovejoy, Gilman, and Chappell had originally planned to store the new press at Roff's store until it could be installed in the *Observer* offices. However, Samuel Roff, who did not want his store wrecked if there were trouble, had strong objections, suggesting instead that it be taken directly to the warehouses of Gilman and Godfrey, only a hundred yards or so from the landing dock. Gilman agreed, and on Monday evening about fifty Lovejoy supporters, many of them carrying guns, gathered at the warehouse. Lovejoy remained at home. At two forty-five, when the watchers at the warehouse heard the steamer whistle in the distance, Gilman went to Krum's house, woke him up, and told him that the press would arrive in a few minutes. Krum dressed and hurried down to the landing just as the crated press was unloaded. There were about twenty of Lovejoy's men with guns there to guard it, he testified later, but no one else present. The men dragged the crate to the warehouse and Krum went home.

The whereabouts of the new press was no secret in Alton. On Tuesday the town buzzed with the news, and a half-dozen armed men stayed in the warehouse through the day. There was no excitement, and Mayor Krum dared to hope that possibly the talk was only that. Nevertheless, he stayed late at his office, and at six o'clock Gilman and Chappell appeared. They had heard rumors, they told him, that the warehouse was to be attacked at midnight. Did they or did they not have the right to defend it "at all hazards"? They did, Krum replied, and if there were such an attack, he himself would call out the militia under his authority to suppress riot—however, he emphasized, only he as Mayor could be "sole judge of the emergency."

Gilman and Chappell, somewhat reassured, returned to the warehouse, where about a dozen men, Lovejoy among them, planned to stay through the night. Gilman and Godfrey's warehouse was in reality two stone buildings, placed side by side on the edge of the town's business district, with windows in the gabled ends but not on the sides. There were vacant lots on three sides of the buildings and the Mississippi in back, so that the building to the south, where the press was stored in the offices on the river side, was easily defensible. It was a clear, cool, moonlit evening.

John Krum stayed in his office after Gilman and Chappell left. Edward Keating remained at his office, about fifty yards from the warehouse, to finish work on a legal brief. Henry West, having just finished his dinner, answered a knock on his door; it was a neighbor to tell him that a mob was being organized to attack the warehouse and that West might like to know. West was not an abolitionist, but he was a peace-loving man and a believer in the Constitution. He put on his coat, started toward town, met Dr. Horace Beal, talked to him briefly about the rumors, got a short answer, and walked on. Samuel Avis, also out walking, met Dr. Beal a few moments later and brought up the same subject. "Every damned abolitionist in town," said Beal, "ought to be killed." Meanwhile West, noting a light in Keating's office, stopped to discuss the matter with his lawyer friend, and the two men agreed that they ought to go to the warehouse, talk to Lovejoy or Gilman, and see if trouble could be avoided.

Mayor Krum, a little after nine, heard loud talk and the rampling of feet in the street. He stepped out to see twenty men passing by; it was too dark to recognize faces, but he saw the moonlight glint on gunbarrels. He called a passerby, sent him to get Justice of the Peace Sherman Robbins and Judge William Martin, and went into his office to wait. At the warehouse the men lounged in Gilman's office, passing the time in idle talk. At about nine thirty, Keating and West knocked at the door, identified themselves, and were admitted. The men in the office were armed, Keating noted, and he talked for a time with Gilman, who seemed to be in charge. Lovejoy was there, Gilman said, but in another room, and if a mob came they intended to defend the press with their lives. Keating left for his office but West stayed, talking to Gilman, until the men heard shouts from outside.

Gilman rushed to the door, looked out, and reported that at least forty men with torches were approaching. Since there were no windows at the side of the building, he ran up the stairs to the attic at the gable end and threw open a window. He heard the men hammering at the door downstairs and called out, "What do you want?"

"The press," someone shouted back.

"You can't have it," Gilman shouted down. "It's our property and we mean to defend it."

The crowd milled uncertainly about the warehouse, shouting and throwing stones. In the light of the torches Gilman thought he recognized James Rock, a local saloon ruffian, but the barrage of stones aimed at his window forced him to keep his head out of sight. Actually, the warehouse was an awkward place to attack. Since the offices where the press was stored was at the rear of the building and there were neither doors nor windows on the sides, the only means of approach lay across forty feet of vacant lot at the south side of the building.

Exactly who fired the first shot no one knows. Mayor Krum, in his official report, claimed that the first shot came from within the building, but Krum was several blocks distant, waiting in his office for Robbins and Martin. Keating, in his office fifty yards away, heard a pistol shot followed by two rifle shots, but he had no way of telling their origin. Henry West, who was inside the warehouse office, testified later that the first shots came from outside—he heard one shot fired from the office but he could not identify the man who fired it. Gilman, at his attic window, said that several shots came first from the crowd, followed by one that came from inside the building below him. Whether it was the first or not, the bullet that came from the warehouse killed Lyman Bishop.

Edward Keating rushed into the street when he heard the shots and ran toward the warehouse, where he met a dozen men carrying a body away. He heard someone shout that Bishop was wounded, watched the crowd disperse, and went back to his office. At the warehouse Gilman, when he saw the mob leave, came down from the attic to join the men in the office. Mayor Krum and Robbins, still waiting for Judge Martin, had already decided to leave without him when they heard the gunshots. Hurrying down the street they met the crowd carrying Bishop's body and tried to find out what had happened. No one seemed able to give a coherent account, so Krum and Robbins ran on to the warehouse.

One man was already dead, and Krum knew that the mob would return for revenge, if for nothing else. He pleaded with Gilman to give up the press, which Gilman flatly refused to do. Lovejoy, who took little part in the argument, simply agreed with Gilman. While Krum pleaded the men heard shouts and gunshots outside and ran out to report a hundred or more men marching on the building with torches, shouting "Kill the damned abolitionists!" "Burn them out!" Krum ran out of the building toward the crowd, trying to find its leaders and shouting for quiet, but it was no use. The bells of Alton, ringing the alarm, brought more men pouring into the crowd surrounding the warehouse and Krum went unheard.

Inside the warehouse the defenders stayed near the windows, firing out now and then as shots came from the crowd. One man, stationed in the attic, ran down to report that someone had placed a ladder against the building and had set fire to the roof. Since the damp shingles smoldered instead of burning, several of the attackers set up the ladder in a different place, hoping to find a drier spot where the flames could catch. Four of Lovejoy's men dashed out, fired at the man on the ladder, missed him, and ran back in. Elijah Lovejoy, who had taken no part in the shooting, opened the door to look out just as a fusillade of shots came from a pile of lumber beyond the vacant lot. Five bullets hit him, three in the chest. He staggered back, fell to the floor, and died almost at once.

Mayor Krum, fighting his way through the crowd, heard someone shouting his name from the warehouse. He ran to the door to find Gilman waiting, and once he was inside, Gilman told him of Lovejoy's death and agreed to surrender. The mob, sensing that something was about to happen, fell silent when Krum emerged. Lovejoy was dead, he told them, and they could have the press. A great roar went up and while the mob rushed into the warehouse Gilman and his men fled into the darkness of the river bank and escaped. The press was dragged to the river, the parts broken up with rocks and hammers, and the whole thing dumped into the Mississippi. The body of Elijah Lovejoy, hidden in the warehouse, remained there all night. At dawn of the next day, November 8, a few of his friends took him home. On November 9, 1837, his thirty-fifth birthday, Elijah Lovejoy's grave, as he had predicted, was made in Alton. The abolition cause had its first martyr.

The town of Alton, shocked at what it had done, tried to pick up the pieces of its shattered community life. Exactly who was responsible to the law, and for what, no one was quite sure, but it was certain that with two men dead someone in Alton should be tried for something. Nobody seemed willing to try anyone for murder, homicide, or manslaughter. The State of Illinois, in the person of Attorney General Linder, decided to prosecute identifiable members of both the mob and defenders of the warehouse under Sections 113, 115, and 116 of Illinois criminal code, relating to riot, unlawful assembly, and entering property with force and violence. The members of Gilman's group were also indicted under Section 117, which concerned the execution of "a lawful act in a violent and tumultuous manner." For the defense, Lawyers Davis, Cowles, and Chickering agreed to serve; for the prosecution, City Attorneys Murdock and Bailey, with Linder as chief counsel. Since the cases involved a large number of Alton citizens, the attorneys decided to choose eleven men from the mob, twelve from the defenders, and to let the decisions rest on one indictment in each group.

On January 16, 1838, Judge William Martin (he for whom Krum had waited) opened court in the case of the State vs. Winthrop Gilman. The trial was orderly and quiet. Keating and West told their stories, Krum told his. Young Anson Platt, who clerked at Roff's store, testified that Gilman and four others had purchased guns and powder on November 6, "to defend their rights." Joseph Greeley, aroused by the bells on the night of November 7, testified he had seen Bishop carried away. The summaries on both sides were reasonable and dignified. Davis, Cowles, and Chickering rested their argument on the constitutional rights of free speech, free press, and defense of one's property. Murdock, admitting those rights, claimed that in their exercise Gilman and his friends had, as the indictment stated, defended their property in a violent and tumultuous manner. Only Linder mentioned abolitionism. No one should forget, he reminded the jury, that "the infatuated Lovejoy . . . intended to preach insurrection and to disseminate doctrines which must tend to disorganization and disunion, to preach rebellion to the slave, to excite servile war, to preach murder in the name of religion." But Linder's attempt at rabble-rousing did not work, for the jury held Gilman Not Guilty and the cases against the others were dropped.

On January 19 Judge Martin heard the indictments read against eleven members of the mob. Linder, now serving as chief counsel for the defense with Samuel Sawyer, faced Murdock and Cowles for the prosecution. Neither side tried very hard. West identified five defendants as members of the mob.

Krum identified seven. Samuel Avis identified five, among them Dr. Beal and James Rock, both of whom he swore had guns; Avis too saw Rock on the ladder with a torch, shouting that "he'd burn down the building and all in it." Webb Quigley saw seven of the defendants in the mob and four other men identified Beal, Rock, Fred Brechy, and Solomon Morgan, who apparently were the ringleaders. Nevertheless, as Linder pointed out, it was impossible to prove that these specific individuals had entered the warehouse and destroyed the press. Someone had, of course, but could it be proved that these men had done it? Cowles, speaking for the prosecution, tried to put the case on constitutional grounds; at stake in the trial, he believed, were "the rights to free discussion, liberty of the press, and freedom of conscience." On January 20 the jury discharged the defendants as Not Guilty.

The tragedy at Alton rocked the North to its foundations. Presses had been wrecked before, and editors roughly handled, but the death of an editor at the hands of an armed mob in a free state was a different matter. That Lovejoy was an abolitionist was one thing; that he died in defense of his right—guaranteed by the Constitutions of the United States and of Illinois—to speak and write, was something quite different. The news from Alton, wrote John Quincy Adams, "gave a shock as of an earthquake throughout this continent," and every editor, preacher, and writer felt the ground tremble a little under his feet. What was involved in the tragedy at Alton was not simply abolitionism, but free speech, free thought, and a free press. With Lovejoy's death they merged into a single cause.

Northern and Southern editors alike joined in condemning the Alton mob. Though a few pointed out that abolitionists invited trouble by agitating the delicate slavery question, most papers agreed with the St. Louis *Commercial Bulletin* that "one wrong is no justification for another." William Cullen Bryant, editor of the New York *Evening Post*, thought that the issue raised in Illinois was not merely "connected with the abolition of slavery in the South, but a question vital to the liberties of the entire Union." Horace Greeley, while admitting "Mr. Lovejoy's errors," believed that they had "nothing to do in any shape with the turpitude of this outrage." If Lovejoy was killed for "resisting public opinion," Greeley reasoned, "then Socrates was an anarchist and Jesus Christ a felon." Of the more than two hundred editorials reprinted by the New York and Boston antislavery papers, all but a dozen or so thought as Greeley did that Lovejoy was "a martyr to liberty."

Since Lovejoy was a minister as well as an editor, the clergy in the North proved particularly sensitive to the implications of the Alton case, which served as the topic of hundreds of sermons for the next year. The Reverend Hubbard Winslow of Boston thought that the mob was "a natural consequence" of Lovejoy's attempt to "oppose the prevailing voice and will," but he was a rare exception. Ralph Waldo Emerson "sternly rejoiced that one was found to die for humanity and the rights of free speech and opinion." William Ellery Channing, who as a pacifist deplored Lovejoy's resort to arms, served on a committee with one hundred prominent Bostonians to call a meeting of protest in Faneuil Hall, New England's cradle of liberty—a meeting which brought golden-tongued Wendell Phillips into prominence as the great orator of the abolition movement.

Editors and ministers, of course, found a special meaning in the death of Lovejoy, but the general public in the North saw a broader implication. To many who had attacked the abolitionists as dangerous radicals, they were now, by Lovejoy's martyrdom, defenders of traditional American rights. And if slavery, to protect itself, must kill its opponents, then slavery had not long to live. As one writer phrased it, Elijah Lovejoy, by "inflexibly maintaining the common rights of every citizen in defiance of the audacious tyranny of the multitude, accomplished more in his death for liberty of thought than a hundred courts, and more for man than a thousand reformers." May the earth of Illinois rest lightly upon the stubborn Yankee's dust.

AND A MIRACLE MAN

★

Phineas Quimby

Phineas Quimby

★

SOME OF HIS CONTEMPORARIES called him a charlatan and talked of putting him in jail. But Phineas Quimby, the New England clockmaker, believed in himself and if he was a fraud, he never knew it. All he said was that illness and disease could be cured, quickly and simply, by using some undefined power that existed in the mind of every person. Others, of course, were saying much the same thing during his time, and others had said it before him. Some of them were quacks, feeding on the ignorant and credulous. Some lost themselves in cults, coteries, and commercial success. Quimby was one of the few who did neither.

The tradition into which Phineas Quimby wandered during the eighteen-forties was a long, if not quite honorable one. The great Cagliostro, who bilked the court of Louis XVI, sold medicinal beds and a bottled "elixir of life" guaranteed to cure everything from gout to sterility. In Cromwell's England, when there were no resident Stuarts to cure the sick by the laying on of royal hands, Valentine Greatrakes made a reputation by touch-healing. In the eighteenth century, science and pseudo-science gave the healer a badly-needed new tool. After the work of Galvani, Volta, and Franklin, the faithhealer went on a scientific basis, for whatever he did, he could say that electricity was responsible and no one could prove him wrong. Dr. Elisha Perkins of Connecticut invented "tractors," a pair of metallic rods, and "drew out" disease by touching them to the body and "generating current." At about the same time an Austrian, Franz Mesmer, announced the discovery of a "universally dispersed magnetic fluid" that produced electric charges in the body; by reversing the charge of "animal magnetism" Mesmer could put a person to sleep and talk to spirits through his mesmerized mind. Such "research," with its promise of finding some sort of cure for the racks and illnesses of humanity, gave the man of 1800 hope for a new kind of life in the century that lay ahead—and incidentally increased his gullibility.

The first half of the nineteenth century developed new "sciences" and new ways to use the old ones. After John Gaspar Spurzheim brought phrenology to America, the Fowler brothers, Orson and Lorenzo, papered the country with bump-charts. Spiritualism, publicized by the Fox Sisters, gained hundreds of converts and produced the "Poughkeepsie Seer," Andrew Jackson Davis, who was guided in hypnotic trances by the shade of Emanuel Swedenborg and who performed the incredible feat of delivering one hundred and fifty-seven lectures (taken down by stenographers) while in a trance. Later he opened a "clairvoyant clinic" and prescribed for illness after consultation with departed spirits. In the forties the "water-cure," an Austrian discovery, came into fashion. From Maine to Louisiana doctors established hydropathic hospitals in which water, "the most powerful of natural elements," was absorbed by "transudation" through the skin from wet clothes, bedsheets, and twenty-three different kinds of baths; Lowell, Longfellow, Harriet Beecher Stowe, James Fenimore Cooper, and others took the treatment.

Quimby's appearance as a faith healer, then, in the midst of all this, was hardly an isolated phenomenon. He had plenty of rivals, but his success depended upon the fact that he had more to offer than the others and that he was obviously honest. His system appealed to the nineteenth century as the kingly touch of the seventeenth and the magic furniture of the eighteenth century never would have. If you wanted a scientific basis for your cure, Quimby had it; if you needed a metaphysical explanation, he had that too. He never became selfish, intolerant, and dictatorial, as had the leaders of so many other mental-healing cults, and most convincing of all, he cared little for money. There was no fraud in him. However he is judged, he must be given credit for that.

Phineas Quimby was born in 1802, one of the seven children of a New Hampshire blacksmith. The family moved to Belfast, Maine, in 1804, where young Phineas learned watch and clockmaking. Until he was thirty-six he lived quietly in Belfast, working at his trade (Quimby clocks may still run in New England), tinkering with inventions, and dabbling with daguerreotypy when that became . popular. He was a small, nervous man with sharp black eyes, talkative, alert, hard to beat in an argument. In spite of his near-illiteracy he was thought by some to have the sharpest mind in town. No doubt he would have gone on making clocks had not a travelling hypnotist named Charles Poyen arrived in Belfast for a "Mesmeric exhibition" in 1838.

Poyen was only one of many such hypnotists on tour in America, but more expert than most. He had made a precarious living as a teacher of French and drawing until 1836, when he took up mesmerism, which he learned in France, to capitalize on the current American fad. At Belfast in 1838, however, he was not successful. His subjects refused to respond properly to his "animal electricity." Possibly to save face he notified the audience that someone among them possessed an extremely powerful magnetic force that was ruining his act. No one was more surprised than Quimby to be identified as the culprit. He talked at great length with Poyen during the rest of his engagement, read a few manuals on mesmerism, and began to practice rather successfully on his neighbors. After establishing a local reputation, Quimby discovered that a Belfast youth named Lucius Burkmar was an almost perfect hypnotic subject, and he decided to tour New England as Poyen did, giving exhibitions of the "science" of mesmerism.

Quimby and Lucius did extremely well on the platform. Quimby explained to his audiences that "animal electricity" passed from himself to Lucius, and that this excess charge in

Lucius magnetized him, making him responsive to the hypnotizer and giving him "vision"—the common interpretation of Mesmer. By fixing his gaze on Lucius and making passes before his eyes, Quimby could hypnotize the lad in a few seconds. Lucius could then read minds, describe persons and places he had never seen, see through wood and metal, and give accounts of happenings far away—he also did a few free autopsies in funeral parlors. Committees of prominent men sat on the stage to prevent trickery, and even Quimby was occasionally surprised by Lucius' clairvoyance.

Lucius seems to have been a pleasant, not overly-intelligent young man. Aware that Quimby possessed some power over him, he cared little about what it was. His diary, kept on their New England tours, showed more interest in "chitchat with a pretty girl" than in mesmerism, and his employer had to watch him rather carefully in the evenings. But he interested Quimby, who actually had little knowledge of the mesmeric theory, and who noted that Lucius did some things not wholly explained by Mesmer's "animal electricity." For a long time it was Quimby's belief that Lucius had sharper "second-sight" during thunderstorms or when grasping a metal rod, since animal electricity, the mesmerists said, was most actively dispersed under such conditions. Yet once when the rumble of passing wagons was mistaken for thunder, Lucius performed at his best. Suspicious, Quimby substituted a wooden stick for the metal rod and found it worked quite as well. These things, and others like them, bothered him.

Perhaps to find out more about mesmerism, Quimby retired from the road and returned to clockmaking in late 1839. Lucius hired out as a subject to another hypnotist, John B. Dods, who had a new twist, the idea that disease originated in "nerve electricity." He would place Burkmar in a trance, during which a spirit (often the reliable and well-known Indian) would diagnose and prescribe for the ailments of members of the audience. Dods also found it profitable to teach Lucius enough Latin to sound medically impressive and enough pharmacy to prescribe medicines which Dods compounded on the spot and sold.

Lucius worked with Dods for nearly a year before Quimby was ready to make another tour. In the meantime he had nearly decided to reject "animal magnetism" as the source of Lucius' power, concluding that there must be some simpler explanation. After Lucius' return, Quimby discovered that the boy could often catch suggestions without the aid of a hypnotic trance. It was not always necessary to give Lucius an oral order, but only a mental one, which he obeyed automatically. If Quimby gave Lucius a six-inch rule while picturing a twelve-inch rule in his own mind, to Lucius the rule was actually one foot; the boy counted off twelve inches on it and measured with it in feet. Puzzling over this, it dawned on Quimby that he was dealing in thought transference. Evidently mind worked on mind, for an idea in Quimby's mind turned up in Lucius' brain without changing an iota.

Another puzzling problem came when Burkmar fell by habit into the routine of "mesmeric diagnosis" taught him by Dods. Quimby had no particular qualms about the medical ethics of the practice, but he noted that Lucius tended to prescribe expensive medicines and often made nonsensical diagnoses. Yet the medicines seemed to satisfy the patient, so Quimby allowed Lucius to continue, ordering him (out of deference to the patient's pocketbook) to restrict himself to common, inexpensive remedies. The range of Burkmar's prescriptions was limited (herb tea, Burgundy patch plasters, poultices, avoidance of cold water) but Lucius happily believed them efficient for anything from dizziness to "lung weakness." A substantial number of his "patients" seemed to think so too.

Quimby tested one of these cures on himself. He had been bothered by kidney pains, which Lucius obligingly diagnosed as ulcerous kidneys. When Lucius cured him by a simple laying on of hands (and Quimby himself felt sure he *was* cured), he tried to puzzle it out. He knew he had kidney pains, yet he knew too that Burkmar's nonsense had not cured them. How then was he cured? He reasoned that (a) his kidneys had been diseased; (b) Lucius made him doubt the fact; (c) doubting the fact made his kidneys get well. Ergo, the kidney trouble was of his own making. To validate his conclusion, he tested it by taking Lucius to visit the sick with local physicians. Lucius made absurd diagnoses and advised more absurd remedies, but nevertheless he had more success than most of the doctors, a fact the doctors themselves grudgingly admitted.

At this point Quimby took a great step, one that lifted him out of the class of ordinary road-show faith-healers. He decided that the benefit of medicine lay in the patient's faith in its power to cure. His next step was equally important. He fired Lucius and gave up mesmerism. The curative process, he believed, was a mental one, not the result of hypnotic suggestion but of faith alone.

Quimby was well aware he was striking out into a new field. He was in the peculiar position of having stumbled on something tremendously important, but something quite beyond his capacity to comprehend. In 1847 he quit the mesmeric circuit and returned to Belfast and clockmaking. Digging into what would today be called psychology, he experimented with the sick, trying to systematize his methods. Most of all, he hoped to find the *why* of his successful cures. Building upon what he already believed, he slowly evolved a body of theory that seemed to account for the results.

Disease, Quimby said, was a false idea, health a true one. "Illness is caused by a disturbance of the mind, which is spiritual matter, and therefore originates there." A false idea could manifest itself outwardly as "real matter"; introduction of a true idea into the mind destroyed the physical manifestation of the false idea, i.e., the disease. "Man is made up of truth and belief," he wrote. "If he is deceived into a belief he has, or is liable to have, a disease, the belief is catching and the effect follows it." Thus a false idea that one had a tumor might "condense" into a solid called a tumor; eliminating the false idea by suggestion therefore dissolved the tumor. How did one suggest? There was really no such thing as "mesmeric" or "magnetic" healing, he knew from his experience with Burkmar, but simply the influence of one mind on another. Therefore Quimby postulated the existence in mankind of an intuitive or clairvoyant principle which was a channel of communication between minds—a power he called variously, "thought," "wisdom," 'the power of progression," or simply "mind." One in whom this principle was highly developed might communicate truth through it to another whose ideas were false.

Quimby worked for nearly ten years developing his theories. Lacking both education and vocabulary, he found it extremely difficult to write coherently or clearly. Furthermore, he kept tinkering with his ideas, adding embellishments to his basic principle that disease was simply a false idea. By the early fifties he had evolved the belief that man existed in double form—an "inward man" (also called a "spirit form") and an outward, physical man. The state of the one governed the health of the other, for "when these are at variance or out of tune, disease is the effect, while by harmonizing them health of the body is the result . . ." Quimby's function was to communicate true ideas to the "spirit form" of his patient through the channel of their common clairvoyant principle. During a consultation, he explained, he "rendered himself absent to everything but the impression of the person's feelings, and these are quickly daguerrotyped on me." By impressing his own feelings back on the patient's mind, Quimby thereby "daguerreotyped" on it his own true ideas of health and harmony. The patient's "spirit-form" (which Quimby thought actually stood beside the patient's sick body) contained the "cause of the grief," and with it, not the patient, he conversed concerning the ailment. He could thus, he believed, actually see and talk with the patient's "inward man," argue with him by thought-transference, change his false ideas to true ones, and cure the physical illness of the "outward man." 'I act as mediator," he said, "bringing his spirit back to harmonize with the body." This was the healing principle of Christ, lost for eighteen hundred years, the secret of Christ's miraculous cures. Yet there was nothing really miraculous about it, Quimby insisted. It was a natural principle, the result of wholly natural forces; its discovery was a fulfillment of Christ's promise of eternal life and proof of God's benevolence. He, Quimby, for some unknown reason, had been chosen to reveal it. This was his mission in the world.

By 1859 Quimby felt confident enough to set up a clinic in Portland, Maine, for the treatment of diseases by the Quimby method. Though the public was nearly out of patience with "cures," his treatment caught on, for it involved no spirits or electricity, diets, health costumes, or gadgets with batteries. Quimby simply sat by his patient, talked to him, occasionally rubbed his head or arm, and explained the mental cause of illness in such a convincing way that the illness itself disappeared, or seemed to. He refused to call himself a messiah and he laid no claim to greatness, pointing out that his only power was a highly developed "natural wisdom" or "clairvoyance" that enabled him to see and explain away the patient's error and substitute truth in its place. Anyone could do it. He made some of his patients promise to learn the Quimby method and teach it to two others in order that the secret would spread until every man was freed from illness. Fees were collected rather casually. A large part of Quimby's practice was with the poor, and he was never known to turn a penniless patient away. "The money will come soon enough," he said, "when people learn." To the accusations of some of the orthodox that he was setting himself up as equal to Christ, Quimby replied heatedly that though his method was Christ's, it was a natural and not a supernatural process. He was willing to teach it to anyone, and discouraged any tendency on the part of the little group which gathered about him in Portland to worship him. He thought of himself as nothing more than a teacher of natural healing.

A good many of his contemporaries classed Quimby with the mesmerists, spiritualists, magnetic healers and others who infested the middle years of the century, but his results could not be lightly tossed off. His records were scanty, but he said in 1861 that he treated about six hundred patients a year, nearly all of them successfully. By treatments ranging in duration from fifteen minutes to two years, he cured "lung weakness," dyspepsia, boils, spinal disease, "optic neuralgia," rheumatism, aphasia, scrofula, "general debility," partial paralysis, blindness, mild insanity, kidney and liver trouble, pneumonia, typhoid, and many other ailments. He was not above curing the smoking habit, nor in one case a peculiar addiction to lemons; after Quimby's conversations with his "inner man", the patient could hardly bear the sight of yellow fruit. Many of his cures were supported by references and sworn testimonials. In 1862 Dr. F. L. Towne, Surgeon, U. S. Army, witnessed and certified the complete cure of a case of dyspepsia and partial blindness in less than six weeks.

The Portland clinic treated children as well as adults, Quimby's theory being that the child absorbed false ideas, and consequently illness, from its parents. A child's mother, for example, fears that it may take cold, a fear that she communicates to the child by constant references to wet feet, sneezes, and coughs. If a child coughs, therefore, "its mind is cognizant of it, and dreads it . . . , and that dread increases the tendency to cough, and thus the disease is produced." To cure childhood illnesses Quimby therefore conversed with both child and parents, ejecting from both the false ideas reflected by the child's ailment. Nor was Quimby averse to long-distance treatment by mail. He sometimes wrote out his talks in letters, making "appointments" to appear to the patient's "inner vision" at a specific time and informing him that the correspondence was directed to the "spirit form" or "scientific man" rather than to the outward addressee. Apparently the suggestive effect was sufficient, for he claimed some successful cures by this method.

Quimby was at his best when working directly with patients and at his weakest when attempting to explain his theories. His lack of education hampered him and his intellectual equipment was not of the best, but he felt that his mission required him to leave for others a record of his discoveries. Running eventually to six manuscript volumes, his writings were diffuse, repetitive, and vague. At times his prose became almost unintelligible, for he had a tendency to borrow from mesmerism, daguerreotypy and electricity, or to coin his own vocabulary wherein "science" equalled "truth," "wisdom" the "clairvoyant principle," "animal spirit" the "inner man," and so on. At other times he entangled himself in a misty philosophical dualism, dividing the world into a "natural world" of opinion and error, and a "real world" of truth and "eternal life"—man's "happiness or misery," he concluded, "depends on which world is uppermost." While he could sometimes explain the mental origins of some illnesses more or less credibly, he had an extremely difficult time with others and went far astray of even the most elementary medical knowledge of his own time.

The origin of all disease lay in mental shock, he believed, for "you cannot move anything unless you start it." The shock was often slight, "a little fright, excitement, pleasure, anything which might produce a disturbance in the system." Thus disturbed, "the natural heat of the body always either increases or diminishes." Feeling hot or cold, the patient imagines himself ill. With the idea giving direction to the fact, he then comes down with a cold, fever, lameness, or some other illness specifically feared and consequently imagined by the patient. A common cold, for example, might come from stooping, which "contracts the stomach and causes an irritation, sending the heat to the head." This heat "excites the glands about the nose, the patient thinks he has a cold," and eventually does have one as the erroneous idea takes outward manifestation. Herein lay the reason for Quimby's great impatience with physicians, who were, "of all mean-looking things, the lowest." The doctor tells you, for example, that you have congested lungs. You believe him, the belief "solidifies" into a congestion, and he gives you medicine which you believe will cure it. It may, if you believe so strongly enough, and the doctor thus collects a fee for causing an illness you need never have had, and for curing it yourself. Far better, reasoned Quimby, that you learn to avoid false ideas.

A small circle of devotees gathered about Quimby at his Portland clinic, to whom it was his practice to dictate his random thoughts on what was beginning to be known as Quimbyism. These manuscripts, some in his own hand, were left open to all patients and reading them served as a preliminary to the actual therapeutic conversations with Quimby. He was never reticent with newspaper interviewers and advertised widely, a practice not unprofessional at the time, so by 1860 his name was well known to the public, which remained divided on the question of whether he was a fake or a near-saint. Among those who read testimonials of Quimby's cures was Mary Baker Glover Patterson, the wife of Dr. Daniel Patterson of Concord, Massachusetts. Afflicted with hysteria since childhood, she suffered from spinal weakness, periods of complete catalepsy, and extreme nervous palsy. Dr. Patterson wrote Quimby early in 1861 to arrange a consultation, but the doctor took a commission in the Union Army, was captured at Bull Run, sent South to prison, and subsequently divorced. It was more than a year before Mary Patterson's plans to visit Quimby crystallized, and then her sister, who mistrusted Quimby, shipped her instead to Dr. Vail's water-cure sanatorium in New York State. By saving pennies from the allowance given her by her sister, she finally obtained the funds to visit Quimby, arriving at his offices in Portland's International Hotel in late 1862.

Quimby's diagnosis was that she was "tied down by her family and physicians"; her disturbed mental state had affected her "spirit," which in turn afflicted her body with spinal disease. After a few consultations she walked without difficulty and slept quietly for the first time in months. Quimby was interested in her as one of his most unusual cases and struck by the obvious intelligence of her conversation. As her treatment progressed, he spent greater amounts of time discussing his theories with her. It was Mary Patterson's belief that God had cured her, and that Quimby was the mediator between herself and God. This supposition brought about long arguments, Quimby maintaining, as he always had, that his method was wholly natural, and Mrs.

Patterson that at the bottom of it lay some divine power vouchsafed to Quimby as a divinely-appointed healer, an idea that confused and embarrassed him. She wrote a sonnet in his praise, published it in a newspaper, and made public testimonials of her cure. Later she wrote to him for absent treatment, returning to Portland briefly in 1864 before beginning a series of public lectures herself on the mental origins of disease.

Phineas Quimby died on January 16, 1866, from an abdominal tumor. He received no medical treatment except his own, though toward the end he allowed his wife to call in a homeopathic physician. One of his adherents, Julius Dresser, and Julius' son Horatio, promised to carry on his work, but it seemed that the vital force of Quimbyism was gone.

As events proved, it was by no means dead. Its most interesting convert, now Mary Baker Eddy after a third marriage, continued to teach his principles until in 1872, while she was lecturing in Lynn, Massachusetts, she began to form her own curative philosophy and to attract a small group of disciples. Three years later she published her book, *Science and Health*. The resemblance of Mary Eddy's "Christian Science" to Quimbyism was quickly noted by the Dressers. George Quimby claimed that the text of *Science and Health* closely paralleled passages in his father's manuscripts, and charges of plagiarism flew back and forth. Mrs. Eddy, admitting her admiration for Quimby in the early sixties, claimed that any manuscripts purporting to express Quimby's ideas were really hers. "I used to take his scribblings," she said, "and fix them over for him and give him my thoughts and language, which as I understood it, were far in advance of his." The fact was, however, that whatever Mrs. Eddy owed to Quimby, her system differed from his on several basic points. Quimby never denied the reality of matter or of disease, emphasizing instead the greater reality of idea, and its corollary, the mental origin and control of physical conditions. For that matter, the principles enunciated by both were neither wholly new nor entirely original, for the ancient and familiar hope of man in his conquest of disease has always been (and will probably continue to be) the discovery of a self-curative principle.

The Dressers, after their somewhat shrill altercations with Mrs. Eddy, gradually diverted Quimbian psychology into a much more generalized system called "Mental Science" and later "New Thought," de-emphasizing its role in curing illness and stressing mental suggestion, personality-building, and "adjustment to life." Whether consciously or unconsciously, the promoters of New Thought struck a note that the generation of the eighteen-nineties found exactly attuned to its ear. The "success formula" of the Gilded Age had already won public acceptance—Andrew Carnegie, Russell Conwell, Horatio Alger and others played variations on the rags-to-riches theme—and society needed a psychological explanation for the ability of one man to outstrip others in accumulation of economic goods. The phrases of Quimby, carried over into New Thought—"personal magnetism," "thought-wave transference," "mental suggestion"—took on new meanings that would have startled him. Employ "thought vibrations," New Thought said, and convince your employer you deserve a raise. Get ahead (as presumably Carnegie and others had done) by mentally impressing your ideas on others; "develop your personality" (a faint echo of Quimby's "inner man") and *think* your way to wealth and influence. If, as Quimby inferred, the mental state governs the physical, nothing is impossible to the magnetic mind. Success was as much a "mental law" as gravity was a law of physics, said Orison S. Marden, whose *Pushing to the Front* sold three million copies after 1894, and "Only by thinking abundance can you realize the abundant prosperous life that is your birthright." A generation later Emile Coué's "Every day in every way I am becoming better and better," a variant of Quimby's familiar self-curative principle, carried on the tradition. Thus did Quimbyism, at second hand, serve as a prop to the cult of high pressure salesmanship, and, in a watered-down version, appear again in the mail-order courses in personality building of today. Nor has the faithhealer, as events in the Netherlands have recently shown, completely disappeared from the contemporary scene.

How should one judge Phineas Quimby? He was sincere, honest, and earnest—but there the list of his virtues should probably end. Though he was no charlatan, the odor of fraud could not help but cling to him; his connections with fad and quackery were unfortunately too close. His excursions into psychology and psychotherapy came far too soon, and were far too amateur, to make any contribution to science. He did have confused glimmerings of what later became psychiatry in other and better adapted hands, for in his Portland clinic he was trying to delve into the dark recesses of the mind, two generations ahead of his time, to find what was there. And in his gropings he did seize upon some significant things. His "clairvoyant principle" and his "inward man" were of course claptrap; yet, when one considers that he was really talking about what later came to be called the subconscious mind, one feels a grudging respect for Quimby's shrewd ability to penetrate even the short distance he did into uncharted territory.

Nor was he so far wrong in tracing the origins of some illnesses to traumatic emotional experience, though he carried his conjectures to absurdity. His treatments of hysteria, sudden blindness, light-sensitivity, "debility and lassitude," dyspepsia, and so on were not so far from the right track. He gradually stumbled his way toward the elements of the psychoanalytic method; the chair in which the patient sat while he looked into Quimby's eyes and told his troubles was not a long step from the psychiatrist's couch. Significantly, about seventy percent of his practice was with women, and probably more than a few of his cases which had failed to respond to standard medical practice hinged upon family troubles, unrequited love, lack of sympathy, and other disturbances of the frustrated nineteenth-century female.

Nor can Quimby's employment of autosuggestion, rudimentary though his method was, be dismissed as sheer fakery.

One cannot be certain that his consultations and his correspondence cures were not at least partially based on a very clever use of that principle. His explanations of the origins of colds, rheumatism, and other minor ailments were nonsense even by the medical standards of his own time. But the patient, believing them, lost his fear of illness and no doubt experienced a great psychological relief. Quimby perhaps knew that his customary prescription of cold water taken at bedtime, and his habit of rubbing the patient's head with one hand, were both valueless. Yet the *placebo* was a stock in trade of the reputable physician in the nineteenth century, nor is its use unknown in the twentieth. Very probably Quimby did not know what he was actually doing. He drew some keen inferences from his observations of illness, but he lacked the capacity to do much with them. Through his inability to explain it or to perceive its scientific value, he buried what he found beneath layers of metaphysical rubble.

Fate, in choosing Quimby the clockmaker for his role in history, played a trick. The principles he popularized were in themselves sound enough, but ironically the man picked to propagate them was incapable of making use of them or of grasping their value. With Quimby science ran down a blind alley; psychology started all over again without him and passed him by without notice. Untrained, uneducated, unable to generalize on any but a vague and naïve level, Phineas Quimby was simply not equipped to meet the responsibilities thrust upon him by accident. Given into the hands of an Emerson, or a James, what might Quimbyism have become?

A NOTE ON SOURCES

★

A Note on Sources

★

The primary sources of information concerning Harman Blennerhassett are W. H. Safford, *The Life of Harman Blennerhassett* (Cincinnati, 1853), and Safford's edition of *The Blennerhassett Papers* (Cincinnati, 1864). Thomas P. Abernathy's *The Burr Conspiracy* (New York, 1954) is the most recent and the best study of Burr's plot and trial, while Nathan Schachner, *Aaron Burr* (New York, 1937), is a trustworthy biography. Accounts of the career of John Fries are found in W. W. H. Davis, *The Fries Rebellion* (Doylestown, Pa., 1899), and W. F. Dunaway, *History of Pennsylvania* (New York, 1948). The stenographic transcript of Fries' trials, Thomas Carpenter's *The Two Trials of John Fries on an Indictment of Treason . . . ,* (Philadelphia, 1800), is a mine of material. A violently partisan account is J. H. Sherburne's edition of *John Wood's Suppressed History of the Administration of John Adams* (Philadelphia, 1846). Horace Binney, "Leaders of the Old Bar of Philadelphia," *Pennsylvania Magazine* XIV (1890), 1-26, adds supplementary information.

Jared Sparks' Life of *John Ledyard* (Boston, 1828), written in charmingly old-fashioned style, is still perhaps the best early biography of Ledyard; Kenneth Munford, *John Ledyard: An American Marco Polo* (Portland, 1939) the best recent account. Henry Beston, *The Book of Gallant Vagabonds* (New York, 1925), contains a chapter on Ledyard, and brief sketches occur in C. B. Moore, "John Ledyard the Traveller," *New York Genealogical and Historical Record* VII (Jan., 1876) 1-13, and H. A. Tirrell, "Ledyard The

Traveller," *Records and Papers of the New London County Historical Society* III (1912) 205-16. A great deal of information on Ledyard's epic journey undoubtedly remains buried in Russian archives, where it is currently unobtainable. Of Edward Bonney no record remains except his own book, *The Banditti of the Prairies* (n.p., n.d.) which apparently was published about 1848 and is extremely rare.

King Strang has had numerous chroniclers, the best of whom is Milo M. Quaife, whose book, *The Kingdom of St. James* (New Haven, 1930) is the definitive account of Strang's life and career. M. L. Loach, "History of the Grand Traverse Region," *Michigan Pioneer and Historical Collections* XXXIII (1902), 14-175, and "A Michigan Monarchy," *ibid.*, XXIII (1891) 628-38; H. E. Legler, "A Moses of the Mormons," *ibid.*, XXII (1902) 180-224; O. Poppleton, "Tales and Traditions" and "The Murder of King Strang," *ibid.*, XVIII (1891) 623-26, 626-27; and J. H. Forster, "Survey of the Northwestern Lakes," *ibid.*, IX (1890) 107-10, all provide contemporary or near-contemporary incidents of Strang's reign. M. M. Quaife, "Polygamy at Beaver Island," *Michigan History* V (1921) 333-35, and M. M. Davis, "Stories of St. Helena Island," *ibid.*, 411-47, are more specialized studies. An interestingly lurid and completely untrue account of Strang's activities is G. G. Bates, "The Trial in this City of King Strang," *Detroit Advertiser and Tribune,* July 12, 1877.

The Oneida Community has been similarly popular with historians and biographers. Charles Nordhoff's *Communistic Societies of the United States* (New York, 1875), Pierrepont Noyes' *My Father's House* (New York, 1937), and G. W. Noyes' *John H. Noyes, The Putney Community* (New York, 1931), all provide first-hand accounts. Robert A. Parker, *A Yankee Saint* (Boston, 1935), is the best biography of Noyes, while excellent studies of Oneida occur in Mark Holloway, *Heavens On Earth* (New York, 1951), Alice F. Tyler, *Freedom's Ferment* (Minneapolis, 1944), and Gilbert Seldes, *The Stammering Century* (New York, 1918).

Consul W. Butterfield, *The History of the Girtys* (New

York, 1890), and Thomas Boyd, *Simon Girty: The White Savage* (New York, 1928), cover Girty's infamous career thoroughly. The major source of information concerning John Murrell is H. R. Howard's edition of Virgil Stewart's account, *The History of Virgil A. Stewart* (New York, 1836), portions of which may be taken with several grains of salt. The relevant chapters in Robert M. Coates, *The Outlaw Years* (New York, 1930) combine most of what is known about Murrell into eminently readable form. Briefer references to Murrell and the Southwest brigands are found in S. C. Williams, *The Beginnings of West Tennessee* (Nashville, 1930); James Phelan, *The History of Tennessee* (Nashville, 1888); Hodding Carter, *The Lower Mississippi* (New York, 1942); and Donald Davidson, *The Tennessee* (New York, 1946). *Niles' Register* for the years 1835-1836 contains a number of items concerning the slave scares, the most complete of which is the account given by the New York *Evening Star,* reprinted October 17, 1835.

The march of Coxey's Army may be followed in the files of any of the metropolitan newspapers of the period. Donald McMurry, *Coxey's Army* (Boston, 1929), remains the best source of information concerning the General and his ideas. Three contemporary estimates are worth reading: W. T. Stead, "Coxeyism," *Review of Reviews* X (July, 1894) 45-59; "The Coxey Crusade," *ibid.,* 63-67; and a symposium, Howard, Byrnes, and Doty, "The Menace of Coxeyism," *North American Review* CLVIII (June, 1898) 687-705. The most fascinating account of Coxey's later years is his own, written for his broadside, *The Big Idea,* Massillon, Ohio, April 16, 1946. James Vallandigham's biography of his brother, *The Life of Clement L. Vallandigham* (Baltimore, 1872) is an excellent though understandably partisan source. Two anonymous pamphlets, *The Trial of the Honorable Clement Vallandigham* and *The Record of the Honorable Clement Vallandigham,* published in 1863 at Cincinnati and Columbus, Ohio, respectively, contain a wealth of additional information. George Fort Milton, *Abraham Lincoln and The Fifth Col-*

umn (New York, 1942), and Wood Gray, *The Hidden Civil War* (New York, 1942) are authoritative studies of anti-war, anti-Lincoln activities during the period, with excellent analyses of Vallandigham's part in them.

W. S. Drewry, *The Southampton Insurrection* (Washington, 1900) is the most detailed study of Nat Turner's insurrection. Much more satisfactory historically is Herbert Aptheker, *American Negro Slave Revolts* (New York, 1943), the best single book in the field. Thomas Gray, *The Confessions of Nat Turner, Leader of the Late Insurrections . . .* (Baltimore, 1831) reprints Turner's own account, while S. B. Weeks, "The Slave Insurrections in Virginia, 1831," *Magazine of American History* 91 (June, 1891) 448-55, and J. W. Cromwell, "The Aftermath of Nat Turner's Insurrection," *Journal of Negro History* V (April, 1920) 208-35, contain pertinent information. For the story of Elijah Lovejoy, Edward Beecher, *Narrative of the Riots at Alton,* (Alton, 1838) and Joseph C. and Owen Lovejoy, *Memoir of the Reverend Elijah P. Lovejoy* (New York, 1838) are indispensable. William S. Lincoln, *The Alton Trials* (New York, 1838) reprints the court records of the two trials. The Alton *Telegraph,* January 24, 1838, and the Cincinnati *Journal,* November 16 and 23, 1837, contain long accounts by witnesses.

Horatio Dresser's edition of *The Quimby Manuscripts* (New York, 1921), Annetta Dresser's *Philosophy of Phineas P. Quimby* (Boston, 1895), and George Quimby's "Phineas Parkhurst Quimby," *New England Magazine,* March, 1888, comprise the main sources of information for the life and ideas of Quimby. The relations between Quimby and Mrs. Eddy, and the controversy between New Thought and Christian Science, are treated by Sibyl Wilbur, *The Life of Mary Baker Eddy,* (New York, 1907).

The author wishes to acknowledge the valuable assistance of Joseph J. Waldmeir in compiling the bibliographies necessary to these studies.